Studies in Contemporary Latin America
JOHN J. JOHNSON, STANFORD UNIVERSITY
GENERAL EDITOR

INTERNATIONAL COMMUNISM IN LATIN AMERICA:
A HISTORY OF THE MOVEMENT, 1917-1963
By Rollie E. Poppino, University of California, Davis

THE ARTS IN LATIN AMERICA
*By Gilbert Chase, Inter-American Institute for Musical
Research, Tulane University*

GOVERNMENT AND POLITICS IN
LATIN AMERICA
*By Philip B. Taylor, Jr., School of Advanced International
Studies, The Johns Hopkins University*

NATIONALISM IN CONTEMPORARY
LATIN AMERICA
*By Arthur P. Whitaker, University of Pennsylvania, and
David Jordan, The Pennsylvania State University*

ORGANIZED LABOR IN LATIN AMERICA
By Robert J. Alexander, Rutgers University

ORGANIZED LABOR IN LATIN AMERICA

Robert J. Alexander

THE FREE PRESS, *New York*
COLLIER-MACMILLAN LIMITED, *London*

To Alex Balinky

Foreword

SINCE WORLD WAR II THE URBAN LABORING CLASSES HAVE BEEN NU-
merically the most rapidly expanding social force in both the
Latin American republics and in the nonrepublican areas of the
Caribbean. Trade Unionism has accompanied the growth of the
urban working elements, and labor organizations now exercise
considerable influence in all of the transitional societies. These
groups, for example, sometimes provide an effective bridge between village social structures left behind and the anonymity of
large factories and cities. A few unions have shunned politics.
Most, however, have associated with political parties. Labor's in-
volvement in politics and its ties with political groups have
tended to embitter relations between the "haves" and the "have
nots." This in turn has tended to distort such national issues as
the role of foreign capital and the distribution of available resources among the several sectors of the economy and the various
elements of society. In three highly perceptive chapters, Professor
Robert Alexander treats those spheres of the labor movement
which lend themselves to generalized discussion.

But if in the Caribbean, Middle America, and South America
labor movements may have much in common, it is no less true
that they may vary greatly from country to country. In certain
republics trade unions have enjoyed considerable freedom of action, in others they have been almost completely dominated by
the national governments. In some republics unions have, on occasion, used the political parties, in others the unions have always
been the vehicles of the parties. Professor Alexander shows that

he recognizes the very great importance of individuality in the labor movement by devoting twelve chapters of his volume to the labor movement in separate countries. Two additional chapters are concerned with the labor movement in Central America and in the nonrepublican areas of the Caribbean, and a final one is concerned with international trade unionism, an important but notably underdeveloped feature of the Latin American labor movement.

The author, Professor Robert Alexander, of the Department of Economics, Rutgers University, needs no introduction to Latin Americanists. For more than two decades now books, articles and reviews have flowed from his pen. He is not only well aware of but sympathetic to the problems of Latin America and he states quite frankly in this volume that he is friendly to labor. As he also notes, that friendship dates back to a time when one could hardly find an article in English on the labor movement in Latin America. There is still a serious dearth of Latin American labor literature in English or for that matter in Spanish or Portuguese. It is with that consideration in mind, plus the knowledge that this is a solid book which covers "all the bases," that I take pleasure in seeing it appear as the second volume in *Studies in Contemporary Latin America*.

JOHN J. JOHNSON

Department of History,
Stanford University,
Stanford, California.

Preface

FOR A QUARTER OF A CENTURY I HAVE BEEN STUDYING THE LABOR movements of Latin America. When I began my researches in this field there was virtually nothing in print in English about this subject. Even today, the only works of significance are Marjorie Clark's study of the Mexican labor movement written in the early 1930's, the small book by Moises Poblete Troncoso and Ben Burnett, "The Rise of the Latin American Labor Movement," and my own study of "Labor Relations in Argentina, Brazil, and Chile." I hope that the present volume will help to arouse further interest in the subject, which is worthy of a great deal more attention than it has hitherto generated.

The lack of interest in Latin American organized labor is only one aspect of the failure of North Americans generally to concern themselves with the problems of the twenty republics to the south. Only when something like the anti-Yankee Castro Revolution of Cuba occurs do the citizens of this country suddenly become interested in Latin America. And then, most of the things which are written or said about Latin America are mistaken or strongly biased, one way or the other.

Frankly, I am sympathetic to Latin American organized labor. Its rise is part of the revolution which is occurring throughout the area. This revolution is seeking to transform the countries of the region from semifeudal, semicolonial nations into full participants in the twentieth century. The labor movement exists because Latin America is participating in the industrial revolution that started in Great Britain two centuries ago. The organized workers are seeking full participation in the economic, political, and social life of their respective countries.

Naturally, I owe many debts of gratitude in connection with this volume. Thousands of Latin Americans have submitted themselves over the years to my persistent questioning. Some of them have become good friends. In addition, numerous North Americans who have had more or less close contact with Latin American organized workers have given me the advantage of their knowledge and opinions about the labor movement of the Latin American countries. I particularly would thank in this connection Serafino Romualdi, for long the Latin American representative of the American Federation of Labor and later of the AFL-CIO, and now director of the American Institute for Free Labor Development. I also owe a special debt to Osmond Dyce, secretary-general of the Caribbean Congress of Labor, who provided me with much up-to-date information on labor groups in and near the West Indies.

I should also thank Professor John J. Johnson of Stanford University, the editor of the series of which this volume is destined to be a part, for inviting me to put my thoughts on Latin American labor together. My appreciation must also be expressed to Mrs. John Carman, who has typed part of the manuscript.

Of course, as most authors, I owe a particular debt to my wife. She, Joan Alexander, and my children, Tony and Meg, have put up with many hours which must have been tedious for them, while I wrote and rewrote this book.

ROBERT J. ALEXANDER

Rutgers University
New Brunswick, N. J.
May 1965

Contents

ORGANIZED LABOR
IN LATIN AMERICA

ONE

Economic and Social Background of Organized Labor

ORGANIZED LABOR IS AN INTEGRAL PART OF THE CONTEMPORARY LATIN American scene. The observer who first begins to study the twenty republics of the area is quickly struck by the prevalence of the trade unions and the ubiquitousness of social and labor legislation in countries where the Industrial Revolution is just commencing.

The early advent of the labor movement in Latin America is due to several factors. In the first place, its presence is explained by the fact that it is an expression of the fundamental social, economic, and political revolution through which the whole area is passing. In the second place, it owes its origins in part at least to the influence of individuals and ideas originating outside of Latin America itself.

THE LATIN AMERICAN REVOLUTION

The forces which are transforming the economy, the society, and the political life of Latin America had their origins in the last decades of the nineteenth century. At that time, a new economy and society began to develop alongside the traditional regimen in the area.

The traditional society was divided sharply into two disparate groups. On top was a small aristocracy, heirs of the Conquest of America by the Spaniards and Portuguese, whose power and influence was rooted in their ownership of the land. These people were principally of European descent, spoke Spanish or Portuguese, and were more or less good Catholic Christians. They had a monopoly of the money income of the national economies, and the educational system existed to train the children of the aristocracy to succeed their fathers as the rulers of Latin American society.

At the other extreme was the great majority of the population, who lived on and worked the land without owning it. They were principally of Indian or Negro ancestry, were largely pagan in religion, and were illiterate. They had little or no participation in the civic life of their respective nations.

There were few middle groups in this traditional society. In the cities and towns there were small groups of merchants, professional men, and artisans, but their political power was small, when it existed at all. They had little sense of separate identity, but were associated more or less closely with the upper- or lower-class groups.

By the last quarter of the nineteenth century this system began to be undermined. The industrializing countries of Europe and North America found that they lacked essential raw materials and foodstuffs. They sought these products outside of their own frontiers. One of the areas in which they looked for them was Latin America, with its extensive agricultural and mineral resources.

European and North American investors soon began to open up mining enterprises and plantations. They also began to finance the construction of railroads to get the products of these mineral and agricultural firms to the ports. They even helped to finance the modernization of port facilities, as well as the public utilities in the growing cities. Finally, they began to develop modern commercial and banking enterprises which could facilitate both the movement of the minerals and agricultural products being exported from Latin America and the importation of the manufactured goods being brought back in payment.

As a consequence of these developments, new classes began to appear upon the scene. One of these consisted of middle-class groups, associated with the new industrial and commercial activities. The other was a wage-earning working class, employed in mines, on plantations and railroads and in public utilities, commercial firms, and the rapidly expanding government services.

The traditional society had had few wage or salary earners, since the great majority of the lower classes were self-supporting tenant or sharecropping peasants. With the growth of a wage-and-salary working class, Latin America had achieved the first prerequisite for an organized labor movement.

These developments brought in their train another phase in the economic development of Latin America, the beginnings of industrialization. The growth of cities and the expansion of those elements in the economy earning a money income expanded the market for handicraft industries, even before World War I greatly expanded the range of manufacturing.

During that conflict, the countries from which the Latin Americans had become accustomed to buying most of their manufactured goods were unable to continue to provide these products; as a result, the Latin American countries were faced with the alternative of going without or producing these goods themselves.

Thus, industrialization, the development of factory industry, received its first major impetus from the First World War. During the succeeding decade, however, many of the industries which had been set up between 1914 and 1918 did badly as a result of renewed competition from the more efficient and more highly organized producers of Western Europe and the United States.

By the advent of the Great Depression, the larger Latin American nations had some light-manufacturing industry. The Depression speeded up the development of these branches of factory production, and also served to convince most Latin Americans in public life of the need for government protection of industry. The Second World War deepened this conviction, saw the foundation of heavy industry in the major countries, and convinced many people of the need for an integrated system of manufacturing.

This development of the industrial sector of the economies of Latin America greatly expanded the urbanized manual and white-collar working class. The stage was thus set for the development of an organized labor movement of significance.

IMPACT OF NATIONALISM

Another aspect of the revolutionary change which has been under way in Latin America during the last three or four generations has been the rise of nationalism. This is undoubtedly the major ideology in Latin America today.

In part, the development of nationalism in Latin America is the reflection of the spread of the idea of loyalty to the nation-state from its original seedbed in Europe to the rest of the world. However, in part, too, the development of nationalism as a popular ideology common to people in all ranks of society is a result of the economic and social changes which we have already noticed.

In the traditional Latin American society, nationalism really had little field for development. The upper classes of this society were more internationalist than nationalist—tending to look abroad to the more highly developed countries for their fashions in ideas and culture as well as in raiment. They felt much more at home with members of their own social class in France or Spain or Italy than they did with their own peons or urban workers.

At the same time, the masses of the people still had a parochial outlook. Their loyalties were to their local tribe or linguistic group, or even to the local plantation owner, rather than to any institution of wider scope. In many cases, they were not even aware of living in a particular nation.

It was not until the rise of the middle groups, both of the strictly middle classes and of the wage-earning workers, that popular nationalism could really take root. These middle groups were cut off to a very large degree from the institutions of the traditional society not being accepted by the upper classes and themselves rejecting association with the lowest groups in the society. They were ripe for attachment to some new concept or institution such as the nation-state, to which they could give their passionate loyalty.

The rise of nationalism played a peculiar role in the development of the organized labor movement. Many of the owners of the railroads, plantations, mines, and factories in which the trade unions first appeared were foreigners. As a result the labor movement was placed in the position of opposing not only the employer but the foreigner as well. Thus, the organized workers often found a much wider degree of sympathy and support among the general population than would have been the case if their opponents had been native business interests.

IMPACT OF OTHER IDEAS

However, nationalism was not the only set of ideas which had its effect on the development of the labor movement in Latin America. From the early days of independence in these countries, the ideas of the French and American revolutions had had their impression on the thinking of literate groups there. These notions were absorbed by the early labor organizations, before World War I, and one finds, for instance, articles written by people using the pseudonyms of "Robespierre," "Danton," and Marat," as well as quotations from Thomas Jefferson and Abraham Lincoln in the early trade-union periodicals.

Furthermore, the immigrants who came to most of the Latin American countries during the last decades of the nineteenth century and the early years of the twentieth played an important role in propagating ideas which were then predominant among workers in the European nations from which they came. Thus the basic idea of trade unionism as well as the related philosophies of anarchism, syndicalism, Marxian socialism, and somewhat later Bolshevism were introduced widely among the nascent working classes of Latin America.

Even as early as the middle decades of the nineteenth century the ideas of the European Utopian Socialists gained certain following in some of the Latin American countries. The names of Francisco Bilbao in Chile and Esteban Echeverría in Argentina are associated with this stream of thought.

Somewhat later, in the 1860's, 1870's, and 1880's important groups of Europeans, some of them refugees from the persecutions that followed the fall of the Paris Commune and from the antisocialist laws of Bismarck, began to popularize the Bakuninist and Marxist ideas which found currency in the First International.

Local groups affiliated with this International were established in Argentina, Uruguay, Brazil, Mexico, and some of the other countries of the area.

In a somewhat different way, anarchosyndicalist ideas were reinforced in Mexico. Starting in the last years of the nineteenth century sizable groups of Mexican workers began to go to the United States in search of work. They tended to concentrate particularly in those unskilled trades in which the Industrial Workers of the World (IWW) centered much of its organizing activity. Some of the Mexican migrants belonged to the IWW, and returned home with its ideas firmly rooted in their consciousness. Once the revolution began in Mexico in 1910, some of these people became leaders of the new labor movement there.

There was also propagation of ideas from one Latin American country to another. Thus the influence of the Socialist and anarchosyndicalist movements of Argentina and Chile found echoes among the workers of Bolivia, Peru, and Paraguay. Likewise, Mexico became a center from which somewhat similar notions were spread to Central America.

THE LABOR MOVEMENT: A PART OF THE LATIN AMERICAN REVOLUTION

Thus from the very beginning, organized labor in Latin America was part of the movement for basic economic, social, and political change in the area. From its inception it was impregnated by ideas of revolution. Furthermore, its very existence was a harbinger of as well as a motivating force for change. It represented a new force on the social scene, and it was inevitable that its members would strive to increase both their civic participation and their share of all the national income of these nations.

The labor movement in Latin America has not only been interested in so-called "bread and butter" issues. It has sought to obtain extensive social and labor legislation to protect its members and their organizations. In fact, it has gone beyond this: it has attempted to bring about a basic change in the structure of the Latin American societies. Thus, it has sought to bring about

agrarian reform, to transfer the land from the traditional aristocracy to those who work it, and thereby to destroy the basis of
power of the oligarchy as well as create potential markets for the
industries in which the trade unionists were employed. It has
supported industrialization so as to gain more jobs for its members and to make possible increases in their level of living.

In pursuance of these broader objectives, the organized labor
movement of Latin America has generally been associated with
political parties and with governments which were pledged to
fundamental alteration of the economic and social *status quo*. We
shall note elsewhere the diversity of political groups which have
been active in the organized labor movement, and some of the
effects of such activity upon the trade unions.

ECONOMIC PROBLEMS OF
LATIN AMERICAN LABOR

The existence of an organized labor movement at an early
stage in the economic development of the Latin American countries has meant that the trade unions there have been faced with
certain very characteristic problems. Two of these are worthy of
particular mention: the tendency toward long-term inflation,
and the issue of employer paternalism.

In a number of the Latin American countries economic development has been accompanied by a high degree of inflation. Furthermore, the rapid rise of prices has continued over several decades in Brazil, Chile, Argentina, and several other nations. The
positions of the workers and of the labor movements have inevitably been effected by this phenomenon.

Long-continuing inflation has meant that the workers have
been faced with a constant battle to maintain their real wages
and levels of living. It has often meant that the trade unions have
been forced to concentrate their efforts on obtaining periodically
very large wage increases, and have given less attention to winning the kinds of fringe benefits which have been of concern to
the labor movement of the United States.

The race between the increase in prices and the ability of the workers to raise their wages has in effect been a struggle over the division of the benefits arising from the process of economic development. Workers who have come from relatively unproductive employment in agriculture to work in manufacturing or other modern forms of urban jobs find that their productivity increases tremendously. However, inflation to a very large degree deprives them of the increased real income which they might otherwise receive from this increased productivity, and thus transfers this income to their employers and other elements in the economy. To the degree that the unions are able to keep wage increases ahead of inflation, the workers are able to share in the benefits resulting from their new kind of employment.

However, labor-management relations in Latin America concern themselves also with other problems arising from the development process. The unions play a very important role in bringing about a change in the psychology of the new industrial worker, which is very necessary if he is to become a full-fledged member of the modern sector of the economy of the Latin American nations.

In the traditional society there was very little social or economic mobility. The chance of an agricultural tenant or farm worker ever becoming a landowner was remote in the extreme. He was born into the lower class of the society and took it largely for granted that it was his lot to live out his life and die in that class.

On the other hand, in the more dynamic society brought into existence by economic development and industrialization, there exists a great deal more mobility. It is possible for a worker to move upward economically and in the social scale. Nevertheless, the worker is often only dimly aware of this fact at first.

The unions play an essential role in acquainting the worker with the social mobility which is available to him. Indeed, sometimes it is almost too successful in this regard, since once awakened to the possibility of changing his status, he becomes anxious to move much faster than the economic situation or his own abilities will permit. Hence, one often finds in Latin American labor relations that the unions make really excessive demands which are impossible for the employers to meet, and they do so not as a bargaining device but in real expectation that they will be able to get these demands fulfilled. Particularly in the early phases of the trade-union movement, this is one partial explanation for the bitterness and violence which often has accompanied strikes and other labor protests.

The employers are not unaware of these problems. Nor are they unaware of another aspect of the environment of the new urban worker recently arrived from the countryside: the fact that as an agricultural tenant or sharecropper, the worker was all but unacquainted with a money income. His income was in kind, and he either grew or made in his home most of the goods necessary to fill his very limited needs.

Once in the city and employed in the modern sector of the economy, the worker finds that he is receiving his income in money. At first the amount he receives appears to be very large, and he tends to spend it foolishly. Even when he becomes aware that his wages really are not ample, he finds it hard to accustom himself to the fact that all his needs must be purchased out of this income.

Hence, employers have frequently found it in their own interests in Latin America to provide a part of the workers' real wages in kind. They may provide the worker through company stores or subsidized cooperatives most of his basic foodstuffs at very low prices. They have provided medical assistance, schooling for the worker or his children, as well as many other sorts of benefits in kind.

Latin American unions have generally had a different attitude toward this employer paternalism than have those in the United States. In Latin America, organized labor has favored paternalism, whereas in the United States it opposed it. In part this is because Latin American paternalism has arisen from the problem of adapting the very backward agricultural laborer to life in an industrial society, rather than from wide use as a union-breaking device. As a result, the unions have tended to regard any sort of augmentation of the workers real wage by payments in kind to be a "conquest" by the worker, and something to be not only maintained but extended.

Summary and Conclusion

Organized labor arrived on the scene early in the process of Latin American economic development. This was due largely to industrialization's relatively late birth in the area, that is, at a time when trade unionism was already well established in some other parts of the world.

Organized labor in Latin America has had an essential revolutionary role. It has been part of the movement for basic economic, social, and political change, and has represented a group which was seeking a larger role in the general life of the community. As a result, it has generally tended to have interests considerably beyond the mere bread-and-butter issues of wages, hours, and working conditions.

Finally, since it arrived relatively early on the scene, organized labor has been presented in Latin America with particular problems. These have included that of a rapid and long-continuing inflation, and of the role which the unions have been called upon to play in helping to transform a backward agricultural tenant or laborer into a modern industrial worker.

Politicalization of Latin American Organized Labor

FROM ITS INCEPTION, ORGANIZED LABOR IN LATIN AMERICA HAS BEEN highly political. Virtually all important trade-union groups of the area have been closely associated with one or another political party or with the government. Frequently, particular labor movements have owed their origin largely to the efforts of a political party or group or of the national government.

Of course, labor movements throughout the world have tended to concern themselves with politics. For example, even the much touted apoliticism of the United States trade unions was rather, in effect, more of a different approach to carrying out political action than a refusal to function in the political field. On the other hand, the distinctive aspect of the relationship of the Latin American labor movements to politics has been that the trade unions of the area have more often than not been dominated by a political party or a government to a greater degree than has been true in some other parts of the world. The labor movement has tended *to be used* by the politicians rather than itself being able basically to use them to serve its own interests.

Organized labor in other parts of the world has sometimes had the same experience as that which has been common in Latin America. In the early deacdes of the United States labor movement there were violent struggles for control of it among various political groups. The same could be said of many if not most of the European labor movements. Subordination of the trade unions to a political party or government has also frequently been a characteristic of the newer nations of Asia and Africa.

13

CAUSES OF POLITICALIZATION OF LABOR

There are many factors which help to explain this phenomenon. In several countries it was due to the influence of politically inclined immigrants in the establishment of the labor movement. Frequently, it was the level of economic development of the various Latin American countries at the time trade unionism began that contributed to politicalization. Likewise, the political circumstances of the individual nations during the formative period of organized labor have been of key importance. The structure of the labor movement in the area has undoubtedly been a contributing cause. Finally, the tradition of strong political bias in the unions has tended to feed upon itself and to be perpetuated.

The labor movements of Argentina, Uruguay, Brazil, and Cuba owed their origin largely to immigrant workers coming from Spain, Italy, Portugal, Germany, and other European countries. Many of these workers had been affiliated both with trade unions and with radical political groups in their native countries, and they tried to establish similar kinds of organizations in the lands to which they had moved. Thus they brought with them to these American countries the various political currents which were prevalent in the European labor movement during the decades preceding World War I. Anarchosyndicalism tended to be the dominant labor philosophy in this period, with Marxian socialism its main competitor. From Argentina, Uruguay, Brazil, and Cuba—and in the unique case of Mexico, from the United States—these ideas tended to spread to other Latin American countries.

The Americanization of the working class of the ABC countries of South America and of Cuba in the interwar period tended to have an important impact on the political loyalties and ideas of the unions. The American-born sons of the immigrants, and the increasing numbers of workers from the interior of the various American countries, to a growing degree came to constitute the urban working class in this period. They either tended to be eager to throw off the "foreign" ideas of the immigrants, or were totally unacquainted with these ideas. Their growing importance thus paved the way for the rise of more indigenous political groups to domination of organized labor. A somewhat similar development was simultaneously taking place in those countries which had never experienced mass immigration.

The low level of economic development of the Latin American countries contributed to the politicalization of their labor movements, and also tended to influence both the *type* of political group which dominated the labor movement in its early years, and the subsequent changes in political control. Organized labor arrived on the scene relatively early, when industrialization was still in its incipient stages—when a large part of the urban working class still consisted of handicraft workers or artisans.

Anarchosyndicalism was a particularly appropriate philosophy for this kind of worker, for he tended to be an individualist, and the extreme individualism of the anarchists was therefore attractive to him. This was at least one of the factors strengthening this political group in the early years of the Latin American labor movement.

Another important aspect of the low level of economic development was the consequent low level of wages which still characterizes most of that area. Together with the fact that Latin Americans in general are not accustomed to paying dues to the organizations to which they belong, low wage levels resulted in the early unions having very small incomes. It was thus very difficult for the labor organizations to obtain the financial resources necessary for adequately carrying on their activities.

The labor organizations had to look elsewhere for the economic resources they needed. A few turned to the employers, but these cases are relatively scarce in Latin America. Much more frequently, the unions sought financial aid from friendly politicians and parties or from friendly governments.

Subsidies are not the only way in which political activity aids the financial situation of the unions. Not infrequently, labor leaders are successful candidates of their respective parties for deputy, senator, or other public office. In these posts they receive salaries, which permit them to spend most of their time on union business. Likewise, they frequently pay part of their salary as public officials into the treasury of their unions.

The state of Latin American economic development, also, helped to contribute to the politicalization of the labor movement. Industry was developing at first in only a handful of cities and towns in each country. Significantly, in addition, there were only relatively few firms in a given industry—with, sometimes, a single enterprise having a monopoly of the production of a given commodity in the early phases of industrialization.

As a result, labor organization, too, tended to be concentrated in just a few places. At first, local unions were formed in individual factories or among workers belonging to a particular trade or craft in a single urban area. The next step in organization was usually the formation of central labor bodies on a city-wide basis in those localities in which the unions existed. National industrial or craft unions tended to come as a later phase in the history of organized labor in these countries. The first national labor confederations tended to be formed by the city central bodies rather than by the national industrial or craft unions.

City-wide labor federations, consisting of unions of workers of different industries and crafts, lent themselves more to political activity than might some other form of organization. Such federations were not particularly well equipped to help their individual affiliates, whose problems varied considerably, to negotiate and enforce collective agreements; nevertheless, these federations could and would serve as a vehicle for achieving unity among their member organizations on a wide range of political issues that were common to all working-class groups. Such political activity in a local community, particularly if it were the capital city, inevitably led to similar participation in politics on a national level, and consequent reliance on leaders and parties which were friendly to organized labor.

Political circumstances at the time of the labor movement's onset also contributed to the politicalization of the trade unions, inasmuch as the leaders and parties which were coming into the political arena were, for one reason or another, depending on the organized workers for support.

Undoubtedly in some cases, political leaders who aided the labor movement did so from opportunistic motives. They realized that the urban workers were an element in the population, which was growing in size and importance; and that when organized into unions the workers were likely to have a degree of discipline and unity which many other parts of the body politic liked. They were therefore worth cultivating, and it seemed worthwhile to give some financial help to their organizations.

Other politicians became interested for other reasons in organized labor. They became impressed with the degree of poverty and oppression which many of the early urban wage earners suffered. They understood that the high degree of militancy which characterized the early labor organizations was often motivated by an equally high degree of resentment upon the part of the workers. Such politicians might well desire to help the workers by sponsoring legislation on their behalf and by aiding their organizations.

Some of the newer parties which appeared on the scene, particularly after World War I, had still other reasons for helping to support—and at the same time to control—the labor movement. These parties were ideologically committed to the cause of organized labor. They sought to bring about the reorganization of the society, economy and political life of their respective countries, and they believed that the organized workers should play an integral part in bringing about this transformation.

Political instability, which is so prevalent in many of the Latin American countries, has likewise contributed to the politicalization of the unions. The workers' organizations realize the necessity of having in power in the nation a government that will provide conditions which will permit them to develop freely, will not regard strikes as subversive by definition, and won't more or less automatically side with the employer in any labor dispute.

Finally, the tradition of politicalization of labor has tended to be self-perpetuating. Political parties and individual political

leaders who have benefited from their control over all or part of
organized labor will not easily give up such control. Furthermore,
the workers' loyalty to such parties and leaders is not easily destroyed, and unless the politicians clearly betray the interests of
the organized workers, the union members are not likely to see
any incompatability between their political and trade-union loyalties.

THE POLITICAL GROUPS ACTIVE IN ORGANIZED LABOR

We have already noted that the first political element to have
a preponderant position in Latin American organized labor consisted of the anarchosyndicalists. Although they claimed to be
"apolitical," they functioned within the labor movement in much
the same way that avowed political parties did then and later.
They sought in several countries to commit the trade unions to
their own political philosophy, which they frequently referred to
as "anarchist communism."

The anarchosyndicalists were believers in "direct action." By
this they meant that the wages, hours, and working conditions of
the workers should be determined unilaterally by them. The unions should present their demands to the employers on a "take it
or leave it" basis. If the demands were agreed to, all was fine; if
they were not, the unions would strike immediately. They usually
refused to have unions under their control sign collective agreements, since they regarded these as limiting the freedom of action
of the workers, and union leaders who would sign such agreements were regarded as betraying the interests of their followers.

The anarchosyndicalist influence in the labor movement
reached its apogee in the years before the First World War. The
growth of factory industry during World War I helped to undermine their positon. The larger groups of workers in the factories,
and the more impersonal nature of labor relations in these enterprises made collective bargaining more necessary than when small
handicraft shops predominated. There was need both for contracts between workers and employers which would establish the

general rules by which their relations would be governed, and for regular grievance procedure to enforce these rules. Hence, political elements which were willing to accept collective bargaining as the basis for trade-union action tended to gain ground on the anarchosyndicalists, who remained committed to "direct action" and continued to regard collective agreements as "class collaboration" and "betrayal" of the workers.

After World War I three kinds of parties were particularly active in the labor movements of Latin America. These were the Socialists, the Communists, and the national revolutionary parties. During the same period, government leaders who were not affiliated with any of these types of political groups also frequently sought to influence or get control of the organized labor movements of their respective countries.

The Socialists were of most significance in southern South America, that is, in Argentina, Uruguay, and Chile. In the first of these countries, they became the single most important element in the labor movement in the early 1920's and were dominant during the decade or more preceding the advent of the Perón regime in 1943. In Uruguay, the Socialists offered more or less important competition to the anarchosyndicalists and Communists in the labor movement throughout the 1920's and 1930's. In Chile, the Socialist party joined the Communist International in 1922, and it was not until 1933 that another one was formed. Between 1933 and 1945, however, this new Socialist party dominated the country's trade unions.

These Socialist parties, and less important ones in Cuba, Peru, Ecuador were generally of the Second International variety, roughly comparable to the British Labor party or the French Socialist party in their ideological orientation. Although they were very active in the labor movements of their respective countries, they professed to believe that the trade unions should have a wide degree of independence not only of employers and governments but also of political parties.

After the Second World War, the Socialist parties declined in importance as a factor in the Latin American labor movements. In Argentina they lost control of the unions with the rise of Juan

Domingo Perón, and after the fall of Perón the Socialists split
into several factions. In Uruguay, too, the Socialists lost most of
their influence in organized labor, and in the 1960's their party
split into two groups. Finally, in Chile the Socialists split several
times during the 1940's and 1950's, and even when they reunited
in a single party in 1957, they were little more than second-class
partners of the Communists in the labor movement.

The Communists were an important element in the labor
movements of Latin America from the time they were organized
in the various Latin American countries. By the late 1950's there
were Communist parties in every one of the twenty Latin American republics, as well as in several of the English-speaking areas of
the Caribbean.

The influence of the Communists in the labor movements of
Latin America has varied greatly from time to time and from
country to country. They reached their apogee during and immediately after the Second World War, when they controlled or
greatly influenced most of the important national trade-union organizations. At that time, too, they controlled the Confederación
de Trabajadores de America Latina, which was until 1948 the
only existing hemispheric labor confederation.

Subsequent to the Second World War, the Communists' influence in the Latin American labor movements declined rapidly.
By the late 1950's the trade-union organizations under their control were only minorities in most of the countries. Only in Chile
and Ecuador were groups dominated by the Communists clearly
the majority elements in the labor movement.

The advent of the Castro regime in 1959, and its turn in a
Communist direction, at first promised to give considerable help
to the Communists in the Latin American labor movement. For
one thing, it restored control of the Confederación de Trabajadores de Cuba to them. For a while the Cuban labor confederation's proposal to form a new "revolutionary" hemispheric labor
group seemed likely to enlist considerable support among noncommunist trade-union organizations; so in 1962, the founding
congress of this new confederation was supposed to be held in
Santiago, Chile, but there was such a disappointingly small rep-

resentation of noncommunist groups at the meeting place that it was decided to hold a further meeting to found the proposed Central Unica de Trabajadores de America Latina. A similar meeting in Belo Horizonte and Brasilia, Brazil, early in 1964 had similar results.

The third major political element in the Latin American labor movements is the group of national revolutionary parties. These include the Aprista party of Peru; the Acción Democrática party in Venezuela; the Liberación Nacional party of Costa Rica; the Popular Democratic party of Puerto Rico; the Movimiento Nacionalista Revolucionario (MNR) of Bolivia; the Partido Revolucionario Dominicano; and the Partido Febrerista of Paraguay. The government party of Mexico, the Partido Revolucionario Institucional is in somewhat the same category.

These are parties which do not belong to any international political movement, such as the Socialist or Communist Internationals. Instead, however, they recognize a kinship among themselves and work together in the hemispheric labor movement. They are parties that have grown up from the particular circumstances of their respective countries, but they share a broadly similar program of support for changing class and race relationships, strengthening the identity and independence of their nations, bringing about rapid economic development, and establishing a firm basis for political democracy.

Virtually from their inception, the national revolutionary parties have had extensive influence in the labor movements of their nations. Thus, the Aprista party controlled the trade unions of Peru in all of the periods in which the party was legal after its foundation in 1930. The Acción Democrática party was the largest element in Venezuelan organized labor after 1944; Liberación Nacional had the backing of most workers of Costa Rica from its foundation in the early 1950's; the MNR grew in influence in Bolivian organized labor during the 1940's, and dominated the unions more or less completely after it gained power in the revolution of 1952.

The Popular Democratic party of Puerto Rico had the support of the overwhelming majority of the organized workers of the island from the establishment of the party in 1937. The Febrerista party has been illegal during most of its career, and it is impossible to measure exactly its influence among the workers of Paraguay, although it is certainly one of the most important elements in organized labor.

The relationship of the Mexican organized workers to the Partido Revolucionario Institucional has been very special. Most of the country's central labor organizations and independent national unions have been directly affiliated with this party since the late 1930's. In some parts of the country, organized labor has been the backbone of the official party.

Since World War II a new political element has gained some influence in Latin American organized labor. This is the Christian Democratic parties. With one or two exceptions these are parties organized since the war, and there are now such organizations in Argentina, Uruguay, Brazil, Venezuela, Peru, Bolivia, Chile, and Paraguay in South America; and in Panamá, Nicaragua, El Salvador, and Guatemala in Central America, and in the Dominican Republic. There also exist Christian Democratic parties among Haitian and Cuban exiles.

Although in most cases, the Christian Democrats have not achieved major influence in the labor movement, such is not the case in Chile and Venezuela. In the former country, the Federación Gremial de Chile, the arm of the Christian Democratic party in the unions, constituted by the early 1960's the strongest single element in the nation's principal central labor body, the Central Unica de Trabajadores de Chile. Although the Communist-Socialist coalition in the CUTCh still controlled a majority of the organization, the Christian Democrats had more than 35 per cent of the delegates to its 1962 congress.

In Venezuela, the growth of the Christian Democrats, organized in the Copei party, was slow in the labor movement. However, during the administration of President Romulo Betancourt (1959-1964), in which the Copei shared governmental responsibility with the president's Acción Democrática party, the Copeyanos for the first time gained extensive influence in organized labor, coming to constitute the second most important political group there.

Apart from these ideological political movements, two individual leaders were able during the 1940's to develop wide support among the organized workers of their respective countries. Their influence persisted two decades later.

These two men were Getulio Vargas of Brazil and Juan Domingo Perón in Argentina. Both were able from positions of power in the government to do enough things for the workers to gain the support of a majority of them and to control the organized labor movement. Both Vargas and Perón organized their supporters into political parties, the Partido Trabalhista in the former case and the Partido Peronista in the latter. In the early 1960's these parties still controlled the largest part of the Brazilian and Argentine labor movements, respectively.

POSSIBLE TRENDS AWAY FROM
POLITICALIZATION

Whether the tendency of the Latin American labor movements to be dominated by political parties and governments continues or is mitigated in the next few decades depends very much upon the political future of these countries. If totalitarian groups such as the Communists and Jacobin Leftists win the struggle for power, the future of the labor movements in the Latin American nations will be the same as it has been in other countries which have fallen under Communist control. They will be converted into nothing more than arms of the government to spy upon the workers and to get them to produce more, as has happened in Castro's Cuba.

On the other hand, if the political instability which has so long characterized most Latin American countries continues, it is all but certain that the labor movements in those nations will continue to be highly political. They will continue to have to associate themselves with those parties and those politicians who are willing to allow the labor movement to function with a relatively wide degree of freedom.

To the degree, however, that the revolutionary changes which are being so widely sought in Latin America come through the democratic process, and that economic progress and political democracy are more or less firmly established, the labor movements are likely to become less concerned with politics. Organized labor will not be so pressed to look for political protection, and economic factors will lessen concern with politics.

As industrialization expands and industries become nation-wide instead of being concentrated in one or two cities, national industrial unions will supersede city central bodies as the typical base of the organized labor movement. In several countries such a transformaton has already taken place.

As national industrial unions become dominant, they will tend to spend an increasingly large part of their time and energies on negotiating collective agreements. The national organizations will also be called upon to provide an increasing range of service to their local affiliates to make sure that the collective contracts are enforced through well-established grievance procedures.

There have been indications during the last couple decades that such trends toward less concern with politics have begun. The Mexican and Argentine national unions have devoted increasingly amounts of time to economic matters. Such was also the case in Cuba before Batista's *coup d'état* of 1952. However, political developments in those countries have hitherto prevented the full development of these tendencies.

Summary and Conclusion

Organized labor in Latin America has been peculiarly prone to political influence and control throughout its history. Few unions are completely free from the control of some party or government. This situation has been caused as much by the political turbulence which has characterized the area during recent decades as by the relatively low state of economic development and the poverty of the workers.

It is by no means clear what the political future of the labor movements will be. This depends both on the rapidity of the economic development of these countries and the future of democracy in the region.

THREE

Collective Bargaining and Its Substitutes

AS IN MOST NONTOTALITARIAN COUNTRIES IN OTHER PARTS OF THE world, organized labor in Latin America has had as one of its basic roles participation in establishing the conditions under which its members would be employed. However, the level of economic development, and the political conditions in the various countries of the area have both tended to influence the way in which the trade unions carried out this task.

Collective bargaining has played an important part in the unions' efforts to determine wages, hours, and working conditions. It has had, though, peculiar characteristics in Latin America. Yet, in some countries its scope has been relatively limited and in most of the countries it has been supplemented by other institutions and procedures.

During the period when anarchosyndicalist elements dominated the Latin American labor movements, the unions often refused to engage in collective bargaining in a real sense. They regarded any agreements signed with an employer to be "class collaboration," since these involved commitments by the union to the employer as well as vice versa. Thus, anarchosyndicalist unions would frequently confine their role to one of confronting the employer with a list of demands which, if he didn't accept them immediately and in full, would be followed quickly by a strike.

Gradually, as power in the labor movement passed from the anarchosyndicalists to other political groups, the idea of real collective bargaining—in which there was negotiation between the two parties toward achieving an agreement to which both could give their consent, and to which they would both generally conform—became more general. Most unions in Latin America today engage in such bargaining with their members' employers.

THE SCOPE OF COLLECTIVE AGREEMENTS

There is great variation in Latin America between different countries insofar as the size and kind of bargaining units which negotiate contracts are concerned. Generally, the extent of economic development, the political history of a country and the national labor law tend to determine such differences. In some cases, however, one finds such variation within a particular country.

In Argentina, the Perón experience transformed the nation's collective bargaining pattern. Whereas before 1943 most negotiation was between individual firms and the unions of their workers, or between regional groupings of employers and the appropriate labor groups, the Perón regime favored the negotiation of nationwide industrial contracts between organizations of employers and the national unions of their workers. By the end of the Perón government in September 1955, the vast majority of workers were covered by such contracts. All attempts substantially to modify this pattern since 1955 have failed. In pre-Castro Cuba the collective bargaining system was generally similar to that of Argentina.

The Chilean situation is in sharp contrast to that in Argentina. There, the law makes it almost inevitable that negotiation should be on the basis of individual firms and local unions. National unions are not provided for in the law, except in a few cases. One of these is the Confederation of Copper Workers, which was given special authorization in a decree-law enacted early in 1956. Nevertheless, even in the copper case, negotiaton by the Confederation is on the basis of the individual companies which operate the country's three largest mines. Only on the railroads and in the maritime industry is there anything approaching industry-wide collective bargaining.

Mexico has still another pattern of collective contract negotiation. There are several national collective agreements of major importance, including those in the petroleum, electric, and railroad industries. In addition, there are many regional and individual-firm contracts. Collective bargaining in most Latin American nations tends to have the diversity of this Mexican pattern.

The kinds of problems dealt with in collective agreements also vary greatly from one Latin American country to the other. As we have noted earlier, in some countries there tends to be a high degree of concentration on the wage problem, because of the tendency of the price level to increase rapidly. Chile is a prime example of such a situation. Collective agreements in that country are largely confined to discussions of increases in basic wage levels and supplementary monetary payments to the workers. There is little or no discussion of such questions as seniority, layoffs, hiring policies, grievance procedures, and similar questions.

In Mexico and Argentina the situation is vastly different from that in Chile. Particularly in the national collective agreements, which are widespread in those two nations and which tend to be quite voluminous, there is ample discussion of virtually all aspects of labor-management relations with which a union negotiator in the United States might be familiar. There are strict seniority rules for layoffs and promotions, there are the equivalent of United States social welfare funds, there are provisions dealing with job classifications. Grievance procedures are outlined in some detail.

In a number of other countries there are individual industries which are covered by contracts as complex as those which are widespread in Mexico and Argentina. A prime example of such an agreement is that between the oil industry of Venezuela and the Federation of Petroleum Workers.

The nature and scope of the collective bargaining agreement depends on various factors, in addition to the existence or absence of severe inflation. One of the most important of these is the ability of the labor organizations to employ the talents of technicians of various kinds to advise them in their negotiation with the employers.

If the unions are going to attempt to deal in labor-management discussions with complicated technical problems of their respective industries, they need the services of economists, industrial engineers, statisticians and other people with specialized knowledge. Of course, their ability to employ such individuals depends upon the financial resources of the unions. It also is determined in part by the relative importance the union leaders attribute to collective negotiation as opposed to political activity and other functions of their organizations. Finally, it depends upon whether or not a nation's labor legislation permits unions to employ outside talent.

Undoubtedly, the labor movements of Argentina, Mexico, Venezuela, and perhaps a few other countries are definitely in a financial and legal position which permits them to employ the kind of technical help which is needed in complicated collective bargaining dealing with technical problems. Definitely, the larger unions in these countries do make use of such personnel, at least during the periods in which collective agreements are being negotiated.

THE ROLE OF LABOR LAW

In most Latin American countries labor legislation limits the scope of collective negotiation to a greater degree than is the case in the United States and most Western European countries. This is because the law covers a much wider range of issues than in the older industrialized nations, thus taking these issues out of the scope of collective negotiation.

Most of the countries have labor codes. These have taken their place alongside the other major divisions into which, in conformity with the traditions of Roman Law, legislation of these nations has been codified. They thus have the same standing as commercial law, criminal law, civil law, and administrative law.

One major field in which legislation sometimes limits the scope of collective negotiation is that of wages. Most of the nations have minimum-wage legislation, and frequently the minimum wages established by the State are in fact maximum wages for a sizable proportion of the nation's wage and salary earners. Thus wage increases for this element of the working population in fact come through government decree. When this does occur, however, it frequently gives rise to negotiation concerning the wage levels of those workers who receive more than the minimum.

Various kinds of fringe benefits that might otherwise be the subject of collective bargaining are sometimes taken out of this field by legislation. For example, when the author was studying labor relations in Chile in 1947 many unions were seeking and obtaining what they called "seven days' pay for six days' work," while employers were seeking to use concession of this extra day's pay as a means of assuring a better attendance record by their workers by tying it to perfect attendance during the six working days. The issue was settled several years later when the Chilean government of President Gabriel González Videla by enacting the "seven days' pay for six days' work" into law, removed it from the bargaining table.

Various other matters that might otherwise be negotiated between management and the unions are dealt with in law in some of the Latin American countries. These include payment for overtime and late shifts, housing to be provided by employers of certain types for their employees, union security, and other questions. Not infrequently, however, the relevant laws merely establish minimum concessions which the employers are supposed to give their workers; so the unions seek, and often obtain, more extensive benefits of the same kind as those provided by legislation.

GRIEVANCE PROCEDURE

In any country the procedure established for workers to present complaints concerning their individual treatment by the employer is as important as the contract that establishes the general conditions under which the workers are to be employed. Generally, the establishment of such machinery is a matter of decision between the employers and the workers; however, as we shall note further on, the governments of the area undertake to deal with certain types of grievances, and in a few countries with most of them.

Argentina has one of the most complete systems of grievance procedure established in collective bargaining agreements. There, shop stewards act on the first stage in the grievance machinery. It is their duty to take up problems with the lower ranks of management. If they cannot be resolved there, the next step is a general factory grievance committee, negotiating with higher management on the local level. The third step is an appeal to an industry-wide parity committee in the Ministry of Labor, consisting of both union and management representatives. Beyond this committee, the only appeal is to government labor courts, which are empowered to use both the law and the collective agreements as a basis for passing judgment.

In most other countries grievances are presented on a rather more *ad hoc* basis than is the case in Argentina. The problem is not usually dealt with in collective agreements; instead, employers and union leaders work out informal procedures for the presentation of individual workers' complaints. Elected local-union officials may be permitted to present grievances to management whenever they arise; or there may be provision for regular meetings between management and union leaders on a weekly or on another periodical basis.

The ultimate step used in grievance procedure in the United States is never used in the Latin American countries, so far as we have been able to determine. We know of no instance in which private impartial arbitrators, completely divorced from direct interest in the conflict at issue, are used as a final court of appeal for individual workers' grievances.

LABOR COURTS

We have noted that labor courts are the last step in grievance procedure in Argentina. This is likewise the case in Mexico; and although such tribunals do exist in most of Latin America, they do not have this role.

In most cases the labor courts can deal only with questions of law, and not with collective agreements. Furthermore, they usually only handle individual cases, and do not intervene in collective negotiations. The role of the unions insofar as the courts are concerned is usually confined to providing their members with adequate legal counsel.

In some instances, though, the unions do have another role in connection with the judiciary: In those countries which provide legislation for representation on the labor courts of the organized workers and the organized employers, the unions have the task of selecting those who are to represent the workers on these tribunals.

In the majority of cases, however, the labor courts consist of professional judges, and the tribunals are regarded as regular parts of the judicial system. Nevertheless, their rules of procedure and their general atmosphere is usually a great deal more informal than is the case with other kinds of tribunals.

In most of the Latin American countries the principal task of the labor courts is the interpretation and application of legislation in the field of labor-management relations and social security. As we have noted, however, in a few countries the labor tribunals also have the task of deciding problems arising under collective bargaining agreements.

THE BRAZILIAN AND CUBAN ALTERNATIVES TO COLLECTIVE BARGAINING

The history of the Latin American labor movement has amply demonstrated that in those countries in which dictatorships exist, the trade unions are either greatly weakened or totally abolished. As a counterpart to this, the process of collective bargaining is either greatly curtailed or is replaced by some other process of settling such labor-management problems as are admitted to exist.

Although most of the Latin American countries have suffered periods of such suppression of trade unionism and undermining of collective bargaining, two cases are particularly worth comment. One took place in Brazil during and after the Vargas dictatorship of 1937-1945, and the other is in Cuba under the Communist regime of Fidel Castro.

During the late 1930's and early 1940's, President Getulio Vargas established what he called "The New State" ("Estado Novo"), patterned after the fascist regimes of Italy and Portugal. The essential element in this system was a complete regimentation of the labor movement and the abolition of collective bargaining. (Elsewhere we discuss the effects of the New State on the unions, but it is worthwhile at this point to note the system which Vargas substituted for collective bargaining during these years.)

Although collective contracts were not formally outlawed, there were virtually none negotiated during the New State period. In their place was established a system of labor courts which both determined wages, hours, and working conditions through so-called "dissidios colectivos" (collective decisions) and heard and settled all individual workers' grievances.

When a union wished to obtain an increase in wages or an improvement in working conditions for its members, it formally presented a request to the appropriate Regional Labor Court, consisting of both professional judges and representatives of the organized employers and the unions. The decisions of these courts were binding on both parties and all strikes and lockouts were outlawed. There was no room in this system for direct negotiations between workers and employers.

Grievances were also handled by the labor courts. When a worker had a complaint against his employer, he brought it before a local Conciliation and Arbitration Board, likewise consisting of a professional judge, a representative of the employers, and a nominee of the unions. The decision of the Board was binding; the only recourse from it being an appeal to the appropriate Regional Labor Court, and such an appeal could only be taken on points of law, not on issues of justice or equity.

As a result of the establishment of the New State there was no collective bargaining in Brazil between the end of 1937 and the first months of 1945. With the relaxation of the dictatorship early in 1945, however, *ad hoc* collective bargaining was revived and there was a wave of strikes which lasted for approximately two years.

In recent years collective bargaining has become the standard method both for establishing general conditions of employment and for handling grievances in the principal industrial centers of Brazil, such as São Paulo, Rio de Janeiro, and Pôrto Alegre. However, the New State labor-management framework has never been formally dismantled, and in those cities where the labor movement remains relatively weak, appeal to the labor courts continues to be the principal means of resolving labor-management disputes. Even in the large industrial cities such recourse is used by those workers who do not have strong or militant unions.

The Castro regime in Cuba, like all Communist governments, has converted the trade-union movement from the defender of the rights and interests of its members into an arm of the regime. As early as June 1960 all wages were frozen by government decree, and all unions were forbidden to demand any further increases. In August 1962 the government established a maximum wage, which resulted in the decline of the income of large groups of workers.

As it took the determination of labor conditions out of the hands of the trade unions, the Castro regime also outlawed the right to strike. In place of their traditional task of seeking improvements in working conditions for their members, the labor organizations were given by the government the task of organizing campaigns of "Socialist competition" among different workers' groups, for the purpose of raising output and productivity.

There is some indication that the Castro regime foresees the complete abolition of the trade unions, and hence the disappearance of any possibility of collective bargaining, even in a disguised form. Minister of Industry Ernesto Guevara announced in February 1962 that "the trade unions must disappear" and that "in the future there will be no labor unions."

Summary and Conclusion

The development of a trade-union movement has brought with it collective bargaining as the means for settling labor-management disputes in most of the Latin American countries; however, in various ways the collective bargaining process differs in Latin America from the way it operates in the United States. Furthermore, to a considerable degree its role has been limited by labor legislation.

The strength of collective bargaining tends to depend to a large degree upon the existence or lack of political democracy. Where dictatorships dominate a country, collective negotiation is weak or nonexistent. In such cases, some other method of settling disputes, under strict governmental control, is substituted for the free negotiation between the parties concerned.

FOUR

Argentine Organized Labor

THE LABOR MOVEMENT OF ARGENTINA IS ONE OF THE OLDEST AND strongest in all of Latin America. In some ways, it is a prototype of organized labor throughout the hemisphere, having passed through all of the phases that have characterized the trade unionism of Latin America.

The earliest trade union in Argentina was probably the Printing Trades Workers' Union of Buenos Aires, founded in 1853. It was originally established as a mutual-benefit society, (a kind of cooperative to provide sick and death benefits) but within a decade was functioning as a real trade union, calling strikes and negotiating with the employers. In a somewhat different form, it continues to exist today.

Yet, in spite of these early beginnings, it was not until the 1880's that a labor movement on a significant scale began to develop in Argentina. By that time, the country was receiving tens of thousands of immigrants each year, from Italy, Spain, Germany, and Eastern Europe. Many of the newly arrived workers brought with them experience with the new labor movements and radical political parties of their native countries. In Argentina they sought to establish similar organizations.

It was during the 1880's that most of the oldest unions of present-day Argentina were established. These included the shipbuilding craftsmen, hotel and restaurant employees, and some of the building-trades workers' unions.

Most of these early organizations were under anarchosyndicalist control; however, one group of workers was unionized under very different auspices. In the year 1885 one of the United States

35

railroad brotherhoods (no one now knows which one, precisely) sent a delegation to South America to help organize their counterparts in these countries. As a result of this delegation's efforts, a union of locomotive engineers, firemen, and washers, known as La Fraternidad (the brotherhood) was established. It was at its inception apolitical, and like the United States railroad unions charged high dues and paid its members benefits when they were sick or unemployed.

Many of these new unions were united in the nation's first central labor organization, the Federación Obrera de la República Argentina (FORA), established as the result of a meeting held on the occasion of the first celebration of May Day in Buenos Aires in 1890. The FORA was launched by a group of Socialist workers, most of them immigrants, and during the decade after its establishment it led a fitful existence. Several times it lapsed into inaction and had to be revived; however, by 1901 the FORA was firmly established as a permanent organization.

Period of Anarchosyndicalist Domination

Two years later, in 1903 the Federación Obrera de la República Argentina was captured by the anarchosyndicalists. In 1905 they changed the name of the organization to Federación Obrera Regional Argentina, reflecting their internationalism, their repudiation of patriotism, and their refusal to recognize anything so *bourgeois* as a republic. They also amended the constitution of the organization to proclaim its ultimate objective to be the attainment of "anarchist communism."

From 1901 until 1910 the labor movement of Argentina was dominated by the anarchosyndicalists. Meanwhile, however, their opponents, the Socialists, established a minority organization called the Unión General de Trabajadores. There were several attempts to reunite the two organizations, one of which, in 1909, resulted in the transformation of the UGT into the Confederación Obrera Regional Argentina (CORA). It soon came under the control of syndicàlists, who copied their organization after the Confédération Générale du Travail of France.

These were the heroic days of the Argentine labor movement.

The anarchosyndicalists believed in "direct action" rather than collective bargaining. This sometimes involved sabotage and very frequently resulted in solidarity strikes and general walkouts.

Both employers and the government looked upon trade unionism as subversive. They did all they could to destroy the labor movement. One of the most potent measures in this direction was a law passed in 1902 which empowered the government to deport any alien whom it felt was a "menace to the security of the state." Hundreds and perhaps thousands of foreign workers were deported during the nearly sixty years that this law remained on the statute books. Native Argentine labor leaders were frequently jailed, and deported to a kind of concentration camp in the Patagonia region of the far south.

The anarchosyndicalists frequently replied in kind to violence used against them. At least one police chief was assassinated by them. Strike breakers and rank-and-file policemen sometimes shared the same fate. Some anarchists preached a veritable cult of violence.

The anarchosyndicalist unions had one other unique characteristic. They did not believe in the employment of full-time union officials. It was held that any worker who lived from the dues contributed by his fellows was betraying them and exploiting them; therefore, throughout its career, the anarchosyndicalist FORA has never had full-time paid leaders.

The anarchosyndicalist domination of the Argentine labor movement ended in May 1910. That was the hundredth anniversary of the independence of the republic, and it was punctuated when the antipatriotic anarchosyndicalists of the FORA announced that they would do their utmost to sabotage the extensive preparations which the government had made to celebrate that event.

About a week before the culmination of the independence celebration, which was scheduled for May 25, mobs of young hoodlums swarmed into the streets of Buenos Aires. They attacked and burned the headquarters of the FORA, the CORA, the Socialist party, as well as the printing plants of the anarchist daily paper *La Protesta* and the Socialist paper *La Vanguardia*.

These hoodlums enjoyed the support of the government, which stepped in to outlaw the FORA. Its leaders were persecuted, many of them were jailed, and some of their non-Argentine leaders were deported. For almost two years the FORA existed only as an underground organization, and as a result lost much ground to its rival, the Confederación Obrera Regional Argentina, which suffered less from the violence of the government.

Attempts To Unify Labor Movement

When the FORA returned to an open existence in 1912, the majority of the organized workers were in the ranks of the CORA. This group took advantage of its position of strength to seek once again the reunification of the national labor movement. This was finally achieved in 1914 at a congress, at which the two groups were merged under the name Federación Obrera Regional Argentina.

However, this new-found unity did not persist for more than a year. In the Ninth Congress of the FORA, held in 1915, the Socialist and syndicalist elements sought successfully to remove from the constitution of the organization its pledge of support for the attainment of anarchist communism. However, this revision was not accepted by the anarchosyndicalists. As a result, they withdrew once again from the united group and re-established their own FORA. For the following seven years the Socialist-Syndicalist FORA came to be known as the FORA of the Ninth Congress, the other one the FORA of the Fifth Congress (the meeting in which the original pledge to anarchist communism was adopted).

In the meantime, the First World War had greatly stimulated the growth of the labor movement. The war also encouraged the development of manufacturing, and at the same time gave rise to considerable inflation. Hence, not only were the employers more of a mind to grant wage increases and other concessions to the workers, but the unions were under considerable pressure from their members to ask for them.

The period was marked by many important strikes. The most significant of these was the 1917 walkout of the railroad workers. It was the first such movement on the part of the non-locomotive employees, who had by this time formed the Federación Ferroviaria.

Another important walkout, which occurred right after the end of the war, took place among packing-house workers in Greater Buenos Aires and near the city of La Plata. Previously, the employers had violently opposed any organization by their workers, but when President Hipólito Irigoyen intervened in this walkout on behalf of the unions, the employers agreed to negotiate. Nevertheless, the strike was finally lost when anarchosyndicalist union leaders rejected completely the intervention of "the State," in the person of President Irigoyen, in the dispute. More than two more decades were to elapse before the packing-house workers were finally unionized.

The end of the First World War brought a decline in the pace of the country's economic development and industrialization. The unions found that they had a much harder time to exact concessions from employers. Furthermore, during the 1920's the labor movement was even more seriously divided than had been the case in previous decades.

For example, another attempt was made in 1922 to merge the two FORAs. However, it failed, as had previous efforts. Nevertheless, as a result of this move the FORA of the Ninth Congress was converted into the Unión Sindical Argentina. The USA was weaker than its predecessor had been, since the two railroad workers unions, La Fraternidad and Federación Ferroviaria, now reorganized as Unión Ferroviaria, refused to affiliate with it.

Four years later, the two railroad organizations took the lead in organizing yet another central labor body, the Confederación Obrera Argentina. It affiliated with the International Federation of Trade Unions, and sought to organize a Latin American Labor Confederation—an effort which failed.

The CGT

In 1929 still another central labor group was established. This was the Comité de Unidad Sindical, which was organized by the Communists. They had formerly worked within the Unión Sindical Argentina, but in 1928 the Communist International adopted the policy of dual unionism: the ordering of each of its member parties to establish separate central labor groups under its own control. The Comité de Unidad Sindical was the Argentine Communists' response to this command.

Yet, the desire for unification of the labor movement persisted. In 1929 the Federación Argentina de Trabajadores de la Imprenta, the national printing trades union, took the lead in fostering negotiations to this end. The leaders of the Unión Sindical Argentina, the Confederación Obrera Argentina, and several independent unions participated in these negotiations. They finally gave rise to the establishment in September 1930 of a new organization, the Confederación General del Trabajo.

Because two weeks before this unity move was completed the armed forces and Conservative party politicians had overthrown the second administration of President Hipólito Irigoyen, and had set up a military dictatorship, the CGT was established by merger of the pre-existing groups without the formality of a congress. In this unification, the principal leaders of the USA were given the main posts in the new CGT, with the leaders of other groups having a somewhat subordinate position.

The old USA leaders were syndicalists, who in principle were opposed to the labor movement's having any close association with a political party. Their partners in the Confederación General del Trabajo were mainly Socialists. The Socialist leaders increasingly pressed the CGT officials to summon the organization's first congress, but each time the proposal was made, the syndicalist leaders suggested reasons why it was not yet propitious to do so.

Finally, in 1935 the Socialist leaders took the initiative. They met and declared that the leaders of the CGT were deposed, organized their own executive committee, and proclaimed themselves to be the true CGT. Rather than fighting this, the syndicalists reorganized the old USA. From then until the advent of Perón, the CGT under Socialist leadership continued to be the country's largest central labor group. Its principal unions were the two railroad-workers' organizations and the General Confederation of Commercial Employees, and it also had affiliated unions of textile workers, municipal employees, shoemakers, trolley-car operators, construction workers, and metallurgical workers. In 1936 the Communists liquidated their Comité de Unidad Sindical and affiliated its unions with the CGT.

The Unión Sindical Argentina continued to be an important minority labor group. Its principal strength was to be found among the maritime workers and telephone employees, although it also had a number of smaller unions associated with it.

Meanwhile, the anarchosyndicalists continued to maintain the FORA. It was very small but militant, and suffered considerable persecution at the hands of successive governments, unlike the other two groups. Its most important unions were the Federation of Ship Builders, the Union of Hotel and Restaurant Workers, and the plumbers' and taxi-drivers' unions of Buenos Aires.

Conditions Leading to Rise of Perón

Until the revolution in 1943 the governments of Argentina paid relatively little attention to the organized labor movement, or to the needs of the workers. Although the extremely hostile attitude of the pre-World War I period no longer prevailed, the governments of the 1920's and 1930's did little or nothing to encourage the labor movement and passed little labor legislation. The railroad workers were the only group of importance able to get the establishment of an extensive social security system; indeed, other aspects of labor legislation lagged far behind that which had become characteristic of the other major Latin American countries by the end of the 1930's.

During these decades there was a change in the nature of the labor movement. The larger unions tended to become bureaucratized and the participation of rank-and-file members became less intensive. Membership in these unions tended to become increasingly a condition for working rather than a privilege.

There was also a change in the nature of the working class itself. The industrialization of the country was much stimulated by the Great Depression. At the same time, immigration from Europe virtually ceased. As a result, the new workers to man the nation's industries were drawn largely from migrants from the interior of the country, and from the ranks of the sons of immigrants.

As a result of this change in the nature of the working class, the ideas which heretofore had dominated the Argentine labor movement lost much of their appeal. The immigrants' sons were anxious to prove to themselves and to others that they were real Argentines. They tended to reject much that was associated with the "foreignness" of their parents, including their loyalties to anarchosyndicalism, syndicalism, socialism, and even communism. The migrants from the interior in many cases had never heard of these ideas.

The Argentine working class, therefore, was increasingly ready to accept a radical leadership that was not associated in their minds with "foreign" ideas. The home training of the sons of immigrants left its residue of allegiance to radicalism, and the natural discontents of the migrants from the interior, arising from their feeling of strangeness in the cities, made them potentially receptive to a radical message couched in specifically Argentine terms.

Peron's Capture of Labor Movement

This change in the Argentine workers was one of the keys to the success of Juan D. Perón after June 4, 1943. His rise to power began as a result of a military *coup d'état* which took place on that day. This revolt had nothing to do with social issues, but was motivated by the fear of the pro-German Argentine army leaders that President Ramón S. Castillo was planning to install a pro-British landowner as his successor in elections scheduled for the end of the year.

However, the leaders of the military regime installed on June 4, 1943, soon found that their regime was unpopular among virtually every civilian group in the country. Some of the younger officers in the group sought to enlist civilian backing. After some fruitless efforts to gain the support of the industrialists, they turned towards the labor movement.

The union leaders were receptive to the overtures of the

young military men, headed by Perón, because of the neglect of labor problems by previous regimes. Although in the beginning they did not promise to support the military regime, they did agree to applaud any pro-labor measures which the government undertook.

Perón's campaign for labor support for the military regime, and within it, for himself, began with his being named Secretary of Labor and Social Welfare in November 1943. He kept this post for almost two years. During this period, he threw his weight, and that of the regime, behind the growth of those segments of the labor movement which were willing to cooperate with him. As a result, the trade unions grew with exceeding rapidity, expanding three or four times over within a couple years.

Perón also brought strong pressure upon employers to grant wage increases and other concessions to the unions. Increasingly, he insisted that important collective agreements be signed in the Secretariat of Labor, with Perón present, and with photographs being taken of the occasion, in which Perón figured prominently.

At the same time, Perón enacted by decree a considerable body of labor and social legislation. Various laws to protect the workers on the job, to increase vacations, grant compulsory periods of rest during the work week were put on the statute books. Most groups of Argentine workers were brought into the social security system.

All these measures served to win for Perón the backing of the majority of the workers of the country. However, those union leaders who refused to cooperate with Perón, accusing him of demagoguery, were dealt with in a ruthless manner: They were jailed, put in a concentration camp in the extreme southern part of the country, were forced to flee into exile or to go into hiding.

To strengthen his control over the unions, Perón enacted a so-called Law of Professional Associations in October 1945. This provided for the first time for legal recognition of trade unions. Ostensibly, the government was supposed to recognize the union in any particular field which had the largest number of workers. In practice, however, Perón tended to extend recognition only to unions which were favorable to him. And only unions which had legal standing were allowed to engage in collective bargaining. As a result, several important old-time unions were destroyed and Peronista unions were established in their stead.

The full extent of working-class support for Perón did not become clear until October 1945. Moreover, although the CGT had declared its backing for the military regime as early as May Day 1944, it was not at all clear for many months thereafter that this action represented the feelings of the majority of CGT members.

On October 9, 1945, Perón was overthrown by a group of officers who were opposed to his growing influence in the military regime. In the week that followed, the head of the revolt, General Avalos, was unable to convince the political parties to form a new government. They demanded as their price for doing so the ousting of President Edelmiro Farrel, and the transfer of the government to the Supreme Court, a very conservative body. Avalos refused.

Within a few days, Perón's labor supporters began to mobilize in his support. They started to "march" on Buenos Aires by bus, truck, and any other means of transport. Mobs of Perón's backers virtually seized control of the city's streets. Although the military could probably have suppressed the Peronistas, they could only have done so at the cost of considerable bloodshed, and they were unwilling to do so at this price.

At a result, General Avalos surrendered to the Peronistas. Colonel Perón was brought back from the Martín García Island prison to which he had been relegated, and on the evening of October 16 triumphantly appeared on the balcony of the presidential palace alongside of President Farrel, and shouted to his massed supporters in the Plaza de Mayo below "I am back!"

With Perón's return to power, a presidential-election campaign began. Perón's candidacy was backed by a new Partido Laborista, established by most of the leaders of the Confederación General del Trabajo. The president of the new party was Luis Gay, head of the Telephone Workers' Federation, and its vice-president was Cipriano Reyes, principal leader of the Packinghouse Workers' Federation, which had been organized largely due to Perón's support.

Two other smaller groups were also organized to back Perón. One was a group of dissident minor leaders of the Radical party, the other a so-called Independent party. All the traditional parties were united, however, in opposition to Perón's candidacy. The Radicals, Socialists, Progressive Democrats, and Communists formed the Democratic Union, which was also backed by the Conservatives.

Perón won the election of February 24, 1946. Although he received only about 54 per cent of the popular vote, his followers won almost two-thirds of the seats in the Chamber of Deputies and all but two seats in the Senate. The Peronistas never allowed the two opposition senators to take their posts.

Labor Under Perón

Perón presided over the government from the day he was inaugurated on June 4, 1946, until he was overthrown on September 16, 1955. During this period, he reduced the labor movement to a status of complete subservience to his government, while picturing himself all the while as the workers savior and sole patron and protector.

During the first six years of Perón's government, labor affairs were principally the province of his wife, Eva Duarte de Perón. She established her headquarters in the Secretariat of Labor, intervened actively in all important collective bargaining negotiations, and held court one afternoon a week for labor people who wanted to bring problems to her attention.

During the first years of the Perón regime, Evita thoroughly purged the labor movement. Virtually all of the leaders who had originally supported Perón, who had organized the Partido Laborista, and who bore much of the responsibility for his election as president were ousted from the leadership of their unions by Perón's wife. Some were jailed, others went into exile, some merely retired into anonymity.

Evita Perón chose the leaders of the individual unions and of the CGT itself. By this time, the CGT had become virtually the only central labor organization in the country. The USA was dissolved, and its member unions joined the CGT. The FORA was driven underground.

The structure of the labor movement was reorganized. All national unions were centralized, and the negotiation of collective bargaining agreements was done almost solely on a national basis. The national unions themselves were completely subordinated to the CGT, which assumed the right to intervene in its affiliates, to remove their leaders, and to replace them with individuals under its control. The CGT even went so far as to oust the leadership of the Packinghouse Workers' Federation in 1951, even though the federation did not belong to the CGT.

The only free elections that continued in the labor movement were those for shop stewards. These elections provided a kind of escape valve for discontent by rank-and-file union members. If, however, shop stewards became too loud in their criticisms, they were removed by higher officials.

The nature of the CGT and its affiliates under Perón was made clear by a new preamble adopted for the constitution of the confederation. It proclaimed that the fundamental purpose of the CGT was to support Perón and to carry out his policies. The CGT insisted that all of its national affiliates adopt similar amendments to their constitutions.

Working-class enthusiasm for Perón had begun to pale by the time he was overthrown. During the preceding half-dozen years the country had experienced an increasing degree of inflation, while Perón had discouraged wage increases sufficient to keep up with the rise in prices. As a result, real wages fell after 1949, and had probably reached about the 1943 level by the time Perón was ousted. In addition, sizable groups of workers had been alienated by the dictatorial methods of the Perón regime.

Furthermore, the corruption and arbitrariness of many of the more important Peronista trade-union leaders had aroused considerable discontent among the workers. Some of the older organized-labor groups, such as the railroad workers and printing tradesmen, likewise resented the intensified regimentation of the workers and the labor organizations.

As a result of all of these factors, there was virtually no trade-union effort to save Perón when the military revolt against his regime began in September 1955. The workers remained more or less passive bystanders during the drama of the overthrow of the dictatorship.

Labor Under the Lonardi Government

The government which immediately succeeded that of Perón, headed by General Eduardo Lonardi, proclaimed the slogan "No victors and no vanquished." This principle was largely applied by the regime insofar as the labor movement was concerned. Although the man who was secretary-general of the CGT at the time of Perón's overthrow. Hugo De Pietri, was forced to resign, the new regime permitted two other Peronistas to assume the leadership of the confederation.

The policy of the Lonardi regime was to allow the workers themselves to carry out the needed purge in the labor movement. General Lonardi and his Minister of Labor Luis Cerutti Costa felt that the disillusionment in Perón and in the more corrupt Peronista labor leaders was sufficiently widespread that, if given a chance to do so, the workers would remove the more undesirable type of Peronista leaders from office in most of the unions.

Therefore, the Lonardi regime did not "intervene" in the CGT or its constituent unions—leaving in charge in most cases the same leaders who had been there when Perón fell. However, the government did call elections to be held in all the unions in the country within 120 days of the date of the decree, and took steps to see to it that these elections would be honest. It seems highly likely that if these elections had been held, the labor movement would have acquired generally new leadership, some of it Peronista and some anti-Peronista.

The development of the general political situation, however, made such a policy as that proposed by Lonardi and Cerutti Costa impossible: A new crisis developed in the government early in November, as the result of which General Lonardi was removed in a palace *coup* and his place was taken by General Pedro Eugenio Aramburu. Admiral Isaac Rojas continued in the post of vice-president, which he had held under Lonardi.

The Peronista leaders of the CGT responded to this *coup*

against Lonardi with an energy which they had lacked at the time of the fall of their own leader. They declared a revolutionary general strike against Aramburu's regime. As a result, the new government was forced to take very stringent measures against the labor leaders. From the nature of these measures and of the men who carried them out came most of the problems of the labor movement in subsequent years.

Labor Under Aramburu

In the face of the CGT-led attempt to overthrow it, the Aramburu regime "intervened" the CGT and all of its national and local unions. Elected officials were removed and "interventors" were placed in charge to run the unions until further notice. A naval officer, Captain Laplacette, as placed in charge of the CGT; and army, navy, and airforce officers were put in charge of most of the constitutuent parts of the confederation.

Although the intervention in the CGT was undoubtedly a political necessity at the time it occurred, and although the generals and admirals in charge of the regime didn't know where to turn except within their own ranks to find people to take over the labor organizations, the long-continued control of organized labor by military officers went far to restore the prestige and popularity of Perón and the Peronistas among the workers. If the military interventors had been succeeded in the unions within the matter of a few days or at most a few weeks by people selected from the ranks of the unions themselves, pending the holding of nationwide union elections, much of this drift back to Perón might have been avoided.

Another fatal error of the Aramburu government in the labor field was the nature of the Ministry of Labor during its incumbency. President Aramburu named as his Minister of Labor a well-known expert on international labor law, who had worked for many years with the International Labor Organization, Dr. Raúl Migone. Unfortunately, he was totally unsuited for the job. What he knew about international labor law he made up for by massive ignorance of the current state of Argentine labor affairs. From the workers' point of view, his incumbency in the Ministry was an unmitigated disaster.

Dr. Migone started out with the totally untenable thesis that it was necessary to "depoliticalize" the Argentine labor movement. This was a pipedream of the rashest sort, under the circumstances. The question at that time was not whether the labor movement was to remain politically oriented or become apolitical —it was certainly going to remain politically oriented. The issue was what its political color was going to be.

As a result of his basic orientation, Dr. Migone refused to work with the anti-Peronista elements in the labor movement. The old Socialists, syndicalists, and early Peronistas who had turned against Perón during his term of office were the only people who, if they had been put temporarily in charge of the labor movement, might have been able to win the masses of the workers away from allegiance to Perón. The proof of this lies in that in the few cases in which such people did act as interventors—the Municipal Workers, La Fraternidad, and the Printing Trades' Federation—the unions remained out of Peronista hands. Most of the others reverted to Peronista control, once the workers were again free to pick their own leaders.

The upshot of this situation was that most Argentine workers felt themselves suddenly abandoned. They no longer had real labor organizations which would support them, they no longer had the backing of the Ministry of Labor, which was largely staffed by Migone (at least in its upper echelons) with the bright young men of the labor relations departments of the country's largest firms. The workers came to feel that to a very large degree the so-called Liberating Revolution of September 1955 had been as much directed against them as it had been against Perón.

All subsequent measures of the Aramburu regime were fruitless in changing this feeling on the part of the workers. In spite of the fact that the military regime established a general minimum wage for the first time, and extended the benefits of labor legislation to groups such as domestic servants which had not previously been covered by it, the sentiment of the workers became increasingly Peronista, the longer the Aramburu regime lasted.

On February 1, 1956, the Aramburu government provided that within 120 days all unions should elect negotiating committees to bargain with employer representatives on new collective agreements, since all labor contracts had expired on that day. It also provided that in the months following the negotiation of these contracts, general elections should be held in the unions. This program was carried out, although in fact the collective bargaining negotiations were in most cases failures, and the government had to step in and decide the conditions of new contracts by compulsory arbitration.

Finally, in September 1957 a convention which was supposed to re-establish the CGT on a normal basis met. This convention broke up, however, in a deadlock, with two opposing groups emerging. One of these, consisting at first of sixty-two unions, was of Peronista persuasion. The other, made up of thirty-two organizations, was anti-Peronista. Subsequently, a third group, drawing away some from each of the others and consisting of nineteen groups, was established under predominantly Communist leadership.

Faced with this failure of the labor leaders to agree among themselves, the Aramburu regime, as one of its last acts, in April 1958, named a committee of anti-Peronista labor leaders to provisionally run the CGT and to call a new congress of the organization; however, soon after taking office, President Arturo Frondizi intervened the CGT once again, and kept it under government control until late in 1961.

Labor and the Frondizi Government

The Frondizi administration was faced with many labor crises, as it was faced with constant threats of rebellion in the military. In part, these labor difficulties were the result of the fact that President Frondizi, who had been elected with the backing of the Peronistas and Communists as well as that of his own party (the Unión Cívica Radical Intransigente), had abandoned the rather demagogic program on which he was elected. Instead, beginning at the end of 1958, the president followed a program of economic stabilization and austerity, which bore down with particular stringency upon the workers. In part, however, his difficulties with labor were politically inspired by both Peronistas and Communists.

The first major crisis occurred in October 1958, with the outbreak of a general strike in the oil fields, which was in part at least politically inspired, in opposition to his decision to allow the entry of foreign firms into the oil industry once again. For the first time, President Frondizi bore down very hard on the strikers, arresting many of their leaders and effectively breaking the strike.

From that time on, Frondizi followed a policy of divide and rule insofar as the labor movement was concerned. He would first make a move to favor the Peronistas, then one to favor the anti-Peronistas, then one to favor the small Communist element, then would repeat the whole process. The labor leaders never knew just where the regime stood, and in the end all factions tended to be hostile to the regime.

One of Frondizi's basic problems with regard to the labor movement was that his party, the Unión Civica Radical Intransigente, was exceedingly weak in the labor movement. There were very few members of the UCRI who hold important posts in the union hierarchy. All factions represented in the union leadership —the Peronistas, the anti-Peronista combination of Socialists, syndicalists, and ex-Peronistas, ànd the Communists—were actually or potentially hostile to the regime. One of the president's fears, therefore, was the possibility of an alliance of all of them against him, which, taken together with the uncertain nature of his support in the armed forces, might have been enough to topple his regime at any time.

Eventually, however, late in 1961, President Frondizi finally did allow the reorganization of the CGT under real labor leadership. A group of leaders representing ten Peronista-controlled unions, and ten anti-Peronista ones (excluding the Communists altogether) was given formal control of the CGT, and the government intervenor was removed. The two groups represented in the CGT agreed that neither would take advantage of any accidental majority at any meeting of the new executive committee to seize full control of the organization. Although the Peronistas undoubtedly continued to have a rank-and-file majority, this agreement was lived up to.

Recent Trends

The labor movement was again a passive bystander at the time of the overthrow of President Frondizi in March 1962. Although he made last minute efforts to rally their support for his regime, the union leaders remained unmoved and did nothing to try and save him from the military coalition which finally overthrew his administration.

During the sixteen months following the overthrow of Frondizi the country was in the grip of economic and political chaos. Prices, which had been brought near to stability in the last year or so of Frondizi's administration, sky-rocketed and the value of the peso on international exchanges plummeted. Economic-development programs of the Frondizi administration came to a virtual halt.

Meanwhile, rival military groups jockeyed for power. During the months following Frondizi's ouster, there were two occasions in which troops of rival groups actually clashed, and hardly a week passed without ultimatums or other moves by one or another faction against the puppet regime of President José Maria Guido. During all of these events, the organized labor movement played little or no active role.

The only significant labor event during this period was the convening of the first post-Perón congress of the CGT, which met in January 1963. Although there was a great deal of jockeying among the three political elements represented in the Confederación in the weeks before the congress, and some fear that the congress itself would break up in disorder, nothing of the sort occurred. The sessions were relatively peaceful, and a new executive committee on which both Peronistas and anti-Peronistas were represented was elected. Again, the Communists were frozen out of the top leadership of the organization, although unions controlled by them participated in the congress and belonged to the CGT.

Thus by the time President Arturo Illía took over in October 1963 as the result of elections held three months earlier, the labor movement continued to be split among three rival and contending elements. The two larger groups, the Peronistas and anti-Peronistas, continued to work together, in somewhat uneasy partnership. The Peronistas remained by all odds the largest political group in the labor movement; nevertheless until that time the Peronista leaders had shown a willingness to compromise with their rivals for the purpose of maintaining the unity of organized labor.

During the first year of the Illía administration, the Peronista labor leaders in the CGT launched what they called the "plan of struggle," designed to force the Illía government to grant sizable wage increases and other demands. The administration rejected the labor demands, fearing that they would ruin its efforts to halt inflation.

The plan of struggle brought new fissures in the labor movement. The anti-Peronistas in the CGT leadership opposed it, and some of the unions under their control flatly refused to participate. At the same time, the extremists among the Peronistas sought to establish rival unions to some of those under anti-Peronista leadership. They were most successful in this among the municipal workers, where a new national confederation, in opposition to that headed by Socialist Francisco Pérez Leirós, was established. When the CGT leadership refused to condemn this dual union group, Pérez Leirós resigned as a member of the Executive Committee of the Confederación General del Trabajo in the middle of 1964.

Meanwhile, the collective bargaining system, as it had been modified by the Perón experience, continued to be the pattern in Argentine labor relations. The Argentine unions continued to be large in membership—perhaps covering some 2½ to 3 million members—and organized labor continued to be one of the country's most potent political forces.

FIVE

Organized Labor in Uruguay and Paraguay

THE LABOR MOVEMENTS OF URUGUAY AND PARAGUAY, THE SMALLEST countries of the Río de la Plata basin, have been decisively molded by the recent economic and political history of their respective nations. Although organized labor in both these republics was in its earliest years greatly influenced by events in Argentina, this has been less the case in recent decades.

THE EARLY LABOR MOVEMENT IN URUGUAY

The first evidences of a labor movement are to be found in Uruguay as early as the 1870's. Largely as the result of the migration there of European Marxists and anarchists, the artisans of Montevideo and one or two other towns began to establish trade unions.

The first such organization of which there is evidence was the Sociedad Tipográfica, established in Montevideo in 1870. Eight years later the first attempt to set up a national labor federation was made with the establishment of the Federación Obrera Regional de la República Oriental del Uruguay. Its existence was of very short duration, however.

As immigration increased in the 1880's, so did the attempts to organize the workers. There were various strikes during the 1880's and early 1890's. By 1895 unions were reported to exist among bricklayers, carpenters, blacksmiths, mechanics, painters, marble cutters, shoemakers, printers, port workers, tobacco workers, sailors, seamstresses, vehicle builders, and watchmakers.

54

With the inauguration of José Batlle y Ordoñez as president of Uruguay in 1903, the labor movement first enjoyed sympathy from the government. As a result, it prospered considerably during the Batlle administration. In 1905 two national union federations were established. One of these was the Federación Obrera Regional Uruguaya, led by anarchosyndicalists and copying its name from a similar group, the FORA of Argentina. The second was the Unión General de Trabajadores, established under Socialist influence, and using the same name as the Socialist-controlled labor group across the Río de la Plata.

During this period, the anarchosyndicalists were the predominant group in the ranks of Uruguayan organized labor. They believed in "direct action," and led many strikes. They published a number of newspapers and within the pages of these, there raged discussions and controversies over issues of concern to the nascent organized-labor movement. One of the most interesting of these polemics centered around the question of whether or not the unions should have full-time paid officials. Those opposed to the idea seem to have had the better of the argument.

With the succession of Claudio Williman to the presidency in 1907, the labor movement met resistance from the government, and entered a period of decline. Most of the organized workers groups therefore welcomed the return of José Batlle to the presidency in the election of 1911.

During the second administration of Batlle (1911-1915), the labor movement was very militant. Strikes took place in the capital among bakers, shoemakers, teamsters, streetcar employees. There was some spread of union organization into the interior. In all of these activities, the FORU played the dominant role, and in its midst a new political element, the syndicalists, who objected to some of the exaggeratedly sectarian attitudes of the anarchists, assumed an increasingly important part.

The Second World War stimulated the growth of the labor movement, both because of the encouragement it gave to the industrialization of the country and of the rising level of prices, which caused not only discontent among the workers but also made it easier for the employers to accede to their demands for

wage increases. During this period of renewed trade-union eu-
phoria, the FORU, which had undergone considerable difficulties
during the 1913-1914 depression, was reorganized and followed a
very militant path. Many new unions were formed, about half of
which joined the FORU immediately, and most of the rest of
which did so in 1920.

One of the most important new unions to be established was
the Federación Obrera Maritima, which remained outside of the
FORU. It was led by a young Socialist, Eugenio Gómez, and
called a general maritime strike in 1919. Although this walkout
was lost, the FOM remained an important element in the labor
movement.

During the 1920's organized labor declined somewhat in
strength, and it was badly divided along political lines. Its membership declined from about ten thousand in 1922 to sixty-five
hundred in 1926. In 1920 the FORU was split, with the antianar-
chist elements in it taking the name of Comité Pro Unidad
Obrera, which in 1923 was converted into the Unión Sindical
Uruguaya, a name borrowed from the Unión Sindical Argentina
across the Río de la Plata.

In the meanwhile, the Socialist party, which grew considerably
during and immediately after World War I, decided in 1921 to
join the Communist International and change its name to Partido Comunista. The trade-union leader, Eugenio Gómez, took a
leading role in carrying out this decision, and ultimately became
secretary-general of the party. A small dissident element, led by
Emilio Frugoni, the founder of the Socialist party, withdrew and
reconstituted that party.

The Communists attempted to work within the Comité Pro
Unidad Obrera, and subsequently within the Unión Sindical
Uruguaya. However, they were ultimately excluded from that
group, and set about establishing their own "autonomous" unions, which were brought together in November 1927 into the
Bloque de Unidad Obrera. For their part, the Socialists had some
supporters in both the USU and the FORU, but were not an
element of great significance in either one of these organizations.

Both the Unión Sindical Uruguaya and the Bloque de Unidad

Obrera were minority organizations in the labor movement in the 1920's. The anarchist-dominated Federación Obrera Regional Uruguaya continued to be the most important element throughout this period.

The splits in organized labor continued during the early 1930's. The Communists in 1929 reorganized their labor followers into the Confederación General del Trabajo, which joined the Red International of Labor Unions, and acted as host to a hemisphere-wide conference of Communist-dominated labor organizations late in 1929. In the next year the Socialists organized a new Unión General de Trabajadores, which maintained friendly relations with the International Federation of Trade Unions. Both the CGT and the UGT appear to have become relatively inactive after the establishment of the dictatorship of President Gabriel Terra late in 1933.

During most of the 1930's the FORU and the USU continued to be the most important central labor groups. In 1938, the Unión Sindical Uruguaya was reported, however, to have only 1,250 members. Most unions did not belong to any central labor organization during this period.

With the end of the Terra dictatorship in 1938, the labor movement became more active. In 1939 a Comité de Unidad y Organización de la Clase Obrera was established, which claimed a membership of fifty unions and some twenty-two thousand workers. As a result of greater freedom to organize and the growing wartime prosperity, a number of important new unions were organized. These included the Sindicato Unico de la Industria de la Construcción, established in 1939 through a merger of ten small unions. The Unión Obrera Textil was established in 1940 with about five hundred members, as were the Organización Obrera del Omnibus, which united most of the bus drivers of the capital, and the Sindicato Unico de la Industria Metalúrgica. In 1942 the trolley-car workers organized the Unión Obrera Tranviaria, the first group in several decades which had been able to resist successfully the constant antiunion pressure of the tramway company.

The most important union to be organized during the first

part of World War II was the Federación de la Industria de la Carne, which was set up in January 1941. This brought together virtually all of the workers employed in the country's most important industry, meat packing.

As a result of the activities of the Comité de Unidad y Organización de la Clase Obrera, a new labor confederation which for the time being brought together most of the country's unions was established early in 1942. This new Unión General de Trabajadores was led by Enrique Rodríguez, a Communist, and included unions under both Communist and Socialist leadership, as well as some which were dominated by other political groups. The FORU and the USU continued their separate existence, but by the early 1940's they had become exceedingly minor influences in the general labor movement.

DIVISION AND REGROUPMENT
IN URUGUAYAN LABOR

The unity established in the Unión General de Trabajadores was short-lived. In January 1943 a bitter strike occurred in the meat-packing industry. The Communist leaders of the UGT opposed this walkout because it was interfering with the delivery of meat to the Soviet Union and its allies. When the Communists denounced the strike leaders as including "Nazi agents," the packing-house unions withdrew from the UGT, and formed a new Federación Autonoma de la Carne as an independent union. They were supported by the Socialists in this attitude, which gave impetus to several other important unions also to withdraw from the UGT. Two years later small groups of unions under the control of members of the Independent Nationalist and Batllista parties also withdrew from the UGT, leaving it a completely Communist-dominated group.

Most of the unions which withdrew from the UGT then came together to form a somewhat loose grouping known first as the Comité Pro-CNT and then as the Comité de Relaciones Sindicales. It was not until 1951 that these unions formally organized a new central labor body. In January of that year the Confederación Sindical Uruguaya was established at a congress attended by delegates from seventeen federations and national unions, including the Railroad Workers, Bank Clerks, Interdepartmental Bus Drivers, Autonomous Construction Workers' Union, Glass Workers' Federation, White-Collar Workers' Federation, Printing Trades' Workers and Brick Makers' Union.

For almost a decade the Confederación Sindical Uruguaya remained the largest union federation in the country. For some time it carried on extensive activities in the fields of labor education, lobbying, and organization. One of its principal accomplishments was a successful unionization campaign among the workers in the nation's sugar industry. The CSU also took an important part in international trade-union activities as a member of both the International Confederation of Free Trade Unions and its regional affiliate the ORIT.

During this period unions affiliated with the Confederación Sindical Uruguaya engaged in numerous strikes, most of which were won. These included walkouts of the interdepartmental bus drivers, sugar workers, maritime and dock workers, and a particularly bitter walkout of railroaders in 1961, which lasted for two months.

In spite of an impressive record of achievement, the CSU declined in the early 1960's. There were several reasons for this. In the first place, the Confederación Sindical del Uruguaya during much of its career was dependent solely upon the financial resources contributed by its affiliates as dues. As a result, it was unable to maintain an adequate bureaucracy to service its various affiliates. In contrast, the unions under the general influence of the Communist party were adequately supplied with funds, a large part of which did not originate in Uruguay.

In the second place, the CSU was the victim of political machinations. During the 1950's and early 1960's, the Socialist party, which had given important support in the early years of the CSU, turned against this group. This was a result of the leadership of the Socialists having been assumed by a group of young people who conceived of themselves as thoroughgoing Marxists and were anxious to demonstrate their ultraleftism. As a result, the party withdrew from the Socialist International in the late 1950's, proclaimed its adherence to Marxism-Leninism and its affinity for the Yugoslav Communist party, and denounced several of the Socialist parties of the Old World.

In terms of internal Uruguayan policy, the Socialist leadership chose to work increasingly closely with the Communists. This trend was particularly noticeable after the victory of Castro in Cuba, whereupon the Uruguayan Socialists proclaimed themselves ardent Fidelistas. The net effect of this trend was to split the Socialist ranks and to bring about a disastrous defeat in the elections of 1962, in which the Socialists for the first time in a generation lost all representation in the national congress.

In the trade-union field, the Socialists cooperated with the Communists, and joined with them in launching still another central labor body. A move in this direction was first taken by the Communists in 1955, when they formed a Committee for Labor Unity, of which the then greatly reduced UGT became a part along with several independent unions. The work of this committee resulted finally in the launching of the Central Unica de Trabajadores del Uruguay in the middle of 1960.

The trade-union situation was complicated by the growing economic and political crisis through which the country was passing in the late 1950's and early 1960's. This crisis had many facets: a decline in the grazing industry; a fall in the price of wool, the country's major export; a slowing down of industrial development; a hugely inflated and highly inefficient government bureaucracy; an excessively expensive and badly administered social security system; and growing inflation.

The inability of the government of the Partido Colorado Batllista to deal with these problems led to the defeat of the Colorados in the election of 1958 for the first time in almost a century. Moreover, the administration of the rival Partido Nacionalista was no more capable of resolving the crisis, and as a result, by the early 1960's there was widespread disillusionment in both major parties, and a growing feeling of frustration and even desperation among wide segments of the electorate.

These circumstances gave growing attractiveness to the ex-

tremism of the Communists and Fidelistas. They made the orthodox trade union approach of the CSU seem increasingly inade-
quate for dealing with the problems facing the workers. This
situation helps to explain the derline of the CSU and the rise of
the so-called Central Unica.

The upshot of all of this was that from its inception the Central Unica de Trabajadores was the dominant element in the
Uruguayan trade-union movement. Outside of it remained a
number of important independent unions, particularly among
government employees, but they also were under Communist and
Fidelista influence. The CSU still claimed a membership of sixty-
eight unions and some seventy thousand members, but was by its
own admission a minority group in the total national labor
movement.

The whole history of the Uruguayan labor movement reflects
the high degree of politicalization which characterizes Uruguay,
as well as reflecting the nature of the country's labor legislation.
Although many of the governments subsequent to that of José
Batlle were friendly disposed towards organized labor, none of
them attempted to impose the kind of controls over the labor
movement which were generally in vogue elsewhere in Latin
America.

As a result, no legal recognition by the government is required in order for a union to function in Uruguay. This is one
of the basic explanations for the tendency for the proliferation of
numerous small labor groups, many of them covering only the
workers of a single factory or workshop—which has always been a
characteristic of Uruguayan organized labor. It also helps to explain the frequent splintering and reunification of unions, not
only on the national central-labor-body level but on the local-
union plane as well.

At the same time, the lack of restrictive legislation has meant
that the Uruguayan labor movement has probably maintained a
wider degree of freedom from government intervention than any
other organized labor group in Latin America. As we have seen,
this fact has had both its advantages and its disadvantages.

THE BEGINNINGS OF PARAGUAYAN LABOR

The comparatively backward nature of the Paraguayan economy has provided relatively little scope for organized labor in that republic. Furthermore, the dictatorial regimes which have plagued Paraguay for much of the twentieth century have tended to stunt the growth of even as much labor organization as might find a foothold in the underdeveloped Paraguayan economy.

The first labor organization in Paraguay was the Federación Obrera del Paraguay, which was established on April 26, 1906. It consisted of a handful of craft unions and rather more mutual-benefit societies. The organization tended to be apolitical and sought to obtain its ends without recourse to strike action. The Federación virtually passed out of existence in 1912.

It was the First World War that tended to provide a spur for the building of the labor movement. At the end of 1914 many of those who had participated in the Federación Obrera del Paraguay organized the Partido Obrero, which sought to organize the workers on a political basis. In 1915 two important organizations were established. The first of these was the Federación Naval, a union of maritime and dock workers. The other was the Federación Obrera Regional Paraguaya, a labor federation of anarchist tendencies, patterned after the FORA of Argentina.

With its revival in 1916, under the stimulus to union organization given by the relative prosperity of the wartime period, the Federacion Obrera del Paraguay succeeded for a few years in organizing groups of workers in most of the important cities and towns of the country. It was syndicalist in its ideological leanings, being somewhat akin to the USA and USU in Argentina and Uruguay.

From the time of the First World War, the maritime workers were the principal nucleus of Paraguayan organized labor. The Federacón Naval conducted a bitter strike in 1920-1921, lasting fourteen months. This walkout received from the FORA of Argentina considerable aid in the form of both money and food for the strikers.

Partly as a result of this walkout, the Federación Naval was split, giving rise to the Liga Obrera Maritima, which not only was the most important organization in the Paraguayan labor movement for several years, but succeeded in 1928 in winning the first important collective bargaining contract in the nation's history. The Liga was moderate in philosophy and was a bitter target for the more-revolutionary political groups which were active in the labor movement.

The Communist party of Paraguay had been formed in the early 1920's and although it was founded largely by university students, its penetration of the labor movement had begun to assume some importance by 1927. The principal leaders of this Communist trade-union effort were Obdulio Barthé and Juan Creid.

In 1930 communists and other elements succeeded in establishing a new Confederación Nacional de Trabajadores which for a short while included most of the country's organized workers in its ranks. When it called a nationwide general strike, however, in 1931, shortly before the outbreak of the Chaco War with Bolivia, the CNT and virtually all of its constituent unions were suppressed.

The labor movement did not revive until after the end of the Chaco War. The resurgence of organized labor was due largely to the revolutionary regime installed in February 1936 under the leadership of Major Rafael Franco, one of the heroes of the Chaco War. This regime, led largely by young intellectuals, started an agrarian reform, enacted extensive labor legislation, and encouraged the growth of the trade unions. During its eighteen months in power it recognized approximately one hundred thirty unions.

During this revolutionary period, the Confederación Nacional de Trabajadores del Paraguay was established under the leadership of Francisco Gaona. He was at the time a Communist; however, in later years he was expelled from the Communist party and became a leader of the Febrerista party, organized by those who had led the 1936 revolution. The CNTP survived the downfall of the Franco regime late in 1937. In 1940 it dropped the word "Nacional" from its title, becoming the Confederación de Trabajadores del Paraguay.

In the meanwhile President Higinio Morinigo became dictator of Paraguay in 1940, and during most of his eight years of rule he persecuted the labor movement severely. The CTP virtually went out of existence, giving way to a semilegal group known as the Consejo Obrero del Paraguay, in which both Febrerista party members and Communists participated, although the latter finally won control of it. In 1944 Morinigo allowed the Communists to revive the CTP, which functioned more or less legally for a short time.

During a short-lived political truce in 1946-1947, during which the Liberal and Febrerista opposition leaders returned to Paraguay and to legal political activity, all four of the parties— the government Colorados, the Liberals, the Febreristas, and the Communists—organized their own following in the labor movement. However, when a month-long civil war brought this truce to an end, all the labor groups except the Colorado party's Organización Republicana Obrera (ORO) were outlawed and suppressed.

Under the succeeding dictatorships of Presidents Natalicio González (1948-1949) and Federico Chaves (1949-1954), the ORO remained the only legal labor organization in Paraguay. In 1950 it was given recognition by the government as a trade-union group, apart from the Colorado party, and in 1951 a convention of the organization renamed it the Confederación Paraguaya de Trabajadores.

The CPT continued to be under the control of elements of the Colorado party, although members of other parties held minor posts in the organization. During the early 1950's the CPT succeeded in establishing a relatively normal system of collective bargaining for a number of its affiliates. Its strongest unions were the organizations of maritime workers and railroaders. There were also organizations of shoemakers, barbers, carpenters, bricklayers, bank clerks, and a few small groups of unionized agricultural workers.

However, what little freedom of action the labor movement had been able to obtain was destroyed in August 1958 by the dictatorship of General Alfredo Stroessner, who had taken over control of the country four years earlier. When the CPT leaders called a general strike for wage increases and other demands, the government intervened the confederation by naming a police official as head of the labor group. The elected leaders of the CPT were deported to Uruguay, where they established a "CPT in Exile." Seven years later, there was still no vestige of an independent labor movement in Paraguay.

Summary and Conclusion

Although both the Uruguayan and Paraguayan labor movements in their early decades tended to reflect what was transpiring in the much stronger trade unions of neighboring Argentina, since the 1920's each has tended to diverge widely from the pattern of Argentine organized labor. The continued political democracy and relative lack of governmental control over unions in Uruguay have tended to encourage splintering of the individual local unions as well as the national labor confederations. On the other hand, the persistent dictatorships and economic backwardness of Paraguay have made it exceedingly difficult for the labor movement to exist at all since the Chaco War; much of the time it has led a semi-legal existence, and it has never been very strong.

SIX

The Organized Workers in Brazil

THE IMPORTANCE OF THE IMPACT OF POLITICAL EVENTS ON THE labor movements of Latin America is nowhere better illustrated than in the case of Brazil. The basic nature of the organized labor movement in that country was altered by the eight-year period of the so-called Estado Novo dictatorship between 1937 and 1945, and nothing that has occurred subsequently has overcome the impact on labor by the attempt at that time to establish in Brazil a fascist-type regime.

BEGINNINGS OF ORGANIZED LABOR

Although Brazil, like Argentina, Chile, and other Latin American countries, had its Utopian Socialist precursors of organized labor during the middle decades of the nineteenth century, there were several factors which hampered the early development of a trade-union movement. Certainly, the most important of these were the continued existence of slavery, which was not abolished until 1888, and the relatively modest state of the country's economic development.

In the turbulent period which followed the abolition of the slave system, a period marked by the overthrow of the monarchy and by authoritarian regimes, there were evidences of some activity among the urban working class. Societies of artisans certainly existed, and some of these issued somewhat romantic political proclamations during the early years of the republic.

These political activities of the early labor groups show a marked influence of intellectual currents coming from Europe.

This tendency was intensified in the decades which followed by massive immigration to Brazil from European countries, notably from Portugal, Italy, Spain, and Germany. It was to a considerable degree these immigrants who made the first serious attempt to establish a trade-union movement.

In the years preceding World War I trade unions were established in various trades and industries in Rio, São Paulo, Recife, Pôrto Alegre, and many smaller cities and towns. In many cases, when there were not enough workers in a locality to form separate organizations according to trade or industry, they would establish Sindicatos de Oficios Varios (unions of workers of miscellaneous trades).

Most of the more important labor organizations of this period were under anarchosyndicalist influence. And it was under this leadership that the country's first national central labor group was established in 1909. This was the Confederacão Operaria do Brasil, which was headed from its inception by a German-born printing-trades' worker, Edgard Leuenroth. It continued in existence for approximately two decades.

The Brazilian anarchosyndicalists differed in a number of ways from their comrades in Argentina and Uruguay. They were considerably less extreme and doctrinaire. They were not averse upon occasion to signing collective agreements. They used the weapon of the general strike very sparingly. They did not believe that a trade-union official who was paid by his union was therefore exploiting its members, and some Brazilian anarchosyndicalist labor organizations had full-time paid officials.

Until after World War I the anarchosyndicalists were not faced with a serious challenge from any other ideological current. There were several attempts made to establish Socialist parties along Marxist lines, and in the state of São Paulo people of this tendency had some influence in the labor movement. The maintenance, however, of such a party on a national basis proved to be too great a task, and the Socialist influence was relatively weak. There was little or no attempt during this period to establish Catholic-workers organizations.

However, after the First World War the anarchosyndicalists

met their first major challenge. It came from their own ranks. Virtually all the Brazilian labor leaders were at first attracted to the Bolshevik Revolution in Russia; however, within two or three years—and particularly after the deportation of anarchist leaders Emma Goldman and Alexander Berkman from Russia in 1921— most of the anarchosyndicalist labor leaders turned against the Bolsheviks.

Nevertheless, a minority did not do so. Particularly among some of the younger anarchosyndicalist trade unionists the enthusiasm for Soviet Russia continued, and in 1922 some of these people established the Partido Comunista do Brasil.

Henceforward, there was waged a bitter struggle for control of the labor movement between the anarchosyndicalists and the Communists. By the end of the decade the Communists had won this struggle, and the majority of the still weak trade-union movement was in their hands or was controlled by elements more sympathetic to them than to the anarchosyndicalists.

In 1929 the Communists succeeded in establishing the country's second significant national central labor body. In a Congress at Rio de Janeiro, which claimed to represent some sixty thousand organized workers, the Confederacão Geral dos Trabalhadores do Brasil was established. It affiliated with the Communists' hemispheric labor group, the Confederación Sindical Latino Americana.

During the 1920's the labor movement as a whole suffered severely at the hands of the government and the employers. One leading official of the government synthesized the attitude of the regime towards the workers movement when he commented that "organized labor is a problem for the police." Strikes were frequently broken by violence, and organized labor found few friends among the politicians of the time.

LABOR AND THE REVOLUTION OF 1930

The Revolution of 1930 represented a sharp break not only in the history of Brazil, but in that of its labor movement. The victory of Getulio Vargas and his installation as president in October of that year began a process of profound and rapid change which is still going on.

This revolution was brought about by a combination of politicians of the old order and young military men. The latter had shown their discontent with the old regime several times during the 1920's by launching insurrections. Although the program of this young military group, known popularly as *os tenentes,* or the lieutenants, was vague in the extreme, and their attempts at revolt were frustrated before 1930, their activities contributed considerably to general discontent with the *status quo.* They preached a program of nationalism and rather confused economic and social reform which found some echo in the humbler ranks of the civilians.

The attitude of the organized workers to the Revolution of 1930 was a mixed one. They had no part in its organization and success. However, in the beginning at least, the anarchosyndicalists were somewhat friendly to the new regime, as were the Trotskyite dissidents from the Communist party. However, the official Communists were exceedingly hostile, since the Communist International had just recently entered its so-called Third Period of extreme sectarianism, and the Communists promptly labelled the revolutionaries of 1930 as "social fascists."

For his part, Getulio Vargas, although an experienced politician of the old regime, was not unaware of the social implications of the revolution which had put him in power. Furthermore, being exceedingly ambitious and anxious to stay in the presidency once he had been placed there, Getulio rode with the mood for change which accompanied the Revolution of 1930.

For the first time, the new president established a Ministry of Labor, Commerce, and Industry. As the first occupant of the post of Minister he named one of his close associates from the state of Rio Grande do Sul, Lindolfo Color.

One of the first acts of the new minister was to issue the so-called Color Law, which for the first time extended legal recognition to the trade unions. With this law, the Brazilian government was transformed from a declared enemy of organized labor into its patron, protector, and domesticator.

The reception of the Color Law by the leaders of the labor movement was generally hostile. Both the Communists and the anarchosyndicalists feared, quite understandably, that legal registration of unions by the government, and the government's insistence that employers deal with recognized unions, would bring in its train possible extensive government control over the labor movement.

Both anarchosyndicalists and Communists therefore opposed having unions under their influence seek legal recognition under the Color Law. In spite of this, thousands of workers groups around the country did seek and obtain legal sanction during the next five years. These constituted a new and important element in the Brazilian labor movement. They engaged in collective bargaining, the signing of collective aggreements, and in a wide range of social welfare work for their members. However, the legal unions did not form any central labor organization, and the Communists succeeded in obtaining influence in a number of them, in spite of government hostility.

Meanwhile, widespread disillusionment with Getulio Vargas and his regime developed among many of those who had supported him in 1930. The Communists succeeded early in 1935 in giving organizational form to this growing discontent, with the establishment under their leadership of the Allança de Liberacão Nacional, with Luiz Carlos Prestes as its president.

Prestes had been one of the leaders of the *tenentes* in the 1920's, but in spite of efforts of the authors of the revolution of 1930 to bring him into their movement, he refused to participate in it, and denounced it after it was successful. Shortly afterwards, he left Buenos Aires, where he had been living in exile, and went to the Soviet Union. There he soon became a member of the Latin American Bureau of the Communist International.

When Prestes returned to Brazil early in 1935 he was a thoroughgoing Communist. His reputation, however, as the hero of the *tenente* struggles of a decade before served to attract many disparate elements to the banner of the National Liberation Alliance.

After carrying on a wide range of activities for almost a year, the Alliance was finally outlawed by President Vargas. Shortly thereafter, it attempted a military insurrection in Rio de Janeiro and Recife, which was unsuccessful, and resulted in the liquidation of the Alliance, and the severe persecution of the Communist party. Prestes was arrested early in 1936 and stayed in jail for more than nine years.

The impact of the failure of the November 1935 uprising upon the labor movement was profound. The Communists and other left-wing elements were purged from the unions, and the militancy of the labor movement was greatly undermined, paving the way for the total reorganization of the trade unions after 1937.

LABOR AND THE ESTADO NOVO

Late in 1937 President Vargas was faced with two serious problems. In the first place, his term was coming to an end, and he faced the unwelcome prospect of having to give up the presidency. In the second place, his regime was being sharply and even violently challenged by a new fascist party known as Acão Integralista. Led by a poet-novelist Plinio Salgado, the Integralistas had all of the trappings of a Fascist party, including green uniform, party salute, and totalitarian philosophy and program. They made little secret of their sympathy for and contact with the Portuguese, Italian, and German Fascists.

Getulio Vargas, in characteristic fashion, solved these problems with two quick strokes. In November 1937 he derogated the Constitution of 1934 under which he was serving, and decreed in its place a new basic document, based on the Italian fascist constitution and proclaimed the establishment of the Estado Novo or New State. Shortly afterwards, he dissolved Acão Integralista and sent its most important leaders into exile.

With the establishment of the Estado Novo, the labor movement was completely reorganized by the government. In conformity with fascist doctrine, the Estado Novo declared that class conflict must cease, that it was the role of the State to resolve whatever differences might arise between workers and employers.

Furthermore, the new form of society was to be based upon the organization of all workers and all employers into organizations which would be at one and the same time organs of class collaboration and the basis of the political structure of the New State.

Although most of the formal organization of the Estado Novo was not established by President Vargas, who continued for almost eight years to rule dictatorially over a very personalist regime, that part of the Estado Novo structure dealing with labor was put into force. The registration of all unions was cancelled, and in order to be re-registered all labor groups had to conform to the rules laid down by the new regime. These rules reduced labor to an innocuous position.

First of all, a union had to conform to the jurisdiction established beforehand by the government. A complicated table of organization was decreed by the Ministry of Labor, breaking down each sector of the economy, and within it each industry, determining which groups of workers within a given industry would be allowed to join together to form a union. Generally, the philosophy adopted by those administering the Estado Novo was to give a union as limited a jurisdiction as possible.

Industrial unions were discouraged by the authorities. When a group existed which had jurisdiction over all of the workers in a locality working in an industry, and a new organization covering only one trade within that industry was organized, the latter would receive control over the more limited group of workers, who would be removed from the industrial union.

The labor legislation of the Estado Novo provided for the establishment of the union covering the workers of a given industry or skill in a municipality as the basic unit of the trade-union structure. These local unions were to be brought together on a state level into federations. The federations were to join to form several different national confederations, such as those of industry, commerce, land transport, banking and insurance, maritime and air transport, and the free professions. As a matter of fact, during the eight years of the Estado Novo no national confederations were ever formed, and the number of state federations was very limited. There was no provision for the establishment of a national central labor organization.

In deciding upon recognition of a union, the Ministry of Labor put primary emphasis on the social welfare program of the organization seeking legalization. Thus, if there were two groups which were seeking recognition, the Ministry had the policy of accepting the group with the more extensive social welfare program, even if its rival had a majority of the workers within the jurisdiction.

The legalized union under the Estado Novo had to submit to very close control over its finances. It was required to spend the major part of its funds on social welfare activities for its members and was forbidden to have strike funds or engage in any other "class warfare" activities.

All workers were required under the Estado Novo to pay the *imposto sindical,* or trade-union tax, consisting of one day's pay per year. This money was divided among the local unions, state union federations, and national confederations, where such existed. Part of it also went to the "social fund," the purpose of which was very vague, and which for many years was used by the government rather than by the workers organizations.

The unions under the Estado Novo were forced likewise to submit to complete government control over their elections. The Ministry of Labor reserved to itself the right to decide whether any given member of the union could be a candidate for office in the organization. Officials of the Ministry observed and supervised the electoral process itself. Finally, once union officers were chosen by the members of the organization, the Ministry retained the authority to veto the election of any victorious candidate.

There were several bases for the government's not allowing a worker to be elected to a post in the unions. These included a criminal record, a case pending before a court of law, or alleged "Communist" inclinations or affiliations of the worker concerned. The last charge was generally leveled against any worker who was known or suspected to be critical of or opposed to the Estado Novo regime. Between 1937 and late 1944, no such person was allowed to hold office in the unions recognized by the Vargas government.

While the unions were subjected to the strictest government control by the Estado Novo, collective bargaining was all but wiped out by it. A system of government labor courts was established to handle not only requests for improvements in wages, hours, and working conditions, but individual workers' grievances as well. The role of the unions in these courts was limited to periodically helping to name workers' representatives on them, and to providing union members with legal help in presenting their grievances before them.

There were three levels of labor courts. The lowest of these was the Board of Conciliation and Arbitration, which was limited to hearing and deciding individual workers' grievances. Above these were the regional labor tribunals, covering a single state or a group of small states. They dealt with appeals from the local boards and with union requests for wage increases and other changes in labor conditions. Finally, there was the Supreme Labor Tribunal, with headquarters in Rio, which was the labor court of highest appeal and which also dealt with certain requests of national union groups for wage increases.

With this system, there was very little direct negotiation between the unions and employers. When a union presented its request for a change in the conditions governing the employment of its members, both it and the employers' groups concerned presented what they considered relevant information to the appropriate labor court. It was the court itself, however, which made the decision concerning what concessions should be made.

This system of control over organized labor and abolition of collective bargaining was supplemented by extensive labor and social legislation. Virtually all urban workers were brought into the national social security system, and elaborate laws dealing with protection of the worker on the job were enacted. Minimum wages were established in 1942.

The political effect of all of this was to build up a wide degree of popularity for Vargas among the country's urban workers. He pictured himself as "father of the poor," and many workers felt that he was just that.

END OF THE ESTADO NOVO

During the last months of 1944 President Vargas began to relax the rigor of the Estado Novo dictatorship. He promised that elections for president, congress, and other offices would be held at the end of 1945, and in the meanwhile allowed a resumption of limited freedom of speech, press, and organization. Opponents of the Vargas regime organized the União Democrática Nacional as a united front, which included as disparate elements as conservative pre-Vargas politicians and the Communists.

One of the first indications of the relaxation of the dictatorship came in union elections during the last half of 1944. For the first time, workers who were critical of the Vargas regime were allowed to run for office and even to be elected in the local unions.

During the early months of 1945 the movement towards liberalization of the regime gained momentum. In May a major step was taken when a general political amnesty was proclaimed by President Vargas, and among those prisoners released from jail were Luiz Carlos Prestes and other Communist leaders.

Between May and October 1945 the freeing of the labor movement from the controls of the Estado Novo proceeded apace. The Communists took the lead in this development. The party, which had been reduced to a few hundred members during the Estado Novo, grew very rapidly, and it became the principal rallying point for those workers who were critical of the Vargas regime.

During this period, the Communists were frequently leaders of strikes, which became numerous and which involved increasingly large numbers of workers. They also took the lead in calling labor congresses.These were organized first on the city-wide level, and subsequently on a statewide basis. Nationally, the Communists established the Movimento de Unidade dos Trabalhadores (MUT), which served as a kind of general staff for their activities in the labor movement, although all members of the MUT were probably not members of the Communist party.

One reason for the ability of the Communists to assume suddenly such an important role in the labor movement was the fact that they were given complete freedom by the Vargas government. Undoubtedly one of the reasons for this liberal attitude by the president was the political position adopted by the Communist party right after Luiz Carlos Prestes' release from prison.

In his first public speech after coming out of jail, delivered at a meeting attended by some one hundred thousand people in the Vasco da Gama stadium in Rio de Janeiro, Prestes adopted the apparently surprising position of urging the president to stay in office "until a new constitution is written." His argument was that any new government which came into power so long as the Estado Novo remained in effect would continue to be a Fascist dictatorship, and that the essential thing was to abolish the regime, not to remove its leader.

The Communists continued to argue this point of view in spite of their serving as the rallying point for most anti-Vargas workers in the labor movement, since there was no other appreciable element which could do so. They took this position because it was the only way in which they could continue to work openly in the labor movement.

Getulio Vargas, though, was not unaware of the progress which the Communists were making in the labor movement. He therefore set about to organize his own labor supporters into a new party, the Partido Trabalhista Brasileiro. It was established under the leadership of officials of the Ministry of Labor and top figures in the unions. José Segadas Viana, the Ministry's director-general of labor, became the first head of the party.

One of Vargas' principal purposes in sponsoring the organization of the Partido Trabalhista was to prepare public opinion for his own continuance in power, in spite of his promises that elections would be held at the end of 1945. The PTB organized mass demonstrations of workers at which the participants shouted "Queremos Vargas" ("We Want Vargas"), as a result of which the members of the party soon came to be known as *Queremistas*. The Communists often cooperated in these meetings.

These efforts of Vargas and his supporters proved fruitless, however. Late in October the president removed João Alberto, an old *tenente*, as chief of the federal police, and put his own brother Benjamin in Alberto's place. The army chiefs interpreted this change as a final move to solidify his position in preparation for canceling the scheduled elections. As a result, on the early morning of October 25, 1945, army tanks surrounded the presidential palace, and forced President Getulio Vargas to resign.

LABOR AND THE DUTRA REGIME

After the overthrow of Vargas, preparations for the election in December went forward as planned. There were three candidates. One was General Eurico Dutra, candidate of the Partido Social Democrático, who had been Vargas' more or less official nominee before October 25. The second was General Eduardo Gomes, former head of the air force, and nominee of the União Democrática Nacional, now transformed into a political party. The third candidate was Yeddo Fiuza, one-time director-general of highways under Vargas, and nominee of the Communist party, although he was not himself a Communist.

Getulio Vargas refused to endorse any of the candidates until shortly before the election; however, he was nominated by the Partido Trabalhista Brasileiro to head that party's ticket (as candidate for senator) in ten states. Finally, he endorsed the candidacy of General Dutra shortly before the polling day. This endorsement was probably responsible for Dutra's rather unexpected victory.

President Dutra took office shortly after his election. For about a year thereafter, there were three elements openly competing for control of the labor movement: the followers of Vargas, the Communists, and elements loyal to or under the control of the Dutra regime and its Ministry of Labor.

The Communists went ahead with their work in seeking to

reorganize the labor movement and to bring it under their control. Their ultimate objective was the establishment of a nation-wide general labor confederation under their sponsorship.

The Communists had made a fundamnetal decision concerning the Estado Novo labor structure. They were faced with the alternative of working within the legally recognized unions or setting up their own workers' organizations parallel to those established by the Vargas regime. They chose the first of these alternatives. This assured them that the income from the *imposto sindical,* which was paid to those unions which they were able to capture, would be at their disposal.

The various state labor congresses that were organized under the sponsorship of the Communists' Movimiento de Unidade dos Trabalhadores all urged the summoning of a national labor congress to establish a Confederacão dos Trabalhadores Brasileiros (CTB). As a final step, the MUT itself issued invitations for such a meeting to convene in September 1946.

At this point, the government of General Dutra intervened. It declared that the plans of the MUT were illegal, and outlawed the MUT itself. At the same time, the Ministry of Labor summoned its own national labor congress for the purpose of carrying out the Estado Novo plans for establishing the various confederations of industrial, commercial, land transport, and other groups of workers.

Subsequently, however, the Ministry of Labor entered into discussions with the leaders of the MUT. As a result, it was agreed that the two groups would jointly sponsor a congress to meet during the first week of September 1946. An accord was also made concerning representation at the meeting, which assured a large representation of elements loyal to the Ministry.

This congress, which the author attended, was marked from the beginning by sharp maneuvering among the three basic elements represented there, that is, the Communists, Vargasistas and Ministry of Labor people. It finally broke up into two separate congresses. One, attended by the Communists and Vargasistas, organized the Confederacão dos Trabalhadores do Brasil; the other, laid the groundwork for the establishment of three of the national confederations provided for in the Estado Novo: those of industrial workers, commercial employees, and land-transport workers.

Under the laws which had established the Estado Novo and which were still in effect the new Confederacão dos Trabalhadores do Brasil was illegal. The Ministry of Labor warned all unions that they were not free to affiliate with the CTB and that if they did so, they would lose their legal recognition. This severely hampered the Confederacão's ability to recruit affiliates.

However, the Confederacão continued to function openly until early in 1947. At that time, the Brazilian Supreme Court declared both the Communist party and the Confederacão dos Trabalhadores do Brasil illegal, wherewith the government arrested a number of Communist leaders in and out of the labor movement. The Communist members of Congress were deprived of their seats and thus no longer enjoyed parliamentary immunity to arrest. Luiz Carlos Prestes went into hiding, and did not again appear in public for a dozen years.

To purge the Communists from the labor movement, those unions under their leadership were "intervened," that is, their elected officials were removed by the Ministry of Labor. All further union elections were canceled, and none was held for the rest of the Dutra regime.

LABOR IN THE SECOND VARGAS REGIME

In the election of 1950, Getulio Vargas was again candidate for the presidency. In his campaign, he had the support of virtually all elements in the labor movement. His own personal supporters, as well as the Communists, and even most of those union officials who had theretofore been loyal to the Ministry of Labor, backed Vargas.

During his campaign, Vargas promised greater freedom for the labor movement than it had enjoyed during most of the Dutra regime. He said that union elections would be renewed, and that the existing confederations would be allowed to join international labor organizations, which they had not previously been permitted to do. Finally, he made a promise to halt inflation and to enact new labor and social legislation.

Vargas was elected overwhelmingly, in a four-cornered race. His regime, however, soon lost much of its popularity. Still, President Vargas did allow a renewal of union elections, and sponsored a law passed by Congress permitting the labor confederations to join the International Confederation of Free Trade Unions and the Inter-American Regional Organization of Workers (ORIT), and the national confederations of industrial, commercial, and land-transport workers did so. However, he had no success in halting inflation, and his administration was generally marked by confusion, inefficiency, and corruption.

In 1952 Vargas named João Goulart, a rich young landholder from the state of Rio Grande do Sul, as Minister of Labor. It soon became clear that Vargas was grooming Goulart as his political successor. Goulart himself made a bid to gain wide labor support.

Goulart's efforts included two tactics. On the one hand, he tended to encourage strikes which he then stepped in and "settled" to the satisfaction of the workers, thus gaining prestige in their eyes. On the other hand, he began a verbal attack on the so-called *pelegos,* the trade-union officials who owed their positions in the labor movement more to the favor of the Ministry of Labor than to the support of the rank and file, and who had generally been loyal to the Ministry in all administrations. Since these officials were widely unpopular among the rank-and-file trade unionists, Goulart's reputation rose among the workers as a whole.

During the second Vargas regime a considerable political vacuum was created in Brazil, particularly among the workers. Vargas' prestige fell rapidly. At the same time, the Communists were unable to capitalize on this fact, and their own prestige declined because the workers became tired of their organizations being used by the Communist party for its own political objectives.

THE LABOR MOVEMENT AFTER VARGAS

Getulio Vargas suddenly recouped his declining reputation by the way in which he died. When he was faced with an ultimatum from the armed forces in August 1954, insisting that he take a "long vacation" until the end of his term, Vargas replied by committing suicide. In doing so, he left behind two letters in which he claimed that he was the victim of the big business and foreign elements which were seeking to oppress the Brazilian workers. He was being forced out of the presidency because he defended the interests of the workers, he claimed.

These spectacular circumstances of Vargas' death sparked a series of demonstrations by workers throughout Brazil. Not only Vargas' own supporters but the Communists participated in these demonstrations.

Vice-president João Cafe Filho succeeded to the presidency upon the death of Vargas. He had been a bitter opponent of Vargas, and had become vice-president on the ex-dictator's ticket in 1950 only because of a political deal. During his year in office, Cafe Filho had the backing of the anti-Vargas elements in the country's political life, and he returned to a certain degree to the labor policies which had characterized the Dutra regime. Many unions were intervened by the Ministry of Labor, and the Ministry would not certify the election of any Communist to office in the labor movement.

Meanwhile, the hold of Getulio Vargas on the imagination of the workers of Brazil was sufficiently great to secure the election of two individuals who had been closely associated with Vargas when the late president's term expired in 1955. Juscelino Kubitschek of the Partido Social Democrático and João Goulart of the Partido Trabalhista Brasileiro became president and vice-president respectively.

During the Kubitschek regime (1956-1961) the labor movement enjoyed unequaled freedom. The government intervened in virtually no unions; the Ministry of Labor did not interfere with union elections. Collective bargaining became more widespread than it had been before. Without modifying the laws which put severe restrictions on the organization of agricultural workers, the Kubitschek regime began in fact cautiously to permit the establishment of unions among them.

During this period, too, the Communists began to make considerable headway once again in the labor movement. This was due at least in part to the fact that Vice-president João Goulart, who was in charge of the administration's labor policy, tended to favor the Communists and their allies over anticommunist elements in the unions. Communist gains among the maritime workers, the bank clerks, and the workers of Rio de Janeiro were particularly notable. A new national labor confederation, that of bank workers, was established under Communist control.

The same trends continued after the end of the Kubitschek regime. After only seven months in office, President Janio Quadros resigned in August 1961, precipitating a constitutional crisis. When the military chiefs attempted to prevent vice-president João Goulart from taking over the presidency, both the Partido Trabalhista and Communists elements helped to mobilize working-class opinion against this maneuver.

With the installation of Goulart in the presidency, the collaboration of his followers and the Communists in the labor movement continued and was intensified. A coalition of these two forces succeeded in early 1962 in ousting the strongly entrenched conservative leadership of the National Confederation of Industrial Workers. Together the two political groups took the lead in organizing the Comando Geral dos Trabalhadores do Brasil, which used the CTB initials in reminiscence of the organization that had been established by the Communists in 1946.

The noncommunist and non-Goulart elements in the labor movement sought to fight back against these groups. In the middle of 1962 they organized their own informal central labor group to rival the CTB. This element found its main support in national confederations of commercial and land-transport workers, affiliated with the International Confederation of Free Trade Unions and the ORIT.

In the meantime, a new element of considerable potential significance had appeared in the labor movement. In the middle 1950's the Confederacão Nacional de Circulos Operarios Catolicos, which theretofore had been largely a confessional organization, conducting catechism classes among workers, began to expand its activities. First in the southernmost state of Rio Grande do Sul, and subsequently in Rio de Janeiro, São Paulo and else-where, the *circulos operarios* began to organize trade-union lead-ership-training classes. In Rio and São Paulo those classes were established in conjunction with the Catholic universities of those two cities.

By the early 1960's the effects of the activities of the *circulos operarios* began to become evident. On the local trade-union level people trained by them began to achieve leadership posts. In several areas they began to organize at least some serious resist-ance to the activities of the Communists and their allies in the labor movement; however, they were very far from constituting a major factor in organized labor.

The overthrow of President João Goulart by the armed forces on April 1, 1964, threw the labor movement into profound confu-sion. Neither Goulart's own supporters nor the Communists were able to mobilize any effective working-class resistance to the mili-tary takeover. The new regime arrested thousands of Communists and followers of Goulart, many of whom were in the labor move-ment. Even many Catholic trade unionists were jailed, since there were elements in the new administration who regarded any mili-tant labor leader as a "Communist."

The noncommunist and anti-Goulart leaders in the labor movement sought to take advantage of the sudden disaster which had overtaken the more extremist leaders. They were able to re-gain control of the Confederacão Nacional dos Trabalhadores na Industria and of many local unions.

Whether or not the nonextremist elements could gain firm control of the Brazilian labor movement depended after April 1, 1964, on the policies of the military regime. If it carried out the reforms which Goulart had used as a demagogic banner—agra-rian, tax, and electoral changes—the position of the moderate elements in the labor movement would be reinforced. However, if the new government took a conservative direction, it would serve to assure the ultimate return of Communist and similar elements to control of Brazilian organized labor.

Summary and Conclusion

The Brazilian labor movement still remains fundamentally within the mold made for it by the Estado Novo. Many unions still present requests to labor courts for changes in the working conditions of their members instead of seeking such changes through collective bargaining. Hundreds of thousands of workers still have their grievances processed in the Boards of Conciliation and Arbitration. The *imposto sindical* remains in force.

However, in the country's major industrial cities the unions have tended to break to some degree with the Estado Novo pattern. They negotiate directly with the employers, sign collective agreements, and handle grievances through union-employer machinery. This tendency has been growing steadily since the end of the Dutra regime.

Several conflicting policial groups have been competing steadily for the control of organized labor since the end of the Estado Novo. These have included three major elements, the Communists, Vargasistas, and agents of the Ministry of Labor. Recently, another element, the Catholic workers' circles has entered the field. During the Goulart regime the Communist and Vargasista groups worked closely together and showed great militancy. Subsequently, however, the military revolution of April 1, 1964, cast great doubt over the future direction of Brazilian organized labor.

SEVEN

The Chilean Labor Movement

THE EARLY ROOTS OF THE CHILEAN LABOR MOVEMENT GO AS FAR BACK as the middle of the nineteenth century. In the 1850's a group of young men, including Francisco Bilbao and Santiago Arcos, who were influenced by the Utopian Socialist ideas then prevalent in Europe, established what they called the Society of Equals. Although this organization was very short-lived and some of its leaders were soon jailed or forced into exile, the ideas which they sowed took root.

One direct result of their activities was the organization in Santiago and other cities of a number of mutual-benefit societies among the artisans and craftsmen. These were a species of insurance society which not only took care of the most pressing financial needs of their members but also engaged in other activities. They undertook the establishment of night schools for their members, and from time to time they even functioned temporarily as trade unions, presenting demands for improvements in working conditions.

It was not, however, until the 1880's that the first serious indications of labor unrest began to become manifest. In 1887 the visit of a delegation from one of the United States railroad brotherhoods was the occasion for the organization of the Federación Santiago Watt, bringing together the locomotive engineers, firemen, and washers on the nation's railroads. Although, like the American railway unions, it was heavily oriented in a mutual-benefit direction, it was also a trade union.

In this same decade there were serious strikes among trolley-car workers and others in the city of Santiago. There also arose a

85

new political party, the Partido Demócrata, which proclaimed itself to be a Socialist organization. For several decades it maintained more or less close relations with the Socialist parties of Europe and was a corresponding member of the Socialist International.

In the 1890's, "resistance societies" began to be formed among the nitrate workers of the northern part of the country. The first strikes in this region also took place in the same decade.

The first decade of the twentieth century was a period of considerable violence in labor-management relations. A maritime workers strike in Valparaiso in 1903 brought about the intervention of the navy to bring it to an end, after there had been some rioting. There were various walkouts in the nitrate fields, and the year 1907 will always be remembered for a brutal massacre of miners which took place in the city of Iquique. At this time, the striking workers, who had been forced to leave their employer-owned homes in the nitrate *pampa* and had congregated in the central square of Iquique, were fired upon point blank by soldiers, who killed scores and perhaps hundreds of them.

In 1909 the country's first central labor group was established, the Gran Federación Obrera de Chile. It was set up upon the initiative of a relatively conservative lawyer who had been associated with the railroad union and who saw in the GFOCh a possibly useful vehicle for his political ambitions.

By this time a position of leadership in the budding labor movement had already been acquired by Luis Emilio Recabarren. A typographer by trade, he had edited several labor newspapers in the nitrate areas, and had come to have a leading role in the Partido Demócrata, of which he served for a time as secretary-general. However, Recabarren and his closest trade-union associates felt that that party had become too conservative, and in 1912 they withdrew to form the Partido Socialista Obrero.

World War I had an important impact on the Chilean labor movement. It served both to stimulate labor organization and activity and to radicalize the trade unions. The wartime period was marked by a number of important strikes in various parts of the country, most of which were successful.

During the early years of the war, the more left-wing unions in the nitrate regions and in Santiago which were under the influence of Recabarren and the PSO joined the hitherto conservative Gran Federación Obrera de Chile. As a result, they were able to capture the organization in its congress of 1916. A year later the name of the group was altered to Federación Obrera de Chile (FOCh), and a new form of organization was adopted, which centralized authority much more highly in the national leadership.

In the meantime, an entirely new labor group was being formed in the nation's principal port cities. This was the Industrial Workers of the World (in Chile the group was known by its English initials as the IWW), which was established as the result of propaganda and organizational efforts of IWW sailors from the United States. By the end of World War I it included virtually all of the nation's maritime and port workers, and had likewise begun to organize in the port cities other groups which were not connected with the maritime-transportation industry.

LABOR AND THE FIRST ALESSANDRI ADMINISTRATION

The expansion of organized labor had important repercussions in the presidential election of 1920. That was a bitterly fought contest between Arturo Alessandri, who was the nominee of all of the more left-wing elements in the country's political spectrum, and Luis Barros Borgoño, the candidate of various right-wing parties. Most of the labor movement enthusiastically supported Arturo Alessandri, who was elected by a very narrow majority.

During his campaign, Alessandri had advocated the enactment of a national Labor Code, which would not only provide protective legislation for the country's workers but would also extend legal recognition to the trade unions for the first time. However, due to congress remaining in the hands of conservative elements, Alessandri was not able to obtain passage of such a code, the elements of which he submitted to congress in 1922.

Meanwhile, the Federación Obrera de Chile continued to

move to the Left, as did the party which controlled it, the Partido Socialista Obrero. In 1922 the latter joined the Communist International, while the Federación joined the newly organized Red International of Labor Unions.

The deep political crisis that had gripped Chile since before the 1920 election came to a head in 1924. In March of that year, the pro-Alessandri forces won control of congress in another bitterly fought campaign. However, the new congress showed itself in no hurry to enact the labor legislation or to adopt the other reforms which Alessandri had suggested to it. Instead, it centered its attention principally on a bill which for the first time would pay salaries to members of congress.

The payment of congress members undoubtedly made good political sense, since the victory of the Left forces in the 1920 and 1924 elections had brought to Parliament many middle- and working-class deputies and senators who needed such compensation if they were to devote their time principally to their parliamentary duties. The move, however, angered government employees, who in recent years had frequently found their pay delayed because of the government's financial crisis arising from the decline in the country's nitrate industry in the wake of German discovery during World War I of means to make artificial nitrates.

Most angry were the army officers. As a result, junior officers demonstrated in the balconies during the discussion of the controversial bill. When President Alessandri demanded that their superiors discipline these young soldiers, the senior officers refused, and the country was faced with a major constitutional crisis.

The military leaders promised President Alessandri that they would end their political activity if congress would pass a long list of laws. The fundamental item in this list, from the point of view of the soldiers, was a pay raise for the military; but for purposes of public relations they also included virtually all the labor and social laws which Alessandri himself had urged during the previous four years.

As a result, on September 8, 1924, virtually all of the fundamental bases of the Chilean Labor Code were enacted into law. However, the soldiers did not thereupon "retire to the barracks" as they had promised the president they would do. Arturo Alessandri therefore resigned, and went into exile in Italy, the land of his forebears.

During the next four months the country was ruled by a junta composed of senior generals and admirals; however, this group became increasingly conservative and as a result discontent arose once again in the ranks of the junior officers. Finally, in January 1925 they organized a new *coup d'état,* led by Lt. Cols. Marmaduque Grove and Carlos Ibañez. The new military-government junta established by this group summoned President Alessandri back from exile, and he returned home in the middle of March 1925.

During these months the labor movement had generally adopted a wait-and-see attitude towards what was occurring in national politics. The only major labor event of importance during this period was the suicide of Luis Emilio Recabarren in December 1924, apparently motivated by personal problems rather than by political considerations.

Upon the return of Alessandri there began a short period of feverish change. A commission was appointed by the president to write a new constitution, on which were represented the country's principal labor organizations as well as the Communist party. This new document separated Church and State, and contained some vague generalizations concerning the "social responsibilities" of property owners, but was not markedly radical on economic and social matters. It was approved by a national referendum, and went into effect in the middle of 1925. This was the first new constitution to be adopted in Chile since 1833, and it is the document which still regulates the general lines of Chilean political and governmental life.

Much more significant than the constitutional change from the labor point of view was the effort of President Alessandri to put into effect the legislation passed on September 8, 1924. The bases for the country's social security system were laid, and the government began to extend legal recognition to unions which conformed to the prerequisites established in the new labor laws.

Both the Communist and anarchosyndicalist trade-union leaders strongly opposed having the unions under their control seek legal recognition. They feared, as in Brazil a few years later under similar circumstances, that legal recognition of the unions would mean extensive government control over the recognized organizations. They were opposed to the powers granted the government in the law to determine union jurisdiction, supervise union finances and elections, and oversee the whole collective bargaining process.

Labor resistance was heightened during the months of the Alessandri period in 1925 by the government not showing very much sympathy for labor's immediate demands for wage and other improvements. Several strikes in the northern part of the country were put down with the intervention of army troops.

President Arturo Alessandri again resigned in September 1925, when his Minister of Interior, Colonel Carlos Ibañez insisted on running for president in elections scheduled for November. Although the popular reaction to the president's resignation was sufficiently strong to induce Colonel Ibañez to withdraw his candidacy, real power in the government was firmly in Ibañez' hands after the departure of President Alessandri. In May 1927 he was finally elected president in an almost uncontested election, and ruled as a dictator until September 1931.

ORGANIZED LABOR AND THE IBAÑEZ DICTATORSHIP

During the period of Ibañez' control of the Chilean government, the process of establishing "legal" unions, organized and recognized under the laws of September 8, 1924, went forward apace. By the end of this period, the majority of the country's unions had legal status.

The Communists and anarchosyndicalists were hampered in their opposition to the legalization of the unions by the fact that they were subjected to continuous though relatively mild persecution by the dictatorship. Many of their leaders were exiled, others were jailed, or were forced to go into hiding. Furthermore, the Communists were wracked during this period with a violent internal feud, as a result of which they emerged from the dictatorship period split into two distinct and separate parties.

The "legal" unions established close relations among themselves. First, there were organized two central labor groups. One of these was the Confederación Nacional de Sindacatos Industriales, including most of the legally recognized unions of factory workers. The other was the Confederación Nacional de Sindicatos Profesionales, including most of the unions of craftsmen and white-collar wokers. Finally, shortly before the overthrow of President Ibañez, the two groups merged to form the Confederación Nacional de Sindicatos Legales.

President Ibañez was overthrown largely because of his inability to deal with the effects of the world economic depression in Chile. His ouster was followed by more than a year of acute political instability and economic crisis.

Two months after Ibañez' fall, elections brought Juan Esteban Montero, a middle-of-the-road Radical-party member, to power. However, his regime of a little more than six months was marked by violent strikes, several revolutionary attempts, and continuing economic and financial difficulties.

THE RISE OF THE SOCIALIST PARTY

Montero was finally overthrown on June 4, 1932, by a coalition of military men, led by Colonel Marmaduque Grove, head of the air force; a group of small Socialist parties which had been organized in the wake of Ibañez' overthrow; some Ibañez followers, led by his ex-Ambassador to Washington, Carlos Dávila; and perhaps including ex-President Arturo Alessandri, although his role has never been very clear. The new leaders proclaimed a Socialist Republic of Chile.

For two weeks the dominant figure in the regime was Colonel Grove. He anounced extensive plans for economic development, for social welfare measures, and other moves. The regime had the enthusiastic support of all radical and labor groups except the orthodox Stalinist Communists, who in conformity with the sectarian line then dominant in the Communist International, denounced Grove and all the other leaders of the regime as "social fascists."

Within two weeks Grove was ousted, and leadership in the Socialist Republic was assumed by Carlos Dávila, who became provisional president. His administration, however, lasted only one hundred days, after which he was ousted by another military coup.

New elections brought Arturo Alessandri back to the presidency, as the candidate of a Center-Right coalition. His principal opponent was Colonel Marmaduque Grove, supported by a coalition of the small Socialist parties and labor groups which had supported the Socialist Republic during the period in which he controlled it.

This coalition, although it failed to elect Grove, was significant because it marked the birth of a new factor of major importance in the country's labor movement and general political life. The elements that backed Grove's Revolutionary and Socialist Alliance in the elections of 1932 joined together early in 1933 to form a new party, the Partido Socialista. From its inception, this party had a majority position in the ranks of organized labor, and was one of the country's largest political organizations.

In the post-Ibañez period, the organized labor movement was split among four principal groups. The Confederación Nacional de Sindicatos Legales was the country's largest central labor organization and was dominated by the Socialists. The Stalinist Communists had reorganized the Federación Obrera de Chile, with Elías Laferte, who had succeeded Recabarren as secretary-general in 1924, back in his old post. The Trotskyite Communists also had a loose grouping of unions under their control, and had considerable influence in the CNSL.

Finally, there was the Confederación General de Trabajadores. This was established by the merger of the remnants of the IWW along the coast, and another anarchosyndicalist group, the Federación Obrera Regional Chilena, which had had a certain membership among the workers of the Santiago area. The CGT was strong principally among port workers, printers, shoemakers, and construction trades' workers.

Following the fall of Ibañez, there was certain sentiment in favor of unification of the labor movement; however, the extreme sectarianism which characterized the Stalinist Communists during this period (the so-called Third Period in the history of the Communist International) made it impossible for them to join their labor forces with those of any other political group. The anarcho-syndicalists also tended to have a very isolationist attitude insofar as other elements in the labor movement were concerned.

In 1935 the Trotskyite Communists dissolved their party and joined the Partido Socialista. As a result, their trade-union groups also merged with those which had hitherto been under Socialist control. This was the first step towards broader trade-union unity.

In 1935 the International Communist line changed to one of alliance with other Leftist groups. In Chile this change was reflected in moves towards further unification of the labor movement and towards establishing a broad Leftist alliance in the general political field.

THE CTCh

After long preliminary negotiations, a labor-unity convention was finally held in December 1936, in which delegates participated representing the Confederación Nacional de Sindicatos Legales, the Federación Obrera de Chile and the Confederación General de Trabajadores. This convention established a new body, the Confederación de Trabajadores de Chile (CTCh). Juan Díaz Martínez, a Socialist, was elected secretary-general of the new group, and Salvador Ocampo, a Communist, was chosen assistant general-secretary. The anarchosyndicalists after some hesitation decided not to merge their trade-union supporters in the CTCh but to maintain the separate existence of the CGT.

Within the CTCh there was great rivalry between Socialist and Communist trade unionists. At the Confederación's second congress in December, 1939, this competition resulted in a split in the organization. Bernardo Ibañez, a Socialist was elected to take the place of Juan Díaz Martínez as secretary-general, whereupon the Communists walked out. They organized a separate group with the same name, making Salvador Ocampo its secretary-general. Nevertheless, a few weeks negotiations brought a resumption of unity within the CTCh, although Socialists-Communist enmity remained intense.

In the meantime, the labor movement had commenced to grow very rapidly. This was due largely to the encouragement which it received from the Popular Front government of President Pedro Aguirre Cerda, who had taken office in December 1938. The Popular Front had been formed several years earlier, and brought together the Socialist, Communist, Democrático, and Radical Socialist parties, as well as the Confederación de Trabajadores de Chile.

President Aguirre Cerda threw all of his government's prestige behind the labor movement, with the result that important employers who had hitherto either refused absolutely to recognize unions or had maintained company-dominated workers organizations within their plants came to terms with the legitimate labor movement. These included the coal-mine operatives, many textile plants, and other important employers.

The only field in which the Aguirre Cerda government did not encourage the formation of unions was agriculture. Although in the first months of the regime there was considerable agitation in the rural areas, and many unions were formed, within six months of taking office, President Aguirre Cerda issued an executive decree prohibiting further recognition of new agricultural workers' groups. This decree reflected the fear of many that the landlords were still powerful enough that, if the government sought to force them to recognize unions of their workers, they might be able to menace the stability of the regime.

However, during the period of the Second World War, virtually all groups of organizable urban workers were brought into the trade-union movement. These included not only factory workers, miners, and railroaders but also such white-collar workers as bank clerks, newspaper employees, and many workers employed in offices and stores. In addition, virtually all workers employed directly or indirectly by the national and municipal governments were unionized. However, only the organizations of those working for semi-autonomous branches of the national government—such as hospital workers and employees of social security institutions—were given legal recognition. Direct government employees were not allowed by law to form organizations which could be formally recognized as collective bargaining agents.

SPLIT IN THE CTCh

Meanwhile, the intense rivalry between different political elements in the labor movement continued. Just after the end of World War II this conflict resulted in an open split in the CTCh. Leaders representing the Communists, Radicals, and Falangistas (Christian Democrats) in the Confederación "expelled" Bernardo Ibañez and other Socialist officials of the organization. They elected in his place Bernardo Araya, a Communist member of the Chamber of Deputies. The Socialists, allied with the small Democrático party, refused to recognize these moves, however, and continued to maintain that theirs was the real Confederación de Trabajadores de Chile.

For six years, between 1946 and 1952, this split in the labor movement continued. In the beginning, the Communist-dominated CTCh was by far the stronger of the two organizations, having in its ranks virtually all the miners, the railroaders, most of the government employees, and a fair number of factory workers' organizations. The Socialist group was centered principally among the factory workers, privately employed white-collar workers, and hospital employees.

For some time, during 1946 and 1947, it appeared as if the Socialist CTCh might disappear. The Communist party had three members in the government of President Gabriel González Videla between November 1946 and April 1947, and at this time the Socialists were very much on the defensive, in the labor movement, and in the general political scene.

Yet, in April 1947 the Communists were forced to resign from

González Videla's cabinet, and they soon declared war on his regime. As a result, González Videla, who had favored the Communist faction of organized labor so long as that party was in the government, switched around to lend his support to the Socialist-led CTCh. Finally, at the end of 1948 he sponsored the so-called Law for the Defense of Democracy, which outlawed the Communist party, and provided for the purging of Communists from leading positions in the labor movement.

The Law for the Defense of Democracy provoked a split within the ranks of the Socialist party, leading to the formation of the Partido Socialista de Chile (PSCh), which supported the law, and the Partido Socialista Popular (PSP), which opposed it. This split weakened the position of the anticommunist element in the labor movement, and in particular weakened the socialist-oriented CTCh.

At the expiration of the presidential term of Gabriel González Videla in 1952, the voters chose ex-dictator Carlos Ibañez to be chief executive once more. Fear of his attitude towards labor served as a catalyst to bring about the reunification of the labor movement once again, this time under the domination of the Communists.

THE CUTCh

Steps had been taken before the election of Ibañez to unify all of the noncommunist elements in the labor movement. The move in this direction was strongly supported by the International Confederation of Free Trade Unions and its American regional affiliate, the ORIT, to which a number of the noncommunist unions belonged. Expectedly, the Communists sought to prevent the formation of a united front against them in organized labor, and they did so by raising the cry of "unity." Playing heavily on the argument that the advent of the Ibañez regime threatened the existence of the labor movement, they insisted that unions under their control be allowed to participate in the labor congress which had been planned with ICFTU and ORIT help.

Against the advice of the international free-trade-union

movement, the noncommunist union leaders of Chile finally agreed to the Communists' terms. The result was as the ICFTU and ORIT leaders had predicted. Although representing in reality only a small minority of the organized workers, the Communists succeeded in dominating the new central labor body which was established, the Central Unica de Trabajadores de Chile.

The Communists were able to achieve such control through various methods. For one thing, they flooded the founding congress of the CUTCh with phantom delegates, representing organizations which existed only in the fertile imaginations of the Communist leaders. In the second place, they succeeded in convincing the noncommunist union leaders that the cause of "labor unity" required that the CUTCh follow fundamentally a Communist line.

As a result of this situation, the CUTCh decided to remain outside of any international labor group, instead of affiliating with the ICFTU and ORIT, as had originally been planned. As a result of this, the CUTCh in subsequent years sent delegates to international labor congresses of all types, sending anticommunists to those of the free labor movement, and Communists to those of the World Federation of Trade Unions and its American affiliate, the Confederación de Trabajadores de America Latina. Whereas the delegates to free labor groups went as "observers," those to the Communist world and hemispheric groups were regularly acepted as "delegates" and made it a point of speaking as if the CUTCh was in fact an integral part of the Communist world labor apparatus.

The opposition of various noncommunist elements to Communist domination was fruitless. The Communist trade-union apparatus in Chile was able to maintain a substantial corps of activists who could work full-time on trade-union affairs; for example, Juan Vargas Puebla, old-time Communist leader in the building trades, and Juan Díaz Iturrieta, one-time Communist miners' union leader, spent most of their time around the headquarters of the CUTCh.

Because of their full-time occupation as "labor leaders," these Communists and others were in a position to deal with any problems which arose in any of the constituent organizations of the CUTCh. They also had firm control of the machinery of the central labor organization. In this work they had the close cooperation for a decade of Clotario Blest, a Catholic, who was known to go to mass regularly—but just as regularly sided with the Communists in the leadership of the labor movement.

During the early years of the history of the CUTCh, the principal opposition to the Communists came from the anarchosyndicalists. The shoemaking, printing, and a few other unions controlled by the anarchosyndicalists had joined the CUTCh, since by 1952 the Confederación General de Trabajadores had for all practical purposes ceased to exist. After putting up fruitless opposition to the Communists within the CUTCh, the anarchosyndicalist unions finally withdrew from it in 1957. Under their leadership a rival organization, the Confederación Nacional de Trabajadores was established a few months later, and it joined the ICFTU and the ORIT. It represented, however, only a small fraction of the Chilean organized labor movement, and was no match for the CUTCh.

During the late 1950's the Christian Democrats came to offer the principal opposition to the Communists within the Central Unica de Trabajadores. The trade-union members of the Christian Democratic party belonged to the Federación Gremial de Chile (FEGRECh) which acted as a faction within the CUTCh. Under the leadership of the FEGRECh the Christian Democrats built up increasing force in the constituent unions of the central labor group.

By 1962 the Christian Democrats represented the single largest political group in the CUTCh. In the congress of the organization in September of that year, the FEGRECh members had more than 35 per cent of the delegates; however, they were still outnumbered by the Communist-Socialist coalition. From the inception of the CUTCh, the Socialists had served as junior partners of the Communists in the organization, and they continued to do so in this congress.

For long the Christian Democrats were under considerable pressure to take their followers out of the CUTCh. The principal labor leaders, though, of the party felt that this would be a mistake, that the pull among the rank and file of the "unity" slogan was too great, and that all of their followers would not abandon the Central Unica de Trabajadores if they were asked to do so.

The labor movement as a whole was considerably weaker in the early 1960's than it had been fifteen years before. In part, this was due to the workers having undergone two decades of continuous inflation, which at times had reached almost galloping proportions.

In addition, the continuous bitter conflicts within the labor movement had made many workers lose faith in the trade unions. This attitude was reinforced by the fact that the Communists had upon many occasions attempted to use the labor movement for their own partisan purposes, calling purely political general strikes. Finally, the employers in some industries had taken advantage of the weakened position of the organized labor movement to reduce their workers' organizations to the status of virtual company unions.

The election of 1964, which brought the Christian Democratic leader Eduardo Frei to the presidency of the republic, is likely to have profound effects on the labor movement. Frei had promised a program of extensive reforms, designed to raise the levels of living of the country's humbler citizens. Although as this is being written it is too early to know the degree to which Frei will be able to carry out his promised reforms, it seems likely that if he succeeds, he will involve the labor movement extensively in the process. Likewise, the advent of the Christian Democrats to power makes likely a shift of power within the ranks of organized labor itself.

Summary and Conclusion

Chile has for several decades possessed one of the most numerous and strongest labor movements of Latin America. Since the early 1940's most organizable workers of the country have belonged to the unions, including industrial, transportation, mining, and white-collar workers, and government employees.

Nevertheless, the labor movement has been weakened by the

fact that it has been sharply split among competing political factions for many decades. During most of the time since World War II, the Communists have been the dominant political element, although there have been various opposing groups which have challenged the Communists' hegemony. This constant political struggle, together with long-continuing rampant inflation, has tended to weaken the economic and political strength of organized labor.

EIGHT

Bolivian Organized Labor

LABOR ORGANIZATION IN BOLIVIA BEGAN BEFORE WORLD WAR I. BOTH anarchosyndicalist and Socialist literature entered the country, principally from Argentina, and visitors from that country also occasionally carried on propaganda in Bolivia. Small groups of Bolivian converts to both anarchosyndicalism and Marxian socialism were established, and they succeeded in organizing a few unions of handicraftsmen in La Paz and one or two other urban centers.

As elsewhere in Latin America, the growth of organized labor in Bolivia was stimulated by World War I. The first important strike among the country's miners took place in 1919. Yet, it was not until 1927 that the first important labor federation, the Federación Obrera Local under anarchosyndicalist influence, was established in La Paz.

During the latter half of the 1920's Communist influence began to compete with that of the anarchosyndicalists in the fledgling labor movement. The chief exponent of left-wing Marxism in these years was Gustavo Navarro, a former member of the Bolivian diplomatic corps, who had become enthusiastic about the Russian Revolution, and who wrote extensively under the pseudonym Tristan Maroff. In this period, however, the anarchosyndicalists continued to be the major influence in the labor movement.

Organized labor was all but destroyed during the Chaco War which Bolivia fought with Paraguay between 1932 and 1935. All elements in the trade unions took an antiwar position, and the

101

government severely persecuted both anarchosyndicalists and pro-communists.

However, the Chaco War marks a major turning point both in the history of Bolivia and in the life of its trade-union movement. The defeat of their country in this conflict aroused widespread discontent among young men of the middle classes with the whole social, economic, and political structure of Bolivia. The end of the war marked the opening of a period of great political turbulence which was to last for more than a decade and a half.

Insofar as the labor movement was concerned, the Chaco War was of major significance because the discontent aroused within the ranks of the younger officers who had participated in the conflict resulted in bringing to power for the first time governments that were sympathetic to organized labor. It was also important for the labor movement because the mobilization of large numbers of Indians to fight in the war had an unsettling effect among the great masses of the indigenous population, exposing them for the first time to a kind of life different from that to which they had been accustomed for hundreds of years. The first evidences of this effect were soon made evident among the workers in the country's all-important tin mines.

THE TORO AND BUSCH REGIMES

In May 1936 a military *coup d'état* installed a government led by Colonel David Toro, which proclaimed Bolivia to be a "Socialist Republic." For the first time, President Toro established a Ministry of Labor, and named a leader of the typographical workers' union of La Paz, Waldo Alvarez as the first person to hold the post. Official encouragement for the first time was shown for the organization of the country's urban workers.

Partly as a result of this official support the country's first really national labor organization was established, the Confederación Sindical de Trabajadores de Bolivia (CSTB). During its first years the CSTB was controlled by the followers of Tristan Maroff, who by this time had adopted an independent leftist position, separate from both Stalinist and Trotskyite Communists, both of whom became active after the end of the Chaco War. The anarchosyndicalist elements remained independent, and their Federación Obrera Local did not become part of the CSTB.

Colonel Toro's government was overthrown in 1937 by another military coup headed by Colonel Germán Busch, a hero of the Chaco War. During his administration, Tristan Maroff had considerable influence in the government, and his followers in the labor movement made the first serious attempt to organize the tin miners. As a result of their efforts, the Federación Sindical de Trabajadores Mineros was established.

The Busch administration was also of considerable significance for the labor movement because it propounded the country's first general labor law, extended legal recognition to the labor movement, and provided for collective bargaining. This was the so-called Busch Labor Code.

President Busch died under mysterious circumstances in the middle of 1939, and for four and a half years thereafter the country was governed by relatively conservative administrations. The only labor events of significance during this period were political in nature. The first was the loss of control of the CSTB by Tristan Maroff's group, now organized into the Partido Socialista Obrero Boliviano, and its capture by members of the newly formed Partido de la Izquierda Revolucionaria, out of which some years later was to emerge the Bolivian Communist party.

The second major labor event was the penetration of the miners' federation by members of another new party, the Movimiento Nacionalista Revolucionario (MNR), headed by Victor Paz Estenssoro, who had been an economic adviser of President Busch.

Another successful military *coup d'état* took place in December 1943. It was organized by a group of young army officers, led by Major Gualberto Villarroel and the MNR. Major Villarroel became president, and remained in power until July 1946.

During the two and a half years of the Villarroel regime, the MNR party consolidated its hold on the miners' unions. A congress of the Federación Sindical de Trabajadores Mineros in the middle of 1945 elected a member of the MNR, Juan Lechin, as the executive secretary of the organization. In alliance with the members of the MNR were the Trotskyites, organized in the Partido Obrero Revolucionario (POR).

The Villarroel government strongly encouraged the growth of the trade-union movement. New organizations were established among the factory workers of La Paz and a handful of other cities, and the already existing union of railroad workers strengthened its position. This government also took the first hesitating steps toward organizing the Indian peasants, calling a Congress of Indians shortly before being ousted from office.

Villarroel was overthrown by an uprising in La Paz in July 1946. During almost six years thereafter, the country was governed once again by relatively conservative elements. During much of this time, the pro-Stalinist Partido de la Izquierda Revolucionaria collaborated with these conservative regimes.

During the whole period between the overthrow of Villarroel and the outbreak of the Bolivian National Revolution in April 1952, the government concentrated considerable attention on trying to destroy the growing influence of the Movimiento Nacionalista Revolutionario on the organized labor movement. However, these efforts failed. The collaboration of the PIR with the conservative governments of the period served to discredit that party almost completely among the workers. Hence, instead of breaking the hold of the MNR on the tin miners, as the government and the PIR had hoped might be possible, they saw the MNR hold fast there and extend its influence to the railroad workers and factory hands, which had formerly been PIR controlled. By April 1952 the MNR dominated most of the labor movement, the only rival of any importance being its ally, the Trotskyite POR.

The revolution of April 9, 1952, put the Movimiento Nacionalista Revolucionario in full control of the government. Miners' chief Juan Lechin became Minister of Mines and Petroleum of the new regime, headed by President Victor Paz Estenssoro. Under Lechin's leadership a new national central labor body, the Central Obrera Boliviana, was organized by the end of April 1952. During the first half-dozen years of the new regime it was officially a "co-government" of the MNR party and the COB—

with the labor organization responsible for choosing four of the members of the cabinet.

The COB did not hold its first convention for a year and a half. During this period it was governed by a committee with a constantly changing membership composed of delegated representatives of its principal affiliates. These included national unions such as the miners, factory workers, and railroaders, as well as the Departmental Federations of Labor, which were soon organized in each of the country's departments or states.

The governing body of the COB met with great frequency, sometimes several times a week, during the early years of the revolution. As a result, it was necessary for the provincial affiliates to name people resident in the capital as their representatives. From this system of deputation there developed an important political struggle between the MNR and the Trotskyites during the first months of the new regime.

The Trotskyites had emerged from the period of conservative reaction stronger in the labor movement than they had ever been before or were ever to be again. The basis of their influence was their alliance with the labor wing of the MNR, and particularly with Juan Lechin, during the period from 1946 to 1952; however, they *had* acquired certain influence of their own among the factory and white-collar workers of La Paz, and to a less degree among the tin miners.

During the early months of the revolution, the principal MNR trade-union leaders were too involved with their responsibilities in helping to administer the new regime to pay the attention they might otherwise have done to the COB. As a result, the Trotskyites were able during this period to get enough of the provincial-labor groups to name members of the POR to represent them in the Central Obrera Boliviana to give the POR control of that organization, at least at certain meetings of its governing body.

The POR leadership tended to regard the Paz Estenssoro government as playing the role of Bolivia's Kerensky, who would "inevitably" be overthrown by the Bolivian Bolsheviks, organized as they saw it in the Partido Obrero Revolucionario. Likewise, they saw in the COB a Bolivian parallel to the Soviets in the Russia of 1917.

As it turned out, the POR leaders proved to be victims of their own slavish belief in historical parallelism. Their position of "critical support" for the Paz Estenssoro regime tended to become increasingly critical and to offer the new government less and less support. Under their editorship, the periodical of the COB became increasingly critical and even disparaging toward the MNR government.

A showdown between the MNR and POR elements in the Central Obrera Boliviana finally occurred early in October 1952. On the 2nd of that month President Paz Estenssoro had nationalized the Big Three tin companies, Patiño, Hochschild, and Aramayo, in a decree which provided for the eventual payment of compensation for the expropriated properties.

The POR had advocated confiscation, with absolutely no payment to the old companies instead of the kind of measure which the MNR regime had decreed. Therefore, in the next meeting of the COB governing body after the issuance of the expropriation decree, the Trotskyites pushed through a resolution denouncing the government's action. This, as it proved, was the beginning of the end of Trotskyite influence in Bolivian organized labor.

The MNR labor leaders immediately went into action. In the provinces where the MNR controlled most of the unions, they secured the deposition of Trotskyite delegates to the COB governing body, and their replacement by people belonging to the MNR. In La Paz they made sure that all unions controlled by the MNR sent MNR delegates to the COB.

As a result, the next meeting of the governing body of the COB reversed the decision to condemn the government's mine-nationalization decree. Furthermore, it deposed Trotskyites from leading positions in the COB itself. Henceforward, the labor movement was solidly in the hands of the MNR.

Meanwhile, organized labor had grown with tremendous rapidity. Virtually all miners, factory workers, railroad workers, and construction laborers were brought into the national unions affiliated with the COB. At the same time most white-collar workers and bank clerks were organized, and national unions of these groups were established, and became part of the Central Obrera Boliviana.

As a result of these developments, both the Confederación Sindical de Trabajadores de Bolivia, under PIR control, and the anarchosyndicalist Federación Obrera Local virtually ceased to exist. The PIR itself went out of existence late in 1952, although out of its remnants was organized a new Partido Comunista de Bolivia.

By the time of the revolution of April 1952 virtually all important trade-union leaders who had formerly belonged to the PIR had joined the Movimiento Nacionalista Revolucionario. After their defeat in the COB, the Trotskyite trade unionists became increasingly alienated from the leadership of their party which was both middle class and very doctrinaire, and in 1954 virtually all leading POR trade unionists likewise joined the MNR.

To a certain degree, the ex-PIR and ex-POR trade unionists carried their old quarrels with them into the Movimiento Nacionalista Revolucionario. The ex-PORistas rallied around Juan Lechin, by 1954 the recognized leader of the so-called "left wing" of the MNR. In contrast, the ex-members of the PIR constituted the core of the opposition to Lechin's influence in the labor movement.

This growing split within the trade-union ranks of the MNR came into the open during 1957. President Hernán Siles, who had succeeded Victor Paz Estenssoro as a result of elections held in the middle of 1956, got congress to enact a stabilization program to combat the sky rocketing inflation, which was threatening to throw the country's economy into chaos. Part of this program was a sizable wage increase for all workers, after which wages were frozen indefinitely.

Juan Lechin took the lead in opposing the Stabilization Program. Under his influence, the COB called a general strike of indefinite duration against the program. However, President Siles appealed over Lechin's head to the workers to support him, and all important unions except the miners finally decided to abandon the strike. The leaders in bringing about this change in heart were the ex-PIR unionists.

Siles then went personally to the country's chief mining centers. There, in spite of threats which had been made against his personal safety, he succeeded in convincing the rank-and-file mineworkers to go along with him, and to repudiate the general strike call.

As a result of this defeat of Lechin, the COB ceased for all practical purposes to be the country's central labor organization. Although few unions formally withdrew, from the middle of 1957 onward, the railroad workers, commercial employees, petroleum workers, and other key groups ceased to participate actively in the work of the COB.

It is probably true that at that point President Siles could have broken Lechin's hold over the miners' federation: for a committee for the reorganization of the federation was established by anti-Lechin elements in the organization, and if it had gotten support from Siles, it could probably have removed Lechin from the leadership. However, the president chose not to push his victory that far. As a result, Lechin remained the leader of the miners.

However, the deep split in the labor movement continued. The Stabilization Program, which was continued by President Victor Paz Estenssoro when he returned to office after the election of 1960, remained anathema to Lechin and his followers. It continued to be supported by his opponents in the labor movement.

Meanwhile, by 1960 the center of gravity of the MNR regime had shifted notably. Whereas, in the early years it had rested largely on the support of the working class and the middle class of the cities, by 1960 it had come to depend largely upon the Indian peasants, before 1952 the forgotten men of Bolivian society. Right after coming to power, the MNR government had thoroughly organized the peasantry into unions, local units of the MNR, and militia groups, armed with weapons formerly in the possession of the army. Thereafter, on August 2, 1953, President Paz Estenssoro had decreed a basic agrarian reform, to transfer the land from the white large landholders to the Indian peasants.

These moves had won the backing of the peasantry for the MNR, but more particularly for Paz Estenssoro and Hernán Siles, who had played the most obvious roles in the agrarian reform. While losing votes in the cities in the elections of 1956, 1958, 1960, and 1962, the MNR maintained solid support among the peasants. This backing freed the Paz Estenssoro group from its previously great dependence upon the urban workers and particularly upon the miners.

The conflict in the labor movement and in the MNR, between the Paz Estenssoro and Lechin wings, came to a head during 1963. In the background to the events of that year was the approaching presidential election campaign of 1964. Juan Lechin was being openly pushed by his supporters to succeed President Paz Estenssoro, who was being backed for re-election by the anti-Lechin elements.

The issue over which the struggle was played out was the problem of reorganizing the mining industry. Several of the bigger government-owned mines were exhausted, the industry was seriously overstaffed, production had been falling since the revolution; and the nationalized tin-mining company, the Corporación Minera de Bolivia, had lost money consistently. Therefore, in 1962 the Paz Estenssoro government entered into an agreement with the Inter-American Bank, the United States Government, and some private West German mining and banking interests to reorganize the country's mining industry with their help.

This reorganization called for the closing down of unproductive mines, exploration for new ones, re-equipment of those mines which were still productive, and the laying off of the COMIBOL's surplus labor force. Juan Lechin's supporters led the resistance to the Triangular Agreement. They urged Lechin, who not only was the vice-president of the republic but was also serving as ambassador to Italy, to return home to lead the struggle. Although he did not do so, the miners' federation finally called a general strike of indefinite duration in August 1963.

The government of Paz Estenssoro refused to budge in the face of this miners' walkout. For the first time, there was a basic showdown between the government and the miners' organization.

The defeat of the miners in this struggle meant the eclipse of the chances of Lechin to become president of Bolivia.

When Juan Lechin sought the MNR candidacy for president against Victor Paz Estenssoro in the 1964 election and failed to receive it, he took his supporters out of the party and organized the Partido Revolucionario de la Izquierda Nacionalista. In a countermove, the followers of President Paz in the labor movement withdrew from the Central Obrera Boliviana and formed the Central Obrera Boliviana Renovada. Lechin's support was limited largely to the miners, and even among them, some local unions balked at Lechin's continuing leadership.

Paz Estenssoro was re-elected president and was inaugurated for a third term in 1964. Before the election, Juan Lechin withdrew from the contest, on the claim that his rights as a candidate were not being respected. Hernán Siles backed up Lechin's claim, and was subsequently expelled from the MNR.

The relations between the government and the dissident elements of the MNR became so strained that Lechin and Siles were accused in September 1964 of having organized a plot to assassinate President Paz Estenssoro. They were deported from the country. Two months later, the opposition of the miners was a key factor in provoking the overthrow of President Victor Paz Estenssoro by the military, led by Vice-President General René Barrientos.

The ousting of Paz Estenssoro brought great confusion to both the organized labor movement and the general political situation. Although Juan Lechin and the miners at first backed General Barrientos, they broke with him within a couple of months of his seizure of power. The realignment of forces in labor and general politics is still not complete as this is being written.

Summary and Conclusion

Thus by the middle of 1965 the labor movement continued to be dominated by the political groups that had led the revolution of 1952. However, the original MNR was seriously divided, and this division was reflected in a split in the labor movement.

The vast majority of the organized workers had been brought

into the labor movement as a result of the National Revolution; but the relative power of the labor movement had declined during the first decade of the revolution, partly because of its own internal feuding, partly because of the growth of the importance of the peasants as a political factor.

Labor relations in Bolivia continue to be plagued by the poverty of the national economy, and of the workers within that economy. Only with the further economic development of the nation would it be possible for the organized labor movement to make any substantial progress in raising the standards of living of its members.

The Labor Movement of Peru

THE KIND OF BASIC SOCIAL REVOLUTION WHICH BEGAN IN BOLIVIA IN 1952 and was well-advanced a dozen years later has only entered its opening phases in neighboring Peru which shares the central part of the Andean range with Bolivia. As a result of these different circumstances, the role of the labor movement has been considerably different in Peru from that in its neighbor.

EARLY YEARS OF PERUVIAN ORGANIZED LABOR

Organized labor in Peru had its origins in the years before the First World War. Anarchosyndicalists and Socialists from abroad, particularly from Argentina, visited the country and spread the ideas of their organizations. At the same time the workers established mutual-benefit societies and a few trade unions in Lima and other important cities during this period.

The majority group in the Peruvian labor movement at that time was the anarchosyndicalists. In 1913 they established a national central labor organization, the Federación Obrera Regional Peruana, the name of which was copied from that of the Argentine anarchosyndicalist group, the Federación Obrera Regional Argentina.

The labor movement of Peru, as those of most other Latin American countries, received a considerable impetus from World War I. The membership of the unions increased rapidly, and their policies were militant during the war years. The high point of this period of the history of Peruvian organized labor was a

112

general strike for an eight-hour day in 1918. The strike was won by the workers, and the government issued a general eight-hour-day law in the following year.

THE BEGINNINGS OF THE APRISTA MOVEMENT

In 1918 the organized labor movement established close contacts with the country's university students. In that year Victor Raúl Haya de la Torre became president of the Federation of Peruvian Students, and under his administration of the federation, it undertook to establish a series of workers-education centers in various union headquarters. These were given the name of Universidades Populares González Prada.

The students also helped the workers in their organizing efforts. Victor Raúl Haya de la Torre, for instance, took a leading part in helping the country's textile workers to establish a national federation for the first time. This was organized in a congress held in Lima, and Haya was one of the principal speakers at this congress. The leader of the new federation was a young anarchosyndicalist, Arturo Sabroso.

This alliance of the workers and students continued for five years. However, the government of the contemporary dictator, President Augusto B. Leguía, was very suspicious of the students activities. He feared that they would lead to conspiracy against his regime. From time to time he closed the "popular universities."

Finally, in May 1923 the students and workers organized an open demonstration against the regime. This took place upon the occasion of a public ceremony commemorating the "dedication of Peru to the Sacred Heart of Jesus" by the Leguía government. Both students and workers, who were anticlerical if not antireligious in their attitudes, felt that this move by the government was not only hypocritical but was designed to give the Church excessive power and influence.

As a result of this demonstration, the principal student leaders were exiled. They stayed abroad for the next seven years, until after the overthrow of the Leguía regime. While in exile, the student leaders established a political organization which they named the Alianza Popular Revolucionaria Americana. They kept in close contact with their labor allies. Haya de la Torre and other student leaders frequently contributed articles to labor periodicals in Peru.

In 1927 the Leguía government cracked down on the organized labor movement. It accused the principal leaders of the trade unions of being "Communists," and arrested many of them. After a short while, most of them were released from prison.

During the 1920's some of the leaders of the students and trade-union leaders who remained in Peru had close associations with José Carlos Mariátegui. He was a young man who had studied in Europe right after the First World War, had been profoundly influenced by the revolutionary atmosphere of the Old World at that time, and had become a convinced Marxist, by his own lights. He published a periodical known as "Amauta," to which not only members of his own group but also Haya de la Torre and his associates contributed.

Mariátegui and his closest associates established the Partido Socialista del Peru, a Marxist party which had "fraternal" affiliation to the Communist International. In 1929 the Comintern ordered it to change its name to Partido Comunista and to repudiate the theories of Mariátegui concerning the need of integrating the Indian into the modern society of Peru, in favor of the then current line favoring the formation of a separate "Quechua republic." Mariátegui died of tuberculosis before he had to make the decision whether or not to accept the Comintern's dictates; however, some of his followers went on and established the Peruvian Communist party, led by Eudosio Rabines as its first secretary-general.

ORGANIZED LABOR IN THE 1930'S

Upon the overthrow of the Leguía dictatorship in 1930, most of the exiled student leaders returned to Peru. There they and the one-time anarchosyndicalists of the labor movement established the Partido Aprista Peruano (a name based on the initials of the Alianza Popular Revolucionaria Americana).

Haya de la Torre returned home in 1931, almost a year after the ousting of Leguía, since the military men in charge would not allow him to go back earlier. He ran against the principal member of the military junta, Colonel Sánchez Cerro, for the presidency in elections held in that year. Although the Apristas claimed that they had won the election, the government counted the votes to show a victory for Colonel Sánchez Cerro.

The emergence of the Aprista and Communist parties led to a split in the organized labor movement. Under Communist leadership, the Confederación General de Trabajadores del Peru was established in 1931. Two years later, however, those unions controlled by the Apristas withdrew from the CGTP to establish a rival central labor group.

The labor movement as a whole led a precarious existence during the 1930's. President Sánchez Cerro established a dictatorship, which was, on one hand, particularly active in persecuting the Aprista party and the unions under its control, and, on the other, much more tolerant of the much smaller Communist party and of the unions which it dominated.

President Sánchez Cerro was assassinated in 1934, allegedly by an Aprista. Power was seized by the country's outstanding military figure, General Oscar Benavides. For about a year he allowed the re-establishment of open-opposition political parties and of the labor movement; however, after that period he again arrested, exiled, and otherwise persecuted the noncommunist part of the labor movement.

President Benavides' term finally ended in 1939. In elections held in that year, he backed Manuel Prado as his successor, against Luis Flores, who had succeeded the late President Sánchez Cerro as head of the fascist-oriented Unión Nacional party.

For the purposes of this election, the dictatorship made an alliance with the Communist party. The Communists supported the candidacy of Manuel Prado, and in return Juan P. Luna, the party's principal labor leader and the head of the Chauffeurs' Federation of Lima, was named as a candidate for the Chamber of Deputies on the Prado ticket.

THE PRADO REGIME AND THE CTP

President Prado relaxed the dictatorship of his predecessor. He allowed a much wider degree of freedom to the organized labor movement. Although the Prado regime favored the Communists and other groups which were opposed to the influence of the Apristas in the organized labor movement, it did allow the Apristas to lead the Textile Workers' Federation and a few other groups in which their predominance could not possibly be questioned.

With wider freedom to organize, the labor movement grew rapidly. Most of the more important groups of regularly employed urban workers were brought into the unions. Existing national industrial federations were strengthened, and several new ones were established during the early years of World War II.

An important event in the labor movement during this period was the visit of Vicente Lombardo Toledano, president of the Confederación de Trabajadores de America Latina, to Peru in 1942. Lombardo talked at length with President Manuel Prado, conferred with most of the country's principal labor leaders, and also met extensively with the leaders of the Peruvian Communist party. He is reported to have urged President Prado to allow the establishment of a new central labor confederation under the leadership of the Communists.

Whether as a result of the influence of Lombardo Toledano or of the general tendency toward relaxation of dictatorial controls, President Prado did allow the re-establishment of a national labor confederation. At a meeting to celebrate the 1st of May 1944, the labor leaders there assembled proclaimed the formation of the Confederación de Trabajadores del Peru.

Subsequently, the structure of the CTP was formalized. Although some Apristas were included in its leadership, Juan P. Luna, the Communist deputy, was chosen as its first secretary-general. His role in the labor movement was peculiarly important throughout the Prado regime. His congressional immunity gave him certain protection during this period, and many important labor meetings took place in his house, which the police did not choose to raid.

From its inception, the CTP was affiliated with Lombardo Toledano's Confederación de Trabajadores de America Latina. Thus, Lombardo's influence continued to be exerted in favor of the Communist leadership of the Peruvian confederation.

So long as the Prado administration remained in power, the Communists continued to dominate the labor movement. In part at least, their leading position was due to the officials of the Ministry of Labor using all their influence to favor the Communists, whom the regime did not fear, against the Apristas, whom it did.

ORGANIZED LABOR IN THE 1945-1948 PERIOD

President Manuel Prado's term came to an end in June 1945. He was forced to hold honest elections to choose his successor. He went so far as to authorize the legalization of the Aprista party, although this was not done in time to permit the party to name its own presidential candidate; however, it did run lists of nominees for both houses of congress. A number of the most important Aprista labor leaders were elected deputies and senators.

The Apristas backed the candidacy of José Luis Bustamante y Rivero, the opposition nominee, who was a former judge and diplomat. During the first months of the Bustamante regime, the Apristas enjoyed a wide degree of power, and for almost a year three members of the party served as ministers in Bustamante's cabinet.

As a result of the election of 1945 and of the legalization of the Aprista party, control of the labor movement changed. The Communists were removed from the leadership of the Confederación de Trabajadores del Peru, and the Apristas took control of the group. Arturo Sabroso, the long-time Aprista leader of the Textile Workers' Federation, became secretary-general of the CTP.

The Apristas also took control of several key federations belonging to the Confederación, which had formerly been in Communist hands, including Juan Luna's Chauffeurs' Federation.

During the three years of President Bustamante's regime, the labor movement was considerably strengthened. Collective bargaining contracts became widespread in urban industries, mining, and the oil fields. Even some of the largest modern agricultural enterprises, such as the sugar plantations, were forced for the first time to deal with their workers' unions.

The change in the political control of the Confederación de Trabajadores del Peru resulted in a withdrawal of the group from the Confederación de Trabajadores de America Latina. The CTP took the lead in helping to establish a rival Inter-American group, the Confederación Interamericana de Trabajadores, the founding congress of which was held in Lima, the Peruvian capital, in January 1948. The action of the CTP in withdrawing from the CTAL served as the excuse for the minority of unions which continued to be controlled by the Communists to withdraw from the Confederación de Trabajadores del Peru and then to establish a short-lived Unity Committee, which affiliated with the CTAL.

LABOR AND THE ODRÍA DICTATORSHIP

Relations between President Bustamante and the Apristas became increasingly strained. On October 3, 1948, a naval mutiny in the port of Callao, led by dissident members of the Aprista party, was used as an excuse by President Bustamante to outlaw the Apristas. Three weeks later, Bustamante himself was overthrown by a military *coup d'état* led by General Manuel Odría, one-time Minister of Defense of Bustamante.

Shortly after the overthrow of Bustamante, the Odría government arrested all of the top leaders of the Confederación de Trabajadores del Peru. They were held in prison for more than a year, when their release was brought about largely by pressure from abroad. The CTP itself was "suspended" by the government.

The Odría regime did not want to allow the free re-establishment of a unified labor movement, fearing quite rightly that it would probably come under the control of the Apristas. There were two principal political groups which were given freedom to act during this period, a Communist faction and the Peronistas.

Juan P. Luna returned to importance in the labor movement during the Odría regime. Officially, he had quit the Communist party a few weeks before the overthrow of the Bustamante government; as a result of which he was eligible under the rules Odría established to run for office in the election that was called in 1950. Luna was chosen a senator on the single pro-Odría ticket which participated in this "contest."

Previously, Juan Luna had succeeded in regaining control of the Chauffeurs' Federation when its Aprista leaders were arrested. Associates of Luna also won influence in the construction workers' and other important unions.

During the late 1940's and early 1950's the Peronistas were attempting to extend their influence in the labor movements of Latin America. In Peru they succeeded in establishing a Committee of Trade Union Unity, headed by a renegade Aprista, Tomás del Piélago, a leader of the Printing-Trades Workers' Federation.

Under the leadership of the pro-Luna Communists and the Peronistas several attempts were made to re-establish the Confederación de Trabajadores del Peru. Yet, in spite of the patronage of these moves, the Apristas tended to have a majority among the union delegates who participated in these meetings. As a result, the government refused to give its approval to the reorganization of the CTP.

In spite of the opposition of the dictatorial government, the Apristas continued to control an important part of the labor movement; e.g., the Textile Workers' Federation, in particular, remained a stronghold of the party among the workers.

The Odría government sought to win over the workers by a labor program of its own. The social security system was extended, special benefits were enacted for some groups of workers, and a sizable low-cost-housing program was carried out in Lima. This program succeeded in gaining for Odría a certain amount of working-class following, particularly in the very poorest working-class wards of Lima and Callao.

LABOR AND THE SECOND PRADO ADMINISTRATION

President Odría's term of office came to an end in 1956. Although he would have liked to have himself re-elected, military and civilian elements associated with his government vetoed this idea, and in the end Odría was forced to call elections.

In the months preceding the election of June 1956, the dictatorship was relaxed, and most Aprista exiles returned to the country. Others were released from jail, and still others who had been politically quiescent in the preceding years returned to party activity. As a result, Aprista influence in the labor movement revived once again.

Odría did not legalize the Aprista party, however, nor allow it openly to participate in the 1956 election. Nevertheless, all three presidential candidates sought the backing of the Apristas. Odría's nominee, Hernando de Lavalle, held long discussions with the Aprista leaders, but they finally refused to back him because his patron refused to legalize their party.

The second candidate was Fernando Belaúnde Terry, one-time ally of the Apristas, while a member of the Chamber of Deputies from 1945 to 1948. He launched his candidacy for president as nominee of the opposition to the dictatorship, and expected to receive Aprista support. The party, however, would not back him because they did not think Odría would allow him to take power, and because he threatened to offer them serious opposition among groups among whom they had always found the bulk of their own support—the workers and urban middle class.

The third candidate was Manuel Prado, the ex-dictator. At the beginning of the campaign, he seemed to have little chance of winning; however, in negotiations with the Apristas, he promised as his first presidential act to legalize their party. As a result, they threw their support to him at the last moment, and thus were responsible for his victory at the polls.

During the six years of the Prado regime, the country enjoyed more political freedom than it had had in any part of its history. The labor movement, in particular, was allowed to organize freely, and to negotiate collective agreements with the employers. Moreover, unions among groups such as the sugar workers, which had been destroyed under Odría, were allowed to reorganize, although some strikes among them were roughly handled by police.

The labor movement was almost completely in the hands of the Apristas during the Prado regime. They completely dominated the Confederación de Trabajadores del Peru, which was reestablished in 1956 under the secretary-generalship once again of Arturo Sabroso. They controlled almost all important national industrial unions, the only important exception being the Federation of Bank Clerks, which was dominated by the Communists and their allies during most of this period.

LABOR AND THE CRISIS OF 1962-1963

Once again in 1962 the advent of a new presidential election provoked a major political crisis, which endangered the labor movement. In the contest to choose a successor to President Prado, there were three major candidates: Victor Raúl Haya de la Torre, founder and chief of the Aprista party; Fernando Belaúnde Terry, repeating his role as opposition nominee which he had had in 1956; and ex-dictator Manuel Odría.

Haya de la Torre got the largest vote in this election, although just short of the number of suffrages necessary to give him the presidency. He would have had enough support in congress to be selected, but the military would not allow this, and they deposed President Prado and canceled the election.

The Apristas sought to use their control of the labor movement to frustrate the military *coup,* but the general strike called by the leadership of the Confederación de Trabajadores del Peru was an almost total failure.

In 1963 elections took place once again, with the same three candidates. This time Fernando Belaúnde Terry was the victor. He took office at the end of July 1963. However, the Apristas elected the largest single group of members of congress, and their successful candidates included nineteen labor leaders.

In spite of their defeats, the Apristas continued in formal control of the organized labor movement. After the inauguration of Belaúnde Terry, they feared that the new government might seriously try to use its influence to break this control. However, two years after Belaúnde took office, the Apristas were still in strong control of the Confederación de Trabajadores del Peru and of most of its affiliates.

Summary and Conclusion

The history of the labor movement of Peru is closely linked with that of the Aprista Party. Many of the anarchosyndicalists who were the first leaders of organized labor became founders of the party, and since World War One it has been the most important factor in the Peruvian trade unions. From time to time the Aprista influence has been challenged by Communists, Peronistas and other rival groups.

The fate of the labor movement has also been closely dependent on the nature of the Peruvian government at any given time. Frequently since the early decades of this century it has been persecuted or even driven underground by dictatorial regimes. However, since the re-establishment of political democracy in 1956 the trade unions of Peru have come to encompass most of the country's regularly employed urban workers, and have been able to engage in orderly collective bargaining.

TEN

Ecuadorean Organized Labor

ECONOMIC DEVELOPMENT AND SOCIAL CHANGE HAVE COME RELA-
tively slowly to Ecuador. The largest part of the population, the
highland Indian people, still work the land under conditions
that have not changed very markedly since the early decades of
the Spanish Conquest in the sixteenth century. It was not until
1964 that a first attempt was made to alter this semifeudal pattern.

Manufacturing is still limited to a few principal cities, and
consists of the production of textiles, some processed foodstuffs,
and scattered building materials and light metal products. A large
part of the urban working class still consists of handicraftsmen
and artisans.

The country from time immemorial has been sharply divided
between the hot, damp coastal regions, and the cool mountain-
ous area, with Guayaquil, the principal port, being the center of
influence of the former, and Quito, the national capital, being
the principal urban center of the latter. These two regions have
differed in racial composition—predominantly Indians in the
highlands, and mainly mulattoes and mestizos along the Coast—
as well as in social customs and outlook.

All of these factors have been reflected in the labor movement
of Ecuador. Even by the 1960's the number of organized workers
was still comparatively small and most of them were concentrated
in the Quito and Guayaquil areas. Ecuador remained one of the
few countries in Latin America in which the differentiation of
mutual-benefit societies (workers cooperatives providing health
and burial insurance) from trade unions was still far from complete.

123

BEGINNINGS OF THE LABOR MOVEMENT

There were a few mutual-benefit societies in existence among the artisans of Quito and Guayaquil as early as the 1870's. The Liberal Revolution of the early 1890's, led by General Eloy Alfaro, resulted in the expansion of this type of workers' organization. In 1905 the mutual-benefit groups of Guayaquil formed a city-wide body, the Confederación Obrera del Guayas, which exists to this day, although it has somewhat changed its character.

However, not only the Liberals were interested in the artisan workers. Their opponent, the Catholic Church, undertook as early as 1902 to begin to establish so-called Catholic Workers' Circles in various parts of the country.

The First World War gave some slight impetus to the development of organizations among the workers of Ecuador. Thus, in 1917 the first recorded strike took place in Quito among the tailors of the city. It was successful, but does not seem to have exerted any major influence on the further development of organized labor in that city.

Most commentators on the Ecuadorean labor movement date the beginning of a modern labor movement to the year 1922. Early in the year anarchosyndicalists among the workers in the two principal cities succeeded in organizing what aspired to be a national labor federation, under the name of Federación Obrera Regional Ecuatoriana. This federation had the distinction of being outlawed by the government in the following year, but was revived in 1924.

Among the affiliates of the FORE was a union of railroad workers. In November 1922 this organization delared the first major strike in the country's history. This walkout was met by repression on the part of the government, and on November 15, 1922, a clash occurred between police, on the one hand, and railroaders and students, on the other, in which several people were killed and wounded.

Soon after this strike a new labor confederation, the Confederación de Sindicatos Obreros was established in Quito. Although it aspired to become a nationwide group, it seems to have been confined largely to the capital city. Its relatively conservative political orientation was shown by the fact that it joined the Pan-American Federation of Labor.

In 1925 a new political element entered the labor movement. A group of young men, headed by Ricardo Paredes, Luis F. Maldonado Estrada and Jorge Carrera Andrade, established a monthly periodical in Quito, known as *La Antorcha* (The Torch), which was broadly Socialist in orientation, although inclined to be friendly to the Soviet Union. Around this periodical there developed a new political party, the Partido Socialista Ecuatoriano, which began to have some considerable influence in the nascent labor movement.

The Partido Socialista continued to move in a procommunist direction, becoming a "fraternal" affiliate of the Communist International in 1928, and changing its name to Partido Comunista in 1929. It was accepted shortly afterwards as a full-fledged member of the Comintern; however, a sizable group of members and leaders, headed by Luis Maldonado Estrada, refused to follow this orientation of the party, and withdrew from it. They finally formed a new Partido Socialista in 1933.

In the meanwhile, the influence of the anarchosyndicalists, which had been very strong in the labor movement, declined; and in 1929 the Federación Obrera Regional Ecuatoriana was reported to have supposedly collapsed—leaving the unions largely under Communist and Socialist leadership. An attempt by the anarchosyndicalists in 1933 to revive their forces, with the founding of the Federación Obrera Regional Local in Guayaquil, had only short-lived success.

The size and militancy of the labor movement grew in the 1930's as industrialization of the country got under way. In the middle of the decade a number of unions began to appear among the industrial workers. In 1936 a Textile Workers' Federation was established; it, too, was short-lived, and was not revived until 1944. The militancy of the new unions was reflected in various strikes in Quito, Guayaquil, and one or two other towns.

Several attempts were made to establish national labor confederations. A congress for this purpose failed in 1935 because of political quarrels among union leaders. In 1937 central labor groups were formed in Quito and Guayaquil: the Unión Sindical de Trabajadores de Pichincha in the former and the Confederación de Trabajadores de Guayaquil in the latter. Socialists and Communists were in the leadership of both of these organizations.

In 1939 a congress called to establish a Confederación General de Trabajadores failed because of political discord and rivalry between unionists of the coastal area around Guayaquil and of the mountain region centering on Quito. In the following year, another congress was called by leading local union leaders in Quito, Guayaquil and other towns for the purpose of establishing a national confederation, the name Confederación Obrera Nacional being used on this occasion but it failed for the same reasons as had earlier attempts to unify the Ecuadorean labor movement.

Although these efforts to set up a national confederation of labor failed, several national industrial federations were established in the late 1930's. These included the Barbers' Federation which was set up in 1937, and the Petroleum Workers' Federation and a new Railroad Workers' Federation founded in 1938 which entered into limited collective bargaining with employers. Again, Socialist and Communist political influences were dominant in these groups.

These political groups were not, however, the only ones active in the organized labor movement. The Catholic Church returned to the field, and in 1938 the First Congress of Catholic Workers was held in Quito. As a result of this meeting, the Confederación Ecuatoriana de Obreros Catolicos (CEDOC) was established. It continued during the following quarter of a century to have some small following in Quito, pariticularly among the artisans of the capital, and most of its affiliates were mutual-benefit societies. However, it did remain a minority group in the organized labor movement.

The government reported in 1942 on the strength of the national labor movement. There were at that time some 451 registered unions in Ecuador, with 22,778 members. Of these, some 6,163 union members were in Quito and 2,951 were in Guayaquil.

These figures perhaps underestimated the total number of unionists in the country, but not appreciably.

THE CONFEDERACIÓN DE TRABAJADORES DEL ECUADOR

Late in 1942 Vicente Lombardo Toledano, president of the Confederación de Trabajadores de America Latina, visited Ecuador. He conferred with President Carlos Arroyo del Rio, and met with the principal Communist and Socialist trade-union leaders. In these conferences, Lombardo Toledano urged the workers to establish a national labor confederation.

Largely as the result of Lombardo Toledano's initiative, a national labor conference was held in Quito in March 1943. The delegates represented unions in all parts of the country, and included people of Communist, Socialist, and anarchosyndicalist persuasion. They elected a Comité Nacional de Trabajadores del Ecuador (National Committee of Ecuadorian Workers), which was instructed to lay the basis for the establishment of a national labor confederation.

The government of President Carlos Arroyo del Rio broke up this March 1943 meeting shortly after the election of the National Committee. Those delegates who were friendly to the government then met separately and organized what they named the Confederación de Trabajadores del Ecuador.

The hostile attitude of the Arroyo del Rio administration toward the Comité Nacional de Trabajadores del Ecuador, and the control of that group by Socialist and Communist elements assured that the Comité would be in opposition to the government. In fact it took a leading part in the plotting which led to the overthrow of Arroyo del Rio on May 29, 1944.

In the provisional government which succeeded the May 1944 *coup d'état,* the Socialist and Communist parties were represented, along with the Liberals and Conservatives. As a result, the new regime was markedly friendly to the organized labor movement. With its endorsement, a new labor congress was called, which met on July 4, 1944. This meeting, which was attended by

1,030 delegates, finally succeeded in organizing a new Confederación de Trabajadores del Ecuador. The organization of the same name which had been established in the previous year disappeared with the overthrow of Arroyo del Rio.

The Communists and Socialists were the principal political factions represented in the new confederation. Not only did a Communist union leader from Guayaquil, Pedro Saad, become president of the founding congress of the CTE, but he also became the first secretary-general of the confederation. Moreover the Communists remained the majority group in the CTE during its first two and a half years; however, they did encounter considerable friction between the Socialists and themselves during these first years of the life of the CTE. In the second congress of the confederation, though, the Socialists succeeded in getting a majority, and they succeeded in ousting Saad as secretary-general of the organization.

Although the Communists were ousted from control of the CTE, the confederation remained affiliated with the Communist-dominated Confederación de Trabajadores de America Latina, even after most of the noncommunist trade-union groups of Latin America had withdrawn from the CTAL. Indeed, the CTE was still a member of the CTAL in the early 1960's, the only ostensibly noncommunist labor-union group in Latin America which remained in that organization.

Throughout the post-World War II period, Communist influence in the Confederación de Trabajadores del Ecuador was maintained largely because of fear of the power of the Right in national politics. The governments of Presidents José Velasco Ibarra (1952-1956), Camilo Ponce Henriquez (1956-1960), and José Velasco Ibarra again (1960-1962) all tended to lean to the conservative side. As a result, the Communists were able to play on the fear of the Socialist union leaders that the government was going to try to destroy the labor movement. In 1960 most Socialist labor leaders supported a joint ticket with the Communists in the presidential elections.

OPPOSITION TO CTE

In the late 1950's there appeared for the first time a sizable group which offered opposition to the CTE in the Ecuadorian labor movement. The base of this anti-CTE movement was the Confederación Obrera del Guayas, one of the country's oldest labor organizations. Although this confederation had traditionally been composed of mutual-benefit societies, by the late 1950's it also included a number of trade unions.

The COG, with the help of the International Cooperation Administration of the U.S. government, established a leadership-training course. Unionists led by the graduates of this training program led a successful fight in the 1960 congressional election to defeat Pedro Saad, who for almost two decades had been senator representing the workers of the coastal region in the national congress.

The culmination of this movement in the Guayaquil area was the establishment of a labor confederation uniting the non-CTE workers' organizations in the coastal region, the Confederación Obrera de Sindicatos Libres de Guayas. This new confederation not only aided its members in their collective bargaining activities but also launched an extensive program of labor education for both leaders and rank and file members of the unions.

Subsequently, other regional labor confederations were organized by the anti-CTE union groups. In the Quito region a confederation was established in 1962. Other similar organizations including the Railroad Workers' Federation, one of the country's most powerful unions, also associated itself with this anti-CTE movement, which had the support of the International Confederation of Free Trade Unions and its regional affiliate, the ORIT.

These efforts in various parts of the country had as their ultimate objective the establishment of a rival national central labor group to the Confederación de Trabajadores del Ecuador. This was finally achieved when the Confederación Obrera Ecuadoriana de Sindicatos Libres was established. It affiliated with the ICFTU and the ORIT.

The overthrow of the government of President Carlos Arosemena in the middle of 1963 brought about a change in the labor movement. The military junta which seized power at that time proclaimed its violent opposition to the Communists, and a considerable number of Communists inside and outside of the labor movement were jailed. It was, however, not only the extreme Left in the labor movement which was adversely affected by the new regime, for the Railway Workers' Federation, too, was reported as being "seriously demoralized" a few months after the junta seized power.

Yet, the moves of the military regime to bring about basic changes in the economic and social structure of Ecuador promised to bring an even more fundamental alteration in the position and role of the organized labor movement. The measure for agrarian reform enacted in the middle of 1964 indicated the possibility of transforming the hitherto landless peasantry into the most powerful element in the nation's political life. Moves to create a more equitable tax system also indicated the likelihood that the position of the traditional wealthy class would be weaker than ever before.

Summary and Conclusion

The labor movement of Ecuador traditionally has been weak. The majority element in the trade unions has been led by Socialists and Communists for three decades, with the latter being the more powerful of the two during most of this period. A Catholic minority group, the CEDOC has existed since the late 1930's, but it has been of relatively little influence in the total workers' movement. Starting in the late 1950's another element appeared in the trade unions, which within half a decade had come to offer serious opposition to the Communist-Socialist controlled Confederación de Trabajadores del Ecuador.

The military *coup d'état* of 1963 showed indications of opening a whole new phase in the history of Ecuadorian organized labor. Not only did it adopt a reserved if not hostile attitude toward all trade-union elements existing at that time, but it also promised fundamental changes in the country's economic and social system. These changes, if carried out, would create entirely new conditions for organized labor, and would undoubtedly bring new political elements to the fore in the trade-union movement.

ELEVEN

Organized Labor in Colombia

AS IN MOST OF THE LATIN AMERICAN COUNTRIES, THERE WERE A number of Utopian Socialists in Colombia during the nineteenth century. Nevertheless, throughout most of this period the country was plagued with political instability, several times resulting in civil war, which served to hinder the nation's economic development, and hence prevented the growth of organized labor.

In the early years of the twentieth century, after three years of bitter civil war, Colombia entered a period of relative political stability. Significantly, although a number of the more important leaders of the country during this period professed to favor the "socialist" reorganization of Colombian society, it was, however, several decades before a genuine labor movement appeared.

During World War I there were several spontaneous strikes. In the following years, workers in the principal urban centers began to form mutual-benefit societies and so-called "resistance societies" (embryonic anarchosyndicalist-led trade unions), a number of which were under anarchosyndicalist leadership. At the same time, local socialist parties appeared in several of the more important cities, and succeeded in electing members to local governing bodies.

THE WORKERS' CONGRESSES OF THE 1920'S

The first attempt to bring the workers' organizations together in a national organization took place in 1924. The First Workers' Congress met in Bogotá, and the delegates represented both mutual-benefit societies and a few scattered trade unions. The

132

general tone of the congress was conservative. No permanent organization resulted from this congress because of disagreements among delegates as to the form it should take.

A year later, the Second Workers' Congress met in the capital. In contrast to its predecessor, it was controlled by anarchosyndicalist elements, who were determined to establish a permanent organization. As a result the country's first central labor organization, the Confederación Obrera Nacional (CON) was founded, with its headquarters in Cali.

Although the anarchosyndicalists controlled the Second Workers' Congress, their influence was not so great in the CON. As a result, anarchosyndicalist unions in the coastal towns and cities withdrew from the organization at the end of 1925 to establish a rival group, the Unión Sindical Colombiana.

In the meanwhile, more conservative elements in the labor movement were centered in the Department of Bolivar. Their stronghold was the Directorio Obrero Departmental de Bolivar, which was affiliated with the Pan-American Federation of Labor, and sent delegates to its congress in Washington, D.C., in 1927.

In 1926 the Third Workers' Congress met in Bogotá. The delegates to this meeting were divided into three discordant groups. The most conservative of these favored the continuation of the Confederación Obrera Nacional as a trade-union group, without any particular political orientation. The extreme Left of the congress proposed that it sponsor the establishment of a Communist party of Colombia, as a full-fledged member of the Communist International. A centrist group, which was dominant in the congress, favored establishment of a workers' political party, but of a more moderate kind. As a result, the Third Workers' Congress set up the Partido Socialista Revolucionario, which was short of a full-fledged Communist party, but joined the Communist International as a "sympathetic member" in 1928.

THE SANTA MARTA BANANA STRIKE

The first major strike in the country's history took place in 1928. The anarchosyndicalists had been active among the banana workers of the coastal region, particularly the employees of the United Fruit Company, for several years. They had succeeded in organizing the workers of the area into unions, although they had not achieved recognition from the company. The Conservative government was hostile to the movement.

Early in 1928 the leaders of the Partido Socialista Revolucionario became interested in the banana workers' organizations. Since some of the PSR members had important contacts in the Liberal party, they succeeded in enlisting some support in the Liberal press of Bogotá and other cities for the trade-union movement among the banana workers.

A strike finally broke out among the United Fruit Company employees in August 1928. Because the company was a foreign-owned enterprise and because many of its activities had been resented by small merchants and other elements in the Santa Marta region, the strike rallied widespread popular support in the banana area. The Liberal press also came to the support of the movement.

One of the reasons for Liberal backing of the banana workers' walkout was the fact that party leaders saw in it an opportunity for embarrassing the Conservative-party government of the day. The administration sent troops into the Santa Marta region, many of the strike leaders were arrested, and the walkout was broken.

This banana workers' strike was one of the important contributing factors in the victory of the Liberal party in the election of 1930—the first time the party had triumphed in the twentieth century. Most of the important leaders of the Partido Socialista Revolucionario rejoined the Liberal ranks from which they had originally come, and they contributed considerably to the Liberal victory.

LABOR AND THE LIBERAL REGIME
OF THE 1930'S

Enrique Olaya Herrera was the first Liberal-party president of Colombia during the twentieth century. His regime assumed a much more sympathetic attitude towards organized labor than had been characteristic of the Conservative administrations. One of its first pieces of legislation was Law 83 of 1931, which provided for the legal recognition of labor unions.

This law provided for three different types of workers' organizations: craft, industrial, and mixed unions. It forced employers to recognize those labor groups which had been granted government recognition. During the period from 1930 to 1937, some 464 unions were recognized. By 1938 there were reported to exist some 319 legally authorized unions, and 201 other groups which did not have such recognition. There were some 82,893 workers reported as belonging to unions at that time.

Both urban workers and agricultural laborers were brought into the labor movement during this period. The Communists were particularly active in trying to establish unions among the rural workers during the 1930's, and in several areas they were sufficiently successful to allow the party to take over political control of local regions.

Under Olaya Herrera's successor, President Alfonso López, who took office in 1934, the labor movement was consolidated. López was strongly prolabor. On May Day 1936 he reviewed the labor parade to celebrate the occasion, along with leading trade-union figures and Gilberto Vieira, secretary-general of the Colombian Communist party.

During the first two years of the López administration, federations of unions were established in most of the country's departments (comparable to states in the U.S.A.), and some national industrial unions were also organized.

The culmination of this process of consolidation of organized labor was the foundation in 1936 of the Confederación de Trabajadores de Colombia. Leaders of the Confederación included Liberals, Communists, Socialists, and at least one anarchist. However, the Liberals and Communists were the two dominant groups in the new organization. For the next decade and a half they were to struggle for dominance in the CTC.

APOGEE AND DECLINE OF CTC

The first serious split between the Liberals and Communists in the Confederación de Trabajadores de Colombia took place in December 1940. At that time, the Liberals favored a position of general support for the Allies in the Second World War, while the Communists, in conformity with the policy of the Comintern, regarded the conflict as an "imperialist" struggle, and favored a policy of neutrality which bordered on outright sympathy for the Axis cause.

As a result of this policy difference between the Liberals and Communists, the Confederación de Trabajadores de Colombia was split. For a year, there were two CTCs. However, after the Nazi attack on the Soviet Union and the consequent change of the Communist position to one of support for the Allies, unity was re-established in the CTC late in 1941.

During World War II the labor movement of Colombia grew rapidly. The country underwent a process of quick industrialization, with a consequent growth of the urban working class. Many of the new city laborers were brought into the labor movement. By late 1943 the Confederación de Trabajadores de Colombia claimed 120,000 members. This was probably the highpoint in the confederation's membership and influence.

The CTC at this time included a number of powerful national unions or federations. The most important of these were the railroaders' federation, and those of the petroleum and maritime workers'. The last two were under Communist control; the former was dominated by the Liberals.

After the war, the rivalry between the Liberals and the Communists in the CTC again resulted in a crisis. In mid-1946 an anticommunist group of Liberal leaders, headed by Juan P. Lara and Bernardo Medina, took the offensive against the Communists, who were already following cold-war policies of enmity against the United States and other American republics. As a result, the CTC split once again.

However, the split in the Confederación de Trabajadores de Colombia, which was generally regarded by public opinion as being dominated by the Liberal party, was inconvenient for the leaders of the party. As a result, unity in the confederation was re-established at the end of 1946, and Victor Julio Silva, Liberal leader of the Railroad Workers' Federation, was elected secretary-general of the CTC. A few months later, Lara, Medina, and other militant anticommunist Liberals were expelled from the ranks of the confederation.

The growth of Communist influence in the CTC helped to pave the way for the establishment of a rival trade-union confederation. The lead in this move was taken by Padre Vicente Andrade, S.J., acting on behalf of the Catholic Social Action Secretariat. As a result of his efforts, the Unión de Trabajadores de Colombia was established early in 1946.

The new UTC profited from the decline of the Confederación de Trabajadores de Colombia, which set in with the defeat of the Liberal party in the election of 1946. President Mariano Ospina Pérez, the successful Conservative-party candidate, did not favor the CTC as his three Liberal predecessors had done. Although the leaders of the Unión de Trabajadores de Colombia refused to allow the Conservatives to control it, they could not help but benefit from the generally hostile attitude of the Ospina Pérez government to the Liberal-controlled labor group.

Late in 1949 President Ospina Pérez established a dictatorship. This resulted in a further weakening of the Confederación de Trabajadores de Colombia, which in the meanwhile was wracked with factionalism. In May 1950 the CTC was again split when the Liberals finally expelled all Communist elements from the organization.

The issue which brought about this division in the ranks of the CTC was that of international affiliation. Until 1950 the Confederación had been a part of the World Federation of Trade Unions (WFTU) and its American regional group, the Confederación de Trabajadores de America Latina. When the principal trade unions of Western Europe as well as the CIO of the United States and its Canadian counterpart, the Canadian Labor Congress, withdrew from the WFTU, the Liberal leaders of the CTC decided that the Colombian group should do likewise. When the Communists resisted this decision at the CTC's May 1950 congress, they were expelled.

For several years, the Communists attempted to maintain their own trade-union group, which they called the Confederación de Trabajadores Independiente; however, the Communists themselves were badly split, and partly as a result of this, their trade-union group was reduced to skeleton proportions within a short time.

LABOR AND THE ROJAS PINILLA DICTATORSHIP

In 1950 Laureano Gómez, most reactionary of the Conservative party's principal leaders, became president of Colombia. During his regime, the virtual civil war between Liberals and Conservatives, which had started with the assassination of the principal Liberal leader, Jorge Eliécer Gaitán, on April 9, 1948, was greatly intensified.

Gómez had supported the Nazis during World War II. As president, he sought to establish a Fascist-modeled corporative-state regime in Colombia. To this end, he named a hand-picked constituent assembly early in 1953 to write a new constitution. However, there was widespread resistance to the fascist plans of President Gómez. Not only were the Liberals strongly against the idea, but it was opposed also by the Ospina Pérez faction of the Conservative party. It likewise met considerable resistance within the ranks of the army.

When Laureano Gómez sought to remove army-commander General Gustavo Rojas Pinilla, because of his opposition to the corporate-state plans of the president, the military deposed Gómez, and Rojas Pinilla was proclaimed provisional president. He remained in power for four years.

In the beginning, the regime of General Rojas Pinilla met with widespread support. It was temporarily successful in putting an end to the violence which had plagued the country for five years or more. It brought about a political truce.

However, after Rojas Pinilla had been in power for a year,

sentiment began to move against his regime. He amplified the membership of the constituent assembly which had originally been established by Laureano Gómez, and its first act was to elect Rojas Pinilla "constitutional president" of the republic. Thereafter, his regime degenerated into a military dictatorship, maintained in power by the armed forces, against the wishes of the country's principal political organizations.

The Rojas Pinilla regime was an inept military dictatorship. It was corrupt, insolent, and obviously self-seeking. However, the president was influenced not only by members of the Socialist party, who looked upon the regime as a way to end the dominance of politics by the two traditional parties, but also by the example of the Perón regime in Argentina.

Rojas Pinilla sought to establish a political base in the labor movement. The first attempt was made to split the Unión de Trabajadores de Colombia. In 1954 a small group of UTC leaders broke away to form the Confederación Nacional del Trabajo. However, this organization, which affiliated with the Peronista-controlled continental confederation, the Agrupación de Trabajadores Latino Americanos Sindicalizados (ATLAS) soon collapsed.

The second move by the Rojas Pinilla government was to split the Confederación de Trabajadores de Colombia. Hernando Rodríguez, secretary-general of the CTC's affiliate in Bogotá, the Federación de Trabajadores de Cundinimarca, first tried to capture control of the Confederación, and when he failed in this, he withdrew his organization from the CTC, and affiliated it with the Peronista-group ATLAS. At the same time, Rodríguez declared his strong support of the Rojas Pinilla regime.

Both the CTC and the UTC opposed the dictatorial actions of the Rojas Pinilla regime. They protested against the government's patronization of pro-Perón dissident groups. They sought to maintain full freedom of collective bargaining. They both participated in the general strike which preceded the fall of the Rojas Pinilla regime.

ORGANIZED LABOR AFTER ROJAS PINILLA

The designs of the Rojas Pinilla regime on organized labor contributed to his overthrow. Early in 1957 the hierarchy of the Catholic Church in Colombia denounced the attempt of the government to undermine the Unión de Trabajadores de Colombia. There is little doubt that the hostility of the Church was a major factor in the growing movement against Rojas Pinilla, which resulted in his overthrow in May 1957.

With the ouster of the Rojas Pinilla dictatorship, the CTC and UTC reorganized their forces. The Confederación de Trabajadores de Colombia again enjoyed official favor with the election of Liberal Alberto Lleras Camargo as president of the republic in May 1958. The Unión de Trabajadores de Colombia also benefited from the greater freedom of labor activity after the fall of the Rojas Pinilla dictatorship.

However, the Communists also returned to trade-union activity. Their party, which had been badly split in the late 1940's, was reunified by the time of the fall of the Rojas Pinilla regime, and began to recoup the ground which it had lost in the labor movement. Gradually, the Communists made particularly serious inroads into the Confederación de Trabajadores de Colombia, such that in 1962 the CTC was forced to expel its Federación de Trabajadores del Valle, centered in the city of Cali, which had fallen under Communist control.

The UTC also felt the weight of the Communists' return to trade-union activity. During the early 1950's they had been able to win control over most of the country's petroleum workers' unions, which in the 1940's had been dominated by the Communists. After the ouster of Rojas Pinilla, however, the Communists again succeeded in getting control of most of these unions, and reorganized the Federation of Petroleum Workers. Although unsuccessful strikes for economic and political issues in the early 1960's weakened the position of the Communists once again, by 1965 a majority of the petroleum workers' unions were still under Communist influence.

After 1951 the Confederación de Trabajadores de Colombia

and the Unión de Trabajadores de Colombia both belonged to the International Confederation of Free Trade Unions and its American regional group, the Organización Regional Interamericana de Trabajadores. Both the ICFTU and the ORIT used their influence to try to bring about the unification of their two Colombian affiliates. In late 1962 the CTC and UTC announced their intention of merging, but they did not establish any definite date for this move. Indeed, by the end of 1965 the much-sought unity had not yet been achieved.

The two central labor groups cooperated in a number of ways. Both groups supported the Liberal-Conservative coalition which governed the country after the fall of Rojas Pinilla. Both supported a program for basic changes in the country's economy and social system, and in particular, the enactment of an agrarian reform.

Subsequently, affiliates of both the UTC and the CTC joined International Trade Secretariats associated with the International Confederation of Free Trade Unions, and both the UTC and CTC affiliates played a particularly important role in the International Federation of Petroleum Workers, both in congresses of the federation and in organizing leadership training activities.

Summary and Conclusion

Organized labor has played an important role in Colombian history for more than three decades. During much of this period, it has been split among two or more central labor bodies. Nevertheless, the majority of the labor movement has sought to establish effective procedures for collective bargaining and to maintain the country's traditional political democracy which has been seriously endangered by right-wing dictatorships and the threat of totalitarian left-wing dictatorship during much of the existence of the organized labor movement.

TWELVE

Venezuelan Trade Unionism

THE TURBULENT POLITICAL HISTORY OF VENEZUELA DURING THE twentieth century has been a source of constant and reiterated trouble for the country's organized labor movement. During only sixteen of the first sixty-five years of the century were the unions able to develop in anything approaching "normality," and even in some of this period the situation would have been considered highly abnormal anywhere but in Venezuela.

Until the end of 1935 the country suffered the severities of the dictatorships of Cipriano Castro and Juan Vicente Gómez. In this period, there was no chance to form trade unions. Although a few mutual-benefit societies maintained a somewhat precarious existence in Caracas and a few other cities, real trade unions were regarded by the government as "subversive" by definition.

Juan Vicente Gómez treated Venezuela as his private hacienda. He took into his own hands and those of his family and close associates, a large proportion of the nation's cultivated land. He lined his pockets in the process of granting concessions in the rapidly growing oil industry. He used the rank and file of the national army as laborers on his estates, and the officers as their foremen. Under such circumstances, there was no place for an organized labor movement.

Gómez died quietly in his bed in December 1935. Within a few days, the foundations of a labor movement were being laid. Some of the workers in the mutual-benefit societies had not been unaware of the existence of trade unionism in other countries. The same was true among the oil workers. Finally, return-

142

ing exiles brought the ideas of organized labor and left-wing political action back home with them.

The first unions appeared among the oil workers and among the skilled craftsmen of Caracas and a handful of other cities. The new unions began to demand the right to bargain collectively with their employers, and some collective agreements were actually negotiated. By the middle of 1937 there were enough unions in existence for the convocation of the First National Workers' Congress. No permanent labor confederation resulted from this congress.

The government of General Eleazar López Contreras, which succeeded that of Gómez, recognized some of the changes which had come about after the death of the dictator. It indicated this by enacting the country's first Labor Law in 1936. This provided for the legal recognition of trade unions, and made such recognition obligatory for any labor organization which wanted to engage in collective bargaining.

Before the end of the López Contreras administration in 1941 two definite political tendencies had begun to develop within the labor movement. One of these was the Partido Democrático Nacional, led by Rómulo Betancourt, a party of the democratic Left. The other was the Partido Comunista de Venezuela, a member party of the Communist International. The latter was the dominant element in organized labor during this period, particularly among the oil-field workers.

In 1941 General López Contreras was succeeded as president by General Isaías Medina Angarita. During his administration, the labor movement enjoyed unaccustomed freedom of action. The number of unions grew considerably, and collective bargaining became widespread.

Perhaps the most significant development during this period was the shifting of political control from the Communists to their opponents, now known as the Partido Acción Democrática. This came about as a result of the Second Workers' Congress, which met in Caracas in the middle of 1944. The Communists had a majority of the delegates at this meeting, which was also attended by Vicente Lombardo Toledano, the procommunist president of the Confederación de Trabajadores de America Latina.

When the issue of electing a national committee for the labor confederation which the delegates proposed to found was raised, an Acción Democrática delegate demanded that the two parties be equally represented. A Communist delegate protested vehemently against this proprosal, and argued that the Communist party should have a majority on the new committee, since it had a majority among the delegates present.

At that point, the Ministry of Labor intervened, suspended the proceedings of the congress, and removed legal recognition from many of the country's Communist-controlled unions. When these unions were reorganized, a majority of them were controlled by Acción Democrática.

Why General Medina Angarita acted in this way remains a mystery. Politically, he was allied with the Communists. Furthermore, this incident was virtually unique during the Medina administration, which interfered very little in the internal affairs of the unions. The net result of this incident was to seriously weaken the Medina administration, since Acción Democrática constituted the principal civilian opposition to Medina's regime.

As President Medina's term of office approached an end, a crisis arose over the succession. Acción Democrática demanded that the president allow popular election of his successor. He refused this, however, and when negotiations between him and Acción Democrática to find a mutually acceptable candidate failed, Acción Democrática accepted an invitation from a group of young army officers to depose President Medina. This *coup d'état* took place on October 18, 1945.

During the following thirty-seven months, Acción Democrática controlled the government. During its administration a process of revolutionary change began, and the labor movement developed very rapidly. The government was presided over by Rómulo Betancourt for most of this period, and by popularly elected President Rómulo Gallegos, also of Acción Democrática, during the last nine months.

The Acción Democrática regime presided over three general elections—for a constitutional assembly; for president, congress, and state legislatures; and for municipal councils. It inaugurated a new oil policy: raising the government's percentage of the profits of the industry from 16⅔ per cent to 50 per cent, and investing these greatly increased revenues in economic development, and raising living standards. Education was greatly expanded, with the number of children in school being more than doubled.

Organized labor benefited greatly from the Acción Democrática regime. The number of legally recognized unions more than quadrupled. For the first time, a large number of agricultural workers unions were organized and were recognized by the Ministry of Labor. The government brought strong pressure on employers to grant wage increases to their workers, while itself spending 100,000,000 bolivars to subsidize foodstuffs and other basic items, so that wage increases did not result in inflation.

Structurally, the labor movement was greatly improved and made more able to carry out effective collective bargaining for its members. National federations, consisting of unions in specific trades and industries, were organized, as were state federations in almost all states. Finally, in 1947 the nation's first central labor organization, the Confederación de Trabajadores de Venezuela, was established by the Third Workers' Congress.

Acción Democrática overwhelmingly dominated the labor movement during this three-year period. The Communists who had been split during the Medina regime over the question of supporting the president, remained divided into two groups: one known as the Reds, and the other known as the Blacks. The unions controlled by the former participated in the Confederación and its affiliates (which were AD controlled), whereas the Black Communists established their own Federation of Workers of the Federal District, which contained a small minority of the unions in the Caracas area.

Many of the policies, however, of the Acción Democrática government, notably its prolabor attitude, disturbed some of the top military men who had originally cooperated with it. As a result, they conspired constantly against the regime. President Betancourt was able to thwart all such conspiracies, but when his successor, President Rómulo Gallegos, was presented with an ultimatum by a group of officers in November 1948, he did not know how to deal with it. As a result, his regime was overthrown on November 24, 1948. Gallegos had refused to call upon the workers to go out on a general strike to thwart the military plotters, and when some unions, particularly in the oil fields, did strike after Gallegos' ouster, their movement was too late and failed.

For more than nine years after President Gallegos was overthrown, the labor movement was severely persecuted by successive military regimes. When a strike broke out in the oil fields early in 1949, the dictatorship dissolved the Confederación de Trabajadores de Venezuela and the Federación de Trabajadores Petroleros, and canceled legal recognition of all oil workers' unions. Subsequently, most other unions were likewise legally suspended.

Yet, although the government allowed the reorganization of most of the unions in urban centers, almost all peasant unions, too, were completely destroyed. In the oil camps and cities, the government decreed that no former union officials could run for office in the unions. So, when political colleagues of the deposed leaders were elected, the government in many cases refused to allow them to take office.

Thus, during most of the more than nine years of dictatorship, the number of unions was very small, and the government did not allow a free central labor organization to function legally. The Acción Democrática, the Red Communists, the Christian Social party, and the Unión Republicans Democrática all maintained informal and illegal groups of the unions under their control.

In fact, the only political group which was allowed to function without interference during most of the dictatorship was that of the Black Communists. Their Federation of Workers of the Federal District was the only such group given legal recognition by the regime, and they were allowed to form another state federation in Anzoátegui, in the eastern part of the country. They held public meetings, and their leaders were allowed for several years to go back and forth to international Communist trade-union meetings. This group was headed by Rodolfo Quintero until the middle of 1954, when he went to Mexico to work as an official of the Confederación de Trabajadores de America Latina.

Starting in 1952 the government began efforts to organize its own *tame* labor confederation which could get control of the workers unions and prevent their being used by parties opposing the dictatorship. A so-called Movimiento Sindical de Trabajadores (MOSIT) was established, and the government constructed a luxurious Trade Union House for it in Caracas, with smaller buildings of the same type in several interior cities. In 1954 the MOSIT was converted into the Confederación Nacional de Trabajadores, which affiliated with the so-called Agrupación de Trabajadores Latino Americanos Sindicalizados, sponsored by Argentine dictator Juan Perón.

This government-sponsored central labor group had few genuine unions affiliated with it. Only a few unions of industrial workers in Caracas and a smattering of groups in the interior were functioning labor groups. The finances of the MOSIT and CNT came almost completely from the government.

The antilabor policies of the dictatorship created serious difficulties for it on the international level. The International Labor Organization, a technical agency of the United Nations, made an investigation of the state of freedom of labor organization in Venezuela in 1950, and issued a scathing attack on the situation.

Several years later, an International Oil Conference sponsored by the ILO met in Caracas. When a workers' delegate from the Netherlands attacked the Venezuelan government's labor policies, he was unceremoniously deported, and the remaining delegates to the conference suspended its sessions indefinitely. Subsequently, dictator General Marcos Pérez Jiménez withdrew Venezuela from the ILO.

Organized labor joined with most of the rest of the civilian population in the final struggle against the Pérez Jiménez dictatorship in January 1958. The tyrant fell on January 23, and almost immediately the work of rebuilding the trade unions got under way.

Labor leaders of all parties agreed that it was necessary to have a united trade-union movement. Party rivalries therefore were muted. A National Committee of Trade Union Unity was established which became the *de facto* central labor body. It consisted of labor leaders from Acción Democrática, the Communist party (now reunited), the Christian Social party Copei, and the Unión Republicana Democrática.

Under the leadership of the National Committee of Trade Union Unity, a campaign was launched to merge the various small rival unions under the control of the various parties which existed in many fields. At the same time, the work of recruiting workers into the newly united unions went forward rapidly.

It was the policy of the National Committee to form national federations covering specific industries and trades, as well as to re-establish state federations. The first national group to be re-established was the Petroleum Workers' Federation.

To assure the continuation of unity, it was agreed that the various parties would not compete in the union elections that were held during the first months after the fall of the dictatorship. Common lists of candidates were agreed upon by the various parties, the representation of the parties being apportioned according to agreed-upon estimates of the relative strength of the parties in the respective unions. The union officials thus elected were to serve for two years.

In this way, Acción Democrática received roughly half of the elective posts in the unions. The Communists were given perhaps a quarter of the positions, and Copei and URD were given the rest, although these two parties had, in fact, relatively little strength in the labor movement.

For almost two years, the unity of the labor movement was maintained. In November 1959 the Confederción de Trabajadores de Venezuela was re-established in a congress in which the Acción Democrática party had a majority. However, in line with the unity program, AD did not receive a majority in the executive of the CTV—the Communists, the Copei, and the URD all being represented out of proportion to their real strength at the congress.

During the first two and a half years after the overthrow of Pérez Jiménez, the labor movement played a key role in preventing ambitious military men from re-establishing a dictatorship. In July and September 1958 groups of officers attempted to oust the provisional government which succeeded Pérez Jiménez. These efforts were countered by the labor movement by general strikes, which were supported also by the organized employers, and were accompanied by violent street demonstrations against the rebellious soldiers.

Again, in April 1960, the administration of prolabor President Rómulo Betancourt, who had been elected in December 1958, was attacked by rebel forces led by General Castro Leon, who had gone into exile the previous year. The general slipped across the border from Colombia and seized control of the city of San Cristóbal, capital of the state of Táchira. His move was met by another general strike, and when other military units failed to join his forces, General Castro Leon attempted to flee. He was captured by a group of armed peasants.

Meanwhile, however, the unity of the labor movement had cracked. The Communist party had become a violent opponent of the Betancourt regime, and had been joined in this attitude by the new Movimiento de Izquierda Revolucionaria, formed by a group of dissident members of Acción Democrática early in 1960.

In November 1960 students under Communist and MIR leadership engaged in serious rioting in Caracas and other cities. In the midst of this rioting, the Communist and MIR leaders called for a revolutionary general strike and urged the people at large to launch a "popular insurrection" against the regime. Both the general strike and the attempted insurrection failed. The Acción Democrática and Copei members of the executive of the Confederación de Trabajadores de Venezuela suspended the Communist and MIR members of that body.

Subsequently, in elections held in the unions throughout

the year 1961, there were rival slates presented by the AD and Copei, on the one hand, and the Communists, the MIR, and the Unión Republicana Democrática, on the other. As a result of these elections, the AD-Copei combination came to control about 85 per cent of the country's local unions, and all the national federations except that of the white-collar workers. They also controlled all but a handful of the state labor federations.

During the two subsequent years, the split in the labor movement widened. A congress of the CTV was held in November 1961, and it removed all Communists and MIR members from the leadership of the Confederación. Subsequently, the unions controlled by the Acción Democrática and Copei proceeded to purge Communists and MIRistas from the leadership. The Communists and MIRistas did the same in unions that they controlled.

No Communist or MIR unions attended the congress of the CTV in 1961, and their unions proceeded to set up what they called the CTV No-Gubernamental. Its ranks were slightly amplified when a few unions controlled by participants in another split in Acción Democrática late in 1961, the so-called ARS, joined the CTV No-Gubernamental.

In April 1963 the trade unionists affiliated with all opposition parties—the Communists, and the ARS, the MIR, and the URD—participated in a congress in Caracas, which established a new central labor organization, the Central Unica de Trabajadores de Venezuela. It claimed "over four hundred unions," of the more than thirty-four hundred legally recognized labor organizations then existing in the country.

Thus, by early 1963 the split in the ranks of Venezuelan labor was complete. Acción Democrática still controlled the great majority of the country's unions, and all but one of the national union federations. The oppositionists in the CUTV controlled scattered unions in various parts of the country, but they were only a small proportion of the total of organized labor. The Confederación de Trabajadores de Venezuela continued to be one of the bulwarks of the democratic regime of President Rómulo Betancourt.

During the Betancourt regime, collective bargaining became the general pattern of labor relations in Venezuela. Almost all the workers in petroleum, mining, manufacturing, and transport industries were covered by collective agreements, as well as many white-collar workers. The great majority of these agreements were negotiated without strikes, in spite of the politically inspired violence which characterized the last two years of the Betancourt administration and the sharp party divisions within the trade unions. According to President Betancourt's final message to congress in March 1964, there had been only 36 strikes during his five years in office, or approximately one for every 100 contracts signed.

With the inauguration of President Raúl Leoni early in 1964, the political alignment within the trade unions was substantially altered. The Copei party did not participate in the government of Acción-Democrática President Leoni, as it had done in that of his AD predecessor, and as a result the alliance of the two parties in the orgainzed labor movement came to an end. URD trade unionists returned to the CTV, while relations between the Copie and AD workers became increasingly difficult.

Summary and Conclusion

Organized labor got a late start in Venezuela, because until the death of dictator Juan Vicente Gómez in December 1935 the government ruthlessly persecuted any attempt to unionize workers. Thereafter the labor movement grew steadily, except for the nine year period of the Pérez Jiménez dictatorship, November 1948-January 1958. Since the overthrow of that regime, the unions have come to include within their ranks most of the country's regularly employed urban workers, as well as large numbers of agricultural laborers and tenants. Collective bargaining has become the standard pattern of Venezuelan labor relations.

Since its inception, the Venezuelan labor movement has been the scene of bitter rivalry among different political groups, but particularly between the Acción Democrática and Communist

THIRTEEN

Cuban Organized Labor

THE BEGINNINGS OF THE CUBAN LABOR MOVEMENT ARE TO BE FOUND in the last two decades that the island remained a colony of Spain. Among the new currents of thought and action which came into Cuba at the time were those of trade unionism and the radical political philosophies associated with it, particularly Marxian socialism and anarchosyndicalism.

During those same closing decades of the nineteenth century the labor movement of Spain was becoming firmly established. This fact had its reflections in the island, and some of the early unions established in Cuba were founded by Spanish immigrants, and may even have been branches of Spanish organizations. The tobacco workers were of particular significance in this early movement.

The first couple decades of independence saw the slow spread of trade unionism, in the face of widespread political strife and disillusionment in the results of independence. The railroad workers and the maritime workers were partly organized, and the tobacco workers continued to figure importantly in the nascent labor movement.

The First World War gave some impetus to the growth of organized labor. One of the most important events of this period was a strike of railroad workers in 1917, which was finally won after contacts made by the strikers with the American Federation of Labor were successful in thwarting the companies' attempts to recruit strikebreakers in the United States. Some attempt was made in this period, also, to organize the sugar workers, although it did not have any marked success.

Although the late 1920's were a period of economic distress

153

and of growing political tyranny under the presidency of Gerardo Machado, it was a period of significant development in the trade-union movement. In 1924 the first national central labor organization, the Confederación Nacional Obrera Cubana, was established. It was originally under the leadership of anarcho-syndicalist elements, but within a few years it came under the control of the young Communist party. It became a part of the Red International of Labor Unions during the famed Third Period of Comintern history.

In 1927 a second central labor body was established, the Federación del Trabajo de Cuba. This organization was led by Juan Arevalo, a Spanish immigrant long resident in Cuba, who had belonged to the Spanish and Argentine Socialist parties before coming to Cuba and had participated in several unsuccessful attempts to establish a Socialist party on the island. This Federación was affiliated with the Pan-American Federation of Labor.

The Communists and other left-wing opponents of Arevalo maintained then and later that the Federación del Trabajo was organized by Arevalo to serve the interests of the dictator Machado. However, in the turbulent days following the fall of the tyrant in 1933, when these charges were publicly aired, and Arevalo was given a kind of trial by the labor movement, he was cleared of all such accusations.

The labor movement generally was strongly opposed to Machado by the late 1920's. He had originally been elected with labor support in 1924, but as his regime degenerated into a dictatorship and inasmuch as he had himself re-elected despite constitutional prohibitions, labor became an important part of the opposition. As the Great Depression became intensified after 1929 this opposition became increasingly severe.

In 1930 there were violent strikes and demonstrations which were suppressed with considerable bloodshed. In this same year the first national sugar workers' union was established under the patronage of the CNOC, with which it affiliated.

The labor movement played an important role in the crisis which led to the ouster of Machado in August 1933. The crisis developed out of a shooting fray between university students and the police, in the process of which several students were killed. The students immediately declared a general strike, and their action was seconded spontaneously by the workers of Havana and other important cities and towns. The movement took on the aspect of a revolutionary general strike against the regime. It was more than a little encouraged by behind-the-scenes maneuvering by United States Ambassador Sumner Welles, who was seeking the ouster of Machado.

At the height of this crisis, there occurred an event which was to set a pattern for many incidents which were to follow in succeeding years. Machado, left virtually without friends or support in the civilian population, and with conspiracies hatching in the armed forces, sought whatever backing he could find. He invited the leaders of the Communist-controlled Confederación Nacional Obrera Cubana to the presidential palace, and offered them a deal. He agreed to legalize their party and their labor confederation if they would call off the general strike against him.

The Communists accepted this offer, and "called off" the general strike. They had little effect, however, upon its progress, since in the last analysis they had had little to do with its occurring in the first place. Nevertheless, their willingness to make a deal with the dictator in this crucial moment was characteristic of the attitude the party was to take in other future crises.

Machado fell in spite of the Communists' last minute attempt to prop him up, and was succeeded by a short-lived government of Carlos Manuel de Céspedes, a highly respected but ineffectual member of a distinguished old family. His regime lasted a little more than three weeks, when it was overthrown on September 4, 1933, by a *coup* organized by noncommissioned officers of the army and university students.

The chief architect of this *coup* was Sergeant Fulgencio Batista. Through his efforts Dr. Ramón Grau San Martín, a professor in the Medical School of the University of Havana, became president in a government made up principally of university students. Batista stood behind the regime so long as it remained in power, as its principal guarantee of power.

The Grau San Martín government was exceedingly radical for its time. It took over the United States owned electric and telephone companies. It drew up a scheme for a vast agrarian reform. It issued a number of pieces of labor legislation, the most important of which was a decree providing that 50 per cent of all employees in any enterprise must be Cuban citizens.

The labor movement generally was enthusiastic about the new regime. Meetings of workers were held all over the country in support of the revolutionary government. There were many strikes during this period, but the government tended more often than not to side with the strikers, solidifying its backing among the workers.

However, the Grau San Martín government had two very formidable enemies. One was the Communist party. The other was the United States Department of State. Together, they were finally able to bring down this government, thus paving the way for the establishment of a new dictatorship which for several years rivaled that of Machado in its ferocity and authoritarianism.

The attitude of the Communists is explainable in terms of the general position of the Communist International at that time. This was the so-called Third Period of the Comintern, during which the Communists everywhere adopted an extremely sectarian position, and categorized all of their opponents as either "fascist" (if they were at all conservative) or "social fascist" (if they were on the Left of the political spectrum). They adopted the latter category for the Grau San Martín government, and they did their utmost to destroy it.

Although the Communists' efforts among the urban workers were not particularly successful, they were more able to influence the rural workers, particularly those in the sugar industry, where they led the only union then in existence. In a number of areas they led these workers in the establishment of "Soviets," which sometimes fought with arms in their hands against the new regime.

These efforts of the Communists fitted very well the attitude and arguments of the U.S. State Department. United States policy in Cuba was being made largely by Sumner Welles, who by this time had been transferred to Washington. He had personally intervened in the establishment of the de Céspedes government and regarded its overthrow as a species of personal insult to him. He was extremely hostile to the Grau San Martín regime as a result. He was successful in preventing the United States from recognizing the Cuban government, using as his excuse the allegation that the Grau San Martín administration did not "effectively control" the country. For this charge, the activities of the Communists supplied a good deal of evidence.

This period is particularly significant because it established the lines of political rivalry which were to predominate in the Cuban labor movement for the following two decades. On the one hand were the supporters of the Grau regime, who were later formally organized in the Partido Revolucionario Cubano (Autentico) and became popularly known as the Autenticos; and on the other hand were the Communists.

United States Ambassador Jefferson Caffrey was finally successful in convincing the now Colonel Batista that the Cuban government would never be recognized by Washington so long as Grau San Martín continued to head it, and that such recognition was essential. As a result, Batista overthrew Grau in January 1934.

Batista's choice for a successor to Grau was Colonel Carlos Mendieta. An old-style politician, of conservative views, he was acceptable to Washington. He was also acceptable to Batista, since he had little power of his own and depended for his tenure of office upon the army led by Batista.

The organized labor movement was unanimously opposed to the Mendieta regime. For a little more than a year it engaged in a series of partial strikes and demonstrations against the regime. Then early in March 1935 there began a revolutionary general strike, which like the one of August 1933, began spontaneously from several smaller economic strikes. It was first backed by the Autenticos, and only a week later by the Communists, who even then tried to call it off before it had finally failed.

As a result of this walkout, the labor movement was decimated. For the following three years the trade unions existed mainly as underground organizations. There was little effective collective bargaining, and most of the more important trade-union leaders were severely persecuted.

By the late 1930's, however, Colonel Batista, after having made and unmade several presidents in succession, decided that he wanted to emerge from being the power behind the scenes and become the constitutional president of the republic. He wished to do this in such a way that his election would appear to be in response to the wishes of the people. As a result, he made overtures to his political opponents, in an attempt to get them to go along with this procedure.

The Autenticos turned Batista down uncompromisingly. He had become their worst enemy by this time, and they were dedicated to the destruction of his power. However, the Communists were much less uncompromising. They accepted Batista's overtures, and as a result, an agreement was made between the dictator and the Communist leaders. They agreed to back his presidential ambitions, and he agreed to legalize their party and to allow them to reorganize the labor movement, and to assure them control of it through governmental action.

This agreement was exceedingly important for the future of the labor movement. Not only did it bring about a considerable period of Communist domination of organized labor, but it set a pattern in labor relations in Cuba which was not ended until the Castro regime during 1960 and 1961 completely destroyed the vestiges of the freedom of organized labor in the island.

The method by which Batista assured the Communists control of the labor movement was through use of the Ministry of Labor. It was staffed by elements friendly disposed to the Communists rather than to their Autentico rivals. At the same time, the pattern was set that all matters of significance in labor relations had to be brought to the Ministry of Labor for resolution, rather than being settled in direct collective bargaining between the two parties. Through this procedure, the influence of the pro-communist officials of the Ministry could always be used in crucial instances on their behalf.

This system did not change after the Communists lost control of the labor movement. The only modification was that the Ministry was staffed by Autenticos instead of by friends of the Communists, but the intervention of the Ministry continued to be of key importance in all important labor disputes. After the overthrow of the Autenticos, the same system continued during the second Batista regime, after a proper reshuffling of posts in the Ministry. Although an attempt was made by the unions during the first months of the Castro regime to substitute real collective bargaining for this system it came to naught because of the totalitarian and procommunist drift of the Castro regime.

The reorganization of the labor movement under Communist aegis was completed in 1938 with the establishment of the Confederación de Trabajadores de Cuba (CTC). Lázaro Peña, a Communist and a leader of the tobacco workers' union, became secretary-general of the new organization. A majority of its leadership was Communist or fellow traveling, although there was a minority of Autenticos and union leaders who were independent of both of these parties.

Throughout the next six years labor relations in Cuba were more or less normalized. Most organizable workers were unionized, including not only tobacco, sugar, railroad, and maritime workers, but also metallurgical workers, commercial employees, bank clerks, many government employees. Collective contracts, usually on a national basis, became the order of the day, although as we have noted, the Ministry of Labor played a major part in determining their conditions, as it did in processing grievances which arose under them.

The CTC itself grew rapidly. National unions or federations were established in about thirty different industries. In addition, local labor federations were established in all six of the provinces and in most important cities and towns. The labor organizations had considerable income, which was of great importance to whatever party was successful in controlling them.

During these years, Colonel Batista realized his ambition. The first step was to call a constitutional convention, which met in 1940 and drafted one of the hemisphere's most advanced constitutions. It included important sections dealing with the working class, assuring it of the right to organize and bargain collectively, and instructing the congress to pass extensive legislation favorable to the workers.

Batista was elected the first president under this new constitution. In the coalition which elected him, the Communists had an important place. They succeeded in electing half-a-dozen members of the Chamber of Deputies, including Lázaro Peña, and several senators. Two Communists, Juan Marinello and Carlos Rafael Rodríguez, served as Ministers Without Portfolio in the cabinet of President Batista in the early 1940's.

In 1944, however, Batista, for one reason or another, was forced to hold honest elections for a successor. His candidate was defeated by the Autenticos' party, headed once again by Dr. Ramón Grau San Martín. This election had an important impact upon the labor movement.

In the beginning President Grau was hesitant about allowing his Autentico supporters to try to take control of the CTC. Right after Grau's election, Lázaro Peña had issued an official announcement to the effect that if Grau "touched" the labor movement, the workers would go out on a general strike. Although such a walkout would undoubtedly not have been general, it might have caused a serious crisis, since Grau did not as yet control either the armed forces or a majority in congress.

Nevertheless, in the congressional elections of 1946 the Autenticos won a sizable majority. Furthermore, by that time the president had been able to make the necessary shifts in the commands of the armed forces to assure the government of a reasonable degree of support from that quarter. As a result, the Autentico party was in a position to take on the Communists in the labor movement.

The occasion for the showdown was the Fifth Congress of the Confederación de Trabajadores de Cuba, scheduled for May 1947. In this congress the two forces were about evenly balanced, with the deciding voice being that of the independents. On this occasion, the independents split among themselves, some siding with the Communists, some with the Autenticos. Cleverly, the

Autenticos made an important maneuver in nominating for secretary-general of the CTC to succeed Lázaro Peña, the head of
the Electrical Workers' Federation, Angel Cofiño, one of the outstanding independent leaders.

The Fifth Congress was the scene of much verbal fireworks,
and some actual shooting by delegates. As a result, the Ministry
of Labor stepped in and suspended its sessions, and, at the same
time, established a supposedly neutral commission to inquire
into the credentials of all who claimed to be delegates. The report of this commission, on which the Communists were a minority, was favorable to the Autenticos, giving them and their supporters a majority. The Ministry then authorized the renewal
of the congress, so that the Autentico and allied independent
elements could, and did, duly meet. However, the Communists
held their own Fifth Congress of the CTC, and as a result, the
organization was split wide open.

Although for a few months the issue seemed in doubt, by
the end of 1947 the Autenticos gained full control of the labor
movement. Then, the Minister of Labor Carlos Prío Socarras
recognized the Autentico controlled faction as the legal Confederación de Trabajadores de Cuba, and turned over to it the
still unfinished Palace of Workers, which the government had
already been constructing for the CTC. Soon thereafter, those independents who had at first sided with the Communists, including the leaders of the powerful Maritime Workers' Federation
and many leaders of the Sugar Workers' Federation, went over
to the Autenticos, taking their unions with them. The Communists
were soon reduced to a small rump organization, which by 1950
had virtually disappeared.

Until 1952, the labor movement was under Autentico control.
In 1949 the Autenticos quarreled with the independents; as a result, the latter launched the Confederación General de Trabajadores, which had a pseudo-anarchosyndicalist tinge, and affiliated
itself with the International Workingmen's Association, the almost nonexistent anarchosyndicalist world trade-union group.
Nevertheless, in 1951, although the two confederations were

reunited, and the principal independent leaders were restored to the leading posts in the CTC, they did not thereby become any more friendly to the Autenticos.

In the meanwhile, Eusebio Mujal had become secretary-general of the CTC at the time of the 1949 split. He had previously been head of the Workers' Bloc of the Autentico party, and had masterminded the seizure of the CTC by the Autenticos in 1947. In the early 1930's he had been a Communist and later a Trotskyite, and had entered the Autentico party when the Trotskyites as a bloc, under the leadership of their principal figure Sandalio Junco, did so in the middle 1930's. Mujal continued to dominate the CTC until the advent of the Castro government on January 1, 1959.

The Autentico years were good ones for the labor movement. The country was very prosperous. It was relatively easy to get good collective agreements. Furthermore, the Autentico labor leaders held important posts in their party, were well represented in congress, and had a powerful voice in the affairs of state.

However, the Autentico regime was overthrown on March 10, 1952. This occurred less than three months before a scheduled presidential election, in which there were three candidates. One was Carlos Hevía, of the Autentico party; another was Roberto Agramonte of the Ortodoxo party, a split-off from the Autenticos which had been formed in protest against the widespread corruption that had characterized the Grau San Martín government. The third candidate was Fulgencio Batista.

Public-opinion polls at the time showed that there was a close race between Hevía and Agramonte, and were in disagreement as to which would win; however, they all agreed that the third candidate, Batista, had no chance at all. Hence, he seized the government by force when it was clear that he had no chance of winning it by election.

Batista's second seizure of power, on March 10, 1952, was engineered by a group of young army officers in Camp Columbia on the outskirts of Havana. However, it succeeded principally because President Carlos Prío Socarras (who had been elected to succeed Grau San Martín in 1948) made little or no effort to fight to maintain his position. Insistent pleas by loyal army officers to let them fight Batista went unanswered. Offers by students to take up arms on behalf of the regime were rejected. The leaders of the labor movement were not even informed of what was taking place until it was too late to call an effective general strike against Batista's seizure of power.

Moreover, it must be recorded that the labor leaders, when they did find out about the general's *coup* did call a general strike. Because the Batista forces by that time already held the radio and television stations, they were only able to get notice of the strike to their followers by word of mouth. In fact, only the bus drivers of Havana carried out an effective walkout, and they went back to work when they found that they had no support from any other quarter.

Batista's *coup d'état* presented a major crisis to organized labor, for the unions were overwhelmingly controlled by members of the Autentico party, which he had overthrown. Even those leaders who were not Autenticos were strongly against Batista. On the other hand, each side realized the power of the other, and neither Batista nor the labor leaders wanted an all-out showdown. As a result, a kind of truce was arranged between the new president and the leaders of the CTC.

On his side, Batista agreed to leave the labor movement alone, and to continue to have the Ministry of Labor cooperate with the leaders of the CTC, although in fact he restored to the Ministry many of those procommunists who had been thrown out when the Autenticos had come to power. On their side, the leaders of the CTC agreed not to use the labor movement as a weapon to overthrow the Batista regime; and also agreed to give nominal representation to Batista's Partido Acción Popular in the leadership of the Confederación de Trabajadores de Cuba.

The labor wing of the Batista party, one of whose members was incorporated in the top leadership of the CTC, was a peculiar group. Most of those who appeared as its top leaders in the days immediately succeeding the *coup,* had until a few days or weeks before been open members of the Communist party. One of these had been a Communist candidate for congress in **the** elections scheduled for June 1952. Others had been Communists some years previously—with no official notification having been given of their ever having ceased to belong to the Communist party.

However, in spite of this incorporation of Batista supporters in the CTC, the labor movement continued during the next six years to be controlled essentially by the same people who had dominated it between 1947 and 1952. A few important Autentico labor leaders, such as Pablo Balbuena of the Printing Trades' Workers, resigned from the CTC leadership, because they could not swallow the agreement with Batista. A few of the independents, notably Angel Cofiño of the Electrical Workers, were ultimately thrown out of their leading positions by Mujal, in part at least because of their opposition to the Batista regime. However, most of the Autenticos and independents who had been the leaders of the CTC on March 10, 1952, were also leaders of the organization on December 31, 1958.

It is fair to say that until November 1956 the relations between the CTC leaders and the Batista government were those of an armed truce. Each side remained cautious with regard to the other, each trying to avoid a showdown which might be fatal for it, and each keeping the other at arms length. This situation, though, did change after the invasion of the island by Fidel Castro and his followers and launching of a civil war in the interior of the republic.

The civil war intensified the brutality of the Batista dictatorship. At the same time, it tended to throw Batista and the CTC leaders closer together. Their objectives became parallel if not the same. Batista naturally feared a revolutionary general strike against his regime, which Fidel Castro twice tried to bring about from the hills. For their part, the labor leaders also feared such a move because they foresaw that if it failed, Batista would ruthlessly suppress the labor movement. Therefore, Batista and the Mujal leadership of the CTC were equally interested in trying to prevent any general movement of the workers against the regime.

In order to assure that the workers would not come under the influence of prorevolutionary elements, Mujal and his associates became increasingly high-handed in their administration of the labor movement. Elections were suspended in several unions, leadership of others was removed arbitrarily. Collective agreements were prorogued instead of new ones being negotiated, and strikes of any kind were strongly discouraged, when not forbidden by the CTC. At the same time, Mujal got the Batista regime to decree compulsory check-off of dues of all unions and the payment of these dues to the CTC instead of to the individual unions. The CTC leadership thus held the power of the purse over all its affiliates.

That these moves were effective in achieving the ends which they sought was demonstrated twice during the two years or more of civil war. In August 1957 and again in April 1958 Castro called for a revolutionary general strike. In both cases it failed almost completely. Both the CTC leadership and the Communists threw their weight against these moves in both instances.

In the meanwhile, however, the urban forces that were allied with the Castro movement in the hills had succeeded in organizing an extensive underground in the labor movement. A few of the top leaders of the CTC were themselves involved in this underground, while others were undoubtedly sympathetic to it. Some of the leaders of the CTC and its affiliates were members of other underground groups not associated with Castro.

By the time the Batista regime was overthrown Castro's movement, called "the 26th of July," had organized groups in most of the country's unions. These underground units were generally very small and were usually made up of very young people, with no experience as trade-union leaders. The coordinator of all of the 26th-of-July labor activities was David Salvador, an ex-sugar worker, one-time local-union official, and one-time Communist, who had left the Communist party in the early 1950's.

When Batista fled on January 1, 1959, the 26th of July underground went into action almost immediately. On that day and the following one it seized most of the union headquarters on the island. It named temporary leaders for all of the unions on a local, regional, and national scale. All of the leaders of the unions as of December 31, 1958, were removed during the next two days. Some of them, including Mujal, sought asylum in various foreign embassies. Others were arrested, and were put on trial later in the year, although most of those tried were acquitted of any wrongdoing. These included Francisco Aguirre, ex-head of the Hotel and Restaurant Workers' Federaction, and Jesús Artigas, who had been treasurer of the CTC between 1952 and 1958.

About ten days after the fall of Batista, the 26th of July labor people held their first public meeting. Those who had led the underground were there introduced to the workers in general. The meeting was also the occasion for these new leaders to lay down the general lines of policy that they proposed for the labor movement to follow in the future.

The most important policy note sounded during this meeting was that of the independence of the labor movement. Various of the new leaders expressed the conviction that the labor movement for twenty years or more had made a mistake in not depending upon direct collective bargaining with the employers instead of upon mediation and arbitration by the Ministry of Labor. They promised that in the future they would follow the path of real collective negotiation and would not call the government into the day-to-day labor-relations picture.

During the months that followed, the new leaders of the labor movement proceeded to reorganize the unions. Within two or three weeks of the overthrow of Batista, membership meetings were held in all local unions. There by show of hands, new temporary officers were elected, usually the same people who had seized the unions in the name of the 26th of July shortly before. In many cases these membership meetings also declared that those who had office in the unions during the two-year civil-war period were to be ineligible for further office in the unions for as long as twenty years. These resolutions applied as much to people like Cofiño, who had gone into exile as to Aguirre, who had held office until the last day of the Batista regime.

During the months of April to June 1959 secret elections were held in all the local unions. In all cases the 26th of July put up tickets, usually consisting of those who were already in effective control of the unions. In many unions, the Communists also put up lists of candidates, who generally were in competition with those of the 26th of July. However, in a very few cases, such as various Hotel and Restaurant Workers' and Textile Workers' locals, the 26th of July leaders agreed to incorporate some Communists in their tickets. Where there were rival Communist tickets, the 26th of July won handily.

Between June and September national conventions of all the labor federations were held, to elect new officers for these groups. Again, the 26th of July had the vast majority of delegates. Thus, in the sugar workers' congress, which included nearly one thousand delegates, only thirty at the most were Communists, perhaps somewhat fewer were Autenticos, and the rest were 26th of July members. All the national federations elected 26th of July executive committees, and the overwhelming majority of the members of these committees were anticommunists, having refused to cooperate with the Communists in the unions.

One problem much debated in the labor movement during these months was that of the international affiliation of the CTC and its constituents unions. The Confederación had been one of the founding members of the Organización Regional Interamericana de Trabajadores (ORIT) and of the International Confederation of Free Trade Unions. In spite of the close collaboration of the Mujal leadership with Batista during the dictator's last two years, demands which had been made by both the Cuban underground and some Latin American affiliates of the ORIT and the ICFTU that the CTC be expelled from those organizations were rejected.

Therefore, once the victory over Batista had been won, there was considerable sentiment among 26th of July labor leaders for the withdrawal of the CTC from both the ORIT and the ICFTU. However, there were long negotiations between the new CTC leaders and the officials of the two international groups, with the result that the Cuban leadership decided to stay in them and to fight there for changes in the Inter-American and international labor organizations. This decision was ratified by a conference of the CTC (second only in power to a national congress) held in September 1959.

In the meanwhile, political events in Cuba had been coming to a climax. The 26th of July Movement had been split since its seizure of power between two groups with different ideologies and different perspectives for the revolution. On the one hand was a faction of democratic revolutionaries, who wanted an agrarian reform that would give the land to the peasants, the development of a planned economy in which the State would have a large role but in which sizable sectors would be left to private enterprise. This same group favored a return, after a period of provisional government, to a democratic regime conforming to the Constitution of 1940, and resulting from popular elections. They were opposed to all relations with the Communists, opposed admitting them to the government in any way, although favoring their free participation in political life.

On the other hand was a group of totalitarian revolutionaries. They supported an agrarian reform based on the Soviet model of collective and state farms, were for a completely socialized economy and for a pro-Soviet foreign policy. They also favored close cooperation with the Cuban Communists, organized in the so-called Partido Socialista Popular.

The overwhelming majority of the 26th of July labor leaders were allied with the democratic faction. This was clearly demonstrated in the elections in the unions, in the national congresses of the federations, and in the national conference of the CTC in September 1959.

Fidel Castro, whose word was law in this early phase of the revolution, did not take a definite stand on either side during the first ten months of the revolution. He gave his followers in the labor movement full support in their refusal to cooperate with the Communists there. On the other hand, when President Manuel Urrutia criticized the attempts of the Communists to infiltrate the regime, he was summarily dismissed by Castro.

The great crisis came at the end of October 1959. At that time, Major Huber Matos, the principal anticommunist figure in the revolutionary army and commander in the province of Camaguey, tendered his resignation in protest against extensive Communist penetration of the armed forces and the civilian branches of the government.

At that point, Fidel Castro threw in his lot definitively and irreversibly with the totalitarians among his followers. Instead of granting Matos his retirement, he himself went to Camaguey, had Matos arrested, and a few days later appeared as principal witness against him in a trial for subversion, as the result of which Matos was sentenced to twenty years in jail. In the midst of these events, Camilo Cienfuegos, commander-in-chief of the armed forces and a supporter of the democratic wing of the 26th of July disappeared under mysterious circumstances, which have not been cleared up to this day.

From the imprisonment of Matos forward, the Castro regime took an increasingly Communist direction. Freedom of the press and of assembly were suppressed. All political groups except the totalitarian faction of the 26th of July and the Partido Socialista Popular were driven underground. The government was purged of all democratic 26th of July elements, and the Communists were given increasingly important positions in the administration.

The impact of this trend of events was felt immediately in the labor movement. The first postrevolutionary congress of the CTC met during the first days of November. As part of the regular agenda they elected a new executive committee for the Confederación, consisting entirely of members of 26th of July. Thereupon, Fidel Castro, Raúl Castro, and the Minister of Labor all appeared before the meeting, demanding that they reverse their action and that they elect a new executive committee in which three Communists would be included.

That particular CTC congress, made up of more than 90 per cent 26th of July members, refused these demands. However, under the threat of the use of military force against them, they agreed to allow David Salvador, the acting secretary-general of the CTC, to select a new executive. They also agreed, as a concession to Castro, to withdraw the CTC from the ORIT and ICFTU, and to take the lead in establishing a new Revolutionary Confederation of Workers of Latin America.

The new executive committee consisted only of 26th of July members, but it had a majority who favored working with the Communists. The most outspoken anticommunists were not appointed. The new executive immediately appointed a three-man "purge" committee, ostensibly to remove from office all of those union leaders who were supporters of Eusebio Mujal. Since in fact, these people had all been removed during the first two days of the revolution, the real purpose of the committee was obviously to remove all who were anticommunist.

Within a year, the secretaries-general of 1,400 of the country's 2,490 unions had been removed by the committee. The leaders of at least half of the nation's thirty-four national industrial federations were also dismissed. One of the most important victims of the purge was David Salvador himself, who was removed in May 1960. Subsequently he was jailed, as were hundreds of other 26th of July labor leaders.

During the two years following the November 1959 congress of the CTC, Lázaro Peña, who had headed the Confederación under Batista and had been a Communist member of the Chamber of Deputies, was given an increasingly large role in the affairs of the Confederación, although he held no official post in it. Finally, in the next congress of the CTC, held in October 1961 and completely dominated by the Communists, Peña was once again reinstalled as secretary-general.

This same congress took all the steps necessary to make the Cuban labor movement conform to the role assigned to organized labor in a Communist regime. The congress declared that it considered null and void most of the principal labor laws as well as key provisions of the collective agreements that had been won during the previous twenty-five years.

Lázaro Peña, in closing the 1961 congress of the CTC proclaimed that the organization was now "a Socialist organization at the service of the Socialist revolution." He added that its basic task "is not the defense of the workers demands, but the defense of the revolutionary and Socialist government."

In conformity with this orientation, the nature of the unions changed fundamentally. As in other Communist countries, their job became that of stimulating production rather than of defending the rights of the workers. In conformity with this objective, the Council of Ministers introduced in 1962 the system of so-called "socialist competition," by which the unions would organize contests to see which groups of workers could produce more.

As the result of the Castro regime, all of the gains which the workers had been able to achieve during the previous quarter of a century were destroyed. In effect, the workers were left virtually without any organization to defend their rights. Their real wages dropped drastically, as the result of increased taxation, "voluntary" contributions that they were forced to pay, price increases, and the rationing of most essential goods. The labor movement, in effect, was turned into an instrument of the all-powerful state and the workers were converted into servants of that same state.

Summary and Conclusion

The Cuban labor movement is one of the oldest in Latin America and for several decades it was one of the best organized. By the 1940's most Cuban workers were unionized and were covered by collective agreements. The unions had considerable property and their leaders played an important role in politics and in the management of the social security system and other government bodies.

Cuban organized labor was long the scene of bitter political struggle among the Communists, Autenticos and other party groups, and had become greatly dependent upon the favors of the government. Although at the beginning of the Castro Revolution there was widespread sentiment both among the leadership and rank and file of the unions for making the labor movement more independent this proved impossible once the Castro regime had begun to move in a totalitarian direction. After ruthlessly purging the unions, the Castro government turned them over to old-line Communist party functionaries, who proceeded to divest them of the last vestiges of independence of either the government or the dominant political party.

FOURTEEN

Labor in Hispaniola

THE ISLAND OF HISPANIOLA, THE FIRST PART OF AMERICA IN WHICH the Europeans made permanent settlements, has been divided for more than a century between the small republics of the Dominican Republic and Haiti. They were the second part of America to achieve independence from Europe, as a result of the turmoil of the French Revolution and the Napoleonic Wars.

The two countries have been jealous, turbulent, and poverty-stricken neighbors. The people of Haiti are overwhelmingly African in descent; whereas most Dominicans are mulattoes. The Haitians speak French and a national language, creole, and most Dominicans speak Spanish. Haiti is tremendously overpopulated, its agricultural resources have been to a considerable extent eroded away, and it has little if any mineral deposits; in contrast, the Dominican Republic has a relatively small population, a rich land, and some appreciable mineral reserves.

However, ever since independence the two countries have been torn by internal strife, and have tended to oscillate between long periods of tyranny and short intervals of chaos. Even today democracy and real political stability remain but aspirations in both republics.

Hence, neither the economics nor the politics of the Dominican Republic or Haiti has been propitious for the development of a labor movement. There have been relatively few workers to organize, and the political atmosphere has seldom been such as to encourage the establishment of strong trade unions even among those workers who might be eligible for membership in them.

173

DOMINICAN LABOR BEFORE AND DURING
TRUJILLO'S REGIME

Small groups of craftsmen began to form unions in the Dominican Republic before World War I, and a few of these groups were affiliated with the United States labor movement. A Federación Local del Trabajo was established in Santo Domingo, the national capital, in 1916, but the conditions under United States Marine occupation were not particularly favorable for its growth, for the unions devoted much of their attention to the struggle against United States military occupation.

After the withdrawal of United States troops, the Confederación Dominicana del Trabajo (CDT) was established in 1929, as the country's first national central labor organization. Within a year, though, the asphyxiating dictatorship of Generalissimo Rafael Leonidas Trujillo was established. During the Generalissimo's thirty-one year domination of the country, there was little opportunity for the development of an autonomous labor movement.

Nevertheless, although Trujillo was one of the worst tyrants that Latin America has seen in the twentieth century, he was anxious to maintain the appearances of presiding over a democratic regime. As a result, at the end of World War II he had enacted a labor code equal, on paper, to those of the most advanced Latin American countries. He also encouraged the establishment of unions among many groups of workers in the country's developing economy, although making sure that these organizations were kept under close control of the secret police. As a result, there were in 1949 some thirteen provincial federations of labor affiliated with the CDT. A few unions had "collective contracts" with the appropriate employers' organizations.

The only period during the Trujillo era when the unions were allowed any appreciable degree of autonomy was a few short months in 1946. At that time, Trujillo was worried by the democratic trends evident elsewhere in Latin America and was preparing an electoral farce to maintain the pretense that his was a popularly chosen regime. For a very short time, therefore, he relaxed the rigors of the dictatorship.

As a result of this comparatively liberal attitude upon the part of the government, the unions achieved a militancy which they had never known before. This was largely due to the work of Mauricio Báez, a sugar worker who had for several years been surreptitiously preparing the ground for real union organization among that group. He became the leader of the sugar workers' unions and finally led them out on strike in the region of San Pedro de Macorís. The walkout had the support of all the unions of that part of the country.

This show of labor militancy frightened Trujillo and troops were sent in to break the strike. Many of the strikers were killed, others were arrested and tortured, and some of them disappeared completely. Mauricio Báez succeeded in escaping the clutches of the soldiers and police and ultimately fled to Cuba. Suddenly, in 1950 he mysteriously disappeared from Havana, and it was presumed by his friends and acquaintances that he had been kidnapped and killed by agents of the Trujillo regime.

During the latter years of the Second World War and the period immediately thereafter, Trujillo was carrying on a flirtation with the Communists. There were reported to have been a corps of Communist delegates to the Sixth Congress of the CDT in 1947, and they joined in the praise of the "progressive" policies of the dictator. At the same time, the CDT figured as a member of the Communist-dominated Confederación de Trabajadores de America Latina.

Unfortunately, Trujillo learned from the events of these years. Never again did he permit the least degree of autonomy upon the part of the organized workers. The secret police kept close surveillance over all their activities; and only a little collective bargaining was permitted, since most of the important industries of the country were owned or controlled by Trujillo or members of his family and since the dictator did not choose to allow "his" workers to negotiate concerning the terms and conditions of their employment.

ORGANIZED LABOR AFTER TRUJILLO

It was not until after the death of Trujillo in 1961 that the beginnings of a free labor movement began to appear. The CDT continued in existence until about half a year after the assassination of the dictator, at which time it was officially declared dissolved by the provisional government of the time. Meanwhile, a number of trade unionists who had not been associated with the apparatus of the dictatorship had established the country's first post-Trujillo independent labor group, the Frente Obrero Unido Pro Sindicatos Autonomos (FOUPSA).

Various factions of the international labor movement, as well as political groups in several countries became interested in the nascent labor movement of the Dominican Republic. Exiled Dominicans of Communist and procommunist persuasion, who had had some experience in labor movements in other countries, returned to the island and entered into both political and trade-union work; while other Dominicans went to Cuba for Communist training in labor, party, and other kinds of activities. However, the Communists had relatively little success in the trade-union field.

Soon after the death of Trujillo, several groups of young Dominicans including both political activists and trade unionists were taken to Costa Rica for a course in the International Institute for Political Education, a school then functioning in that republic under the control of several Latin American parties of the democratic Left. At the same time, sizable numbers of Dominicans were also taken to Venezuela, for training in a Christian Democratic trade-union institution recently created in that country's capital.

Finally, the Inter-American Regional Organization of Workers (ORIT) sent a resident representative to the Dominican Republic at the end of 1961 to help in the work of reconstructing the Dominican labor movement. The ORIT office extended considerable moral, organizational, and other kinds of help to the unions.

Within a short while, the labor movement was divided into several rival central labor organizations. The FOUPSA soon split, with a majority of its affiliates breaking away to form the so-called FOUPSA Libre, which in 1962 was converted into the Confederación Nacional de Trabajadores Libres. This emerged as the largest single trade-union group in the country. It affiliated with the ORIT and the ICFTU.

The original FOUPSA continued in existence, and for some time was closely associated with the Unión Civica Nacional party, the country's second largest political group. A second faction broke away from FOUPSA to establish the Confederación Sindical de Trabajadores Dominicanos, which was reported to have only half-a-dozen unions by the middle of 1962. The Communists also had a trade-union group at this time, which had even less unions affiliated with it.

Finally, there was established in 1962 the Confederación Autonoma de Sindicatos Cristianos (CASC). This group not only was aided considerably by the Christian Social Copei party of Venezuela but it also, from its inception, undertook a slow and patient work of training rank-and-file leadership. By 1964 the CASC was certainly the second largest central labor group and was bidding fair to challenge the predominant position of the CNTL. It was a member of the International Federation of Christian Trade Unions and its regional grouping, the Confederación Latino Americana de Sindicalistas Cristianos.

The election of the first democratic constitutional government in a generation promised a new day for trade unionism in the Dominican Republic. The victor in the December 1962 election was Juan Bosch, nominee of the Partido Revolucionario Dominicano, the party to which the largest segment of the country's trade-union leaders belonged. Bosch was committed to a program of political democracy, social reform, and economic development. During his short administration, President Bosch encouraged free trade unionism and collective bargaining.

However, the Bosch government lasted only some seven months, being overthrown at the end of September 1963. It was ousted by a military *coup d'état,* supported by the Unión Civica Nacional, which had lost the election in the previous year. Although the provisional government established at that time did not prove to be particularly hostile to organized labor, as some had feared it might, the labor movement was nonetheless adversely influenced by the *coup d'état* of September 1963. Programs for economic development which were being planned by the Bosch regime were largely abandoned by its successor, thus intensifying an already difficult unemployment situation. In addition, the instability of a *de facto* military government such as that which ruled for several years after the fall of the Bosch regime limited the freedom of action of the organized labor movement.

The future of the Dominican organized labor movement will undoubtedly depend upon the general political future of the country. A new conservative dictatorship of the Trujillo kind would have little room for a real trade-union movement. A victory for left-wing totalitarianism would convert the nascent labor movement into little more than a tool of the government. Only the firm establishment of a progressive democratic regime would assure a strong future for a really independent free labor movement.

THE LABOR MOVEMENT OF HAITI

Haiti has had only a very narrow economic base for any labor movement at all. In addition, except for a short period in the late 1940's and early 1950's the country's political situation has provided no encouragement for even the small labor movement which the national economy might have permitted.

A small Fédération Ouvrière d'Haiti was reported to belong to the Pan-American Federation of Labor during the 1920's. It apparently devoted much of its energies to opposition to the occupation regime established by the United States Marines, who had taken over the country during World War I.

The occupation regime was succeeded in the 1930's by the government of Stenio Vincent. During his administration and that of Elie Lescot, which ruled from 1941 until it was overthrown in January 1946, the government ruled with an iron hand and did not permit the development of any organized labor movement.

The provisional government and the administration of President Dumarsais Estimé which succeeded the Lescot administration within a few months were the first Haitian regimes to give full encouragement to organized labor.

Trade unions were established among various workers' groups soon after Lescot was ousted. In October of the same year the Fédération des Travailleurs Haitiens was established by unions of mechanics, electricians, chauffeurs, and maritime workers. This group soon claimed some fifty-one unions in its membership.

However, the FTH soon split. In March 1948 many unions withdrew from this federation, claiming that it was controlled by the local Communist party, which operated under the name of Parti Socialiste Populaire. The seceding unions established the Fédération Haitien du Travail, which soon became the country's largest central labor organization. It included most of the unions in small factories in Port-au-Prince and other major towns, as well as port workers and other transportation employees. The FHT became a member of the Inter-American Confederation of Workers, the predecessor of the ORIT.

An entirely separate central labor group was established under the leadership of Daniel Fignolé, who had been for a short while a member of the government of President Estimé. He established both a political party, the Mouvement Ouvrière Paysan, and a labor federation, the Union Nationale des Travailleurs Haitiens. Its principal strength was among sugar workers, white-collar employees, and scattered industrial workers' groups.

The Haitian labor movement reached its apogee in 1948. At that time, the Ministry of Labor reported that there existed 153 unions in the nation, of which 53 per cent were located in the capital. Port-au-Prince. After 1948 the trade unions began a slow decline which was intensified in the 1950's.

In the meantime, the Estimé government developed a modern

labor policy such as no previous Haitian regime had ever followed. A Ministry of Labor was established, a minimum-wage law was enacted, and the foundations were laid for a social security system. At the same time, the government frankly encouraged the development of trade unions, and their engaging in collective bargaining with the employers.

One cause of decline was continued splitting in the labor movement. In August 1949 the Fédération Haitien du Travail was divided when a small group of unions withdrew to form a new group, the Fédération Sindical d'Haiti. A year later, the FSH changed its name to Confédération Générale du Travail and became the Haitian affiliate of the short-lived Peronista hemispheric federation, the Agrupación de Trabajadores Latino Americanos Sindicalizados.

Another factor in the decline of the Haitian labor movement was the re-establishment of a dictatorship. President Dumarsais Estimé was overthrown by a military *coup* late in 1949. After a short period of provisional government, General Paul Magloire was elected president, and ruled as a more or less benevolent dictator until shortly before the end of 1956.

Although the Magloire government continued the social security and housing programs which had been started by the Estimé government, Magloire exercised close control over the labor movement. Daniel Fignolé's Union Nationale des Travailleurs Haitiens was virtually unable to function during the Magloire administration. Other labor groups were less roughly handled.

In August 1950 the Fédération Haitien du Travail began a move to unify the country's labor movement. The federation was joined in its efforts by the hitherto independent Chauffeurs' Federation. As a result of those efforts, a Committee of Trade Union Coordination of Haiti was established. This was later transformed into the Union Nationale du Travail d'Haiti. It became affiliated with the ORIT and the ICFTU. Its principal centers of strength were the port workers and chauffeurs.

During 1956 and 1957 the country's political difficulties again endangered the labor movement. President Magloire's efforts to have himself re-elected were resisted by employers, workers, and the military, and as a result, he was overthrown in November 1956. From then until September 1957 the country underwent a period of rapidly changing regimes and growing chaos. Among those who served temporarily as president of the republic during this period was Daniel Fignolé, who occupied the office for about three weeks in May 1957.

This period of instability was ended in September 1957 with the election of President François Duvalier. There was no opposition nominee to Duvalier, who had been chosen by the armed forces as their way out of the political crisis.

Duvalier moved quickly to establish a rigorous personal dictatorship. He set about to destroy all political and social groups which might interfere with his aspirations to be absolute ruler of his unfortunate country. All parties were outlawed; freedom of press, speech, and assembly was completely suppressed; all of the country's churches were curbed. Even the army was decimated, with most of its officers being jailed, exiled, killed, or otherwise disposed of.

In such an atmosphere, it was impossible for any kind of a free labor movement to survive. The Union Nationale du Travail was soon suppressed, and most of its leaders were forced into exile. There they established a unit abroad which carried on active propaganda against the Duvalier regime—to which end the unit received extensive cooperation from the ORIT and the ICFTU.

Within a few months of the advent of the Duvalier regime, the labor movement had been totally destroyed. It seemed unlikely that the workers would again be able to organize in defense of their own interests until a constitutional and at least semi-democratic regime had been restored to Haiti.

Summary and Conclusion

Weak economic development and tyrannical governments have hampered the development of organized labor in both the Dominican Republic and Haiti. In the former country, although dictator Trujillo organized puppet trade unions during the

1940's, it was not until after his assassination in May 1961 that a real labor movement was able to develop. In Haiti, the only period during which the workers were able to organize with any effectiveness was in the decade 1946-56, when the governments of Estimé and Magloire enacted some modest labor legislation and permitted trade unions to function.

FIFTEEN

Labor and the Mexican Revolution

THE RISE OF THE TRADE UNIONS OF MEXICO IS CLOSELY ASSOCIATED with the development of the Mexican revolution of 1910. Although there were some beginnings of an organized labor movement as early as the middle decades of the nineteenth century, the unions established at that time were effectively destroyed by the dictatorship of Porfirio Díaz.

The outbreak of the revolution against Díaz in 1910 made possible the emergence once again of organized labor, and in the decades which have transpired since then, the trade-union movement has been an integral part of those forces which have supported and pushed forward the development of the revolution.

ORIGINS OF MEXICAN ORGANIZED LABOR

In the middle of the nineteenth century groups of European exiles and Mexicans established in Mexico groups which were influenced by the ideas of utopian socialism then prevalent in Europe. Somewhat later, in the 1860's and early 1870's, similar elements established local units of the International Workingmen's Association, the First International of Karl Marx and Michael Bakunin.

At the same time, groups of artisans in Mexico City and other important urban centers organized mutual-benefit societies and various kinds of cooperatives. Some of these organizations functioned as trade unions and a number of strikes occurred. The

183

workers' groups in the capital city were organized into a Cemtro de Sociedades Obreras.

There was a very active press associated with this incipient labor movement. It generally supported the Reform forces led by Presidents Benito Juárez and Sebastian Lerdo de Tejada, but it was ideologically varied. It included periodicals of Marxist orientation, others which were more sympathetic to the revolutionary anarchist philosophy of Michael Bakunin, and still others which remained loyal to one or another of the Utopian Socialist schools.

During the first years of the regime of General Porfirio Díaz, who seized power from President Lerdo de Tejada in 1876, the labor movement continued to grow. A national confederation of workers, with the grandiloquent name of the Gran Confederación de Asociaciones de Trabajadores de la República Mexicana, was established during the first months of the Díaz regime. It proposed a varied program of activities including trade unionism, the establishment of producers' and consumers' cooperatives, and political activities designed to establish a "working-class republic."

By the late 1880's the dictatorship of Porfiro Díaz would no longer brook the kind of opposition and potential "sedition" represented by the labor movement. Its press was suppressed, and the labor organizations themselves found it increasingly difficult to carry on their activities. Strikes were ruthlessly suppressed.

However, in spite of the oppressiveness of the Díaz regime, the activity of organized labor began to reappear in the years immediately preceding the outbreak of the Mexican revolution. It received its inspiration from the Partido Liberal, an organization of anarchosyndicalist tendencies in spite of its name. This was headed by the Flores Magón brothers, who spent much of their time in exile in the United States, but who were able to extend the network of their organization among important groups of workers and young professional people in the country's major cities.

The most outstanding labor events during the years just preceding the revolution were two strikes in the year 1907. These took place in the important Cananea copper mines in the North, and among the textile workers of Puebla in the South. Although the strikes were lost, they contributed considerably to the development of labor discontent against the Díaz regime.

LABOR AND THE MADERO REGIME

There was widespread support among the workers for the revolutionary movement launched by Francisco I. Madero in 1910. When the Madero forces were successful, the workers of Mexico City began to establish their own organizations, and their lead was soon followed in other parts of the republic.

The first organization set up by the workers was the Casa del Obrero Mundial. It undertook the organization of the workers into unions. Moreover, most of those who organized the Casa had been associated with the Partido Liberal, and at least some of them had participated in the Industrial Workers of the World, while working in the United States.

Although all of the Casa leaders were at first sympathetic to President Madero, many soon became disillusioned in the revolutionary leader, for the Casa del Obrero Mundial urged upon Madero the necessity for a broad program of legislation on behalf of the working classes which had supported his revolution. President Madero, however, apparently had little realization of the depth of social protest which had been let loose by his movement to overthrow the Díaz dictatorship. Thus he failed to launch the kind of reform programs which were being urged upon him in the labor field by the Casa del Obrero Mundial and in the agrarian field by Emiliano Zapata, an important revolutionary leader operating southwest of Mexico City and distributing large landholders' estates among landless peasants. Consequently there were some strikes during the Madero period. So, although at first giving the Casa full freedom to conduct its activities, Madero tended to become impatient with it in the last months of his administration.

LABOR AND THE REVOLUTIONARY
CIVIL WAR

In January 1913 President Francisco Madero was assassinated and the presidency was seized by General Victoriano Huerta, an officer of the old Díaz army. Huerta's *coup d'état* served to unite all of the conflicting revolutionary elements in a struggle against the new dictatorship. Huerta's opponents were divided into three armies: those of ex-Governor Venustiano Carranza, which were strongest in the northeastern part of the country; of Francisco Villa, in the Northwest; and of Emiliano Zapata in the Southwest. At least temporarily, all forces recognized the supremacy of Carranza as "First Chief" of the revolution.

By the last months of 1914 the anti-Huerta forces were victorious: they occupied the capital city. However, this victory was only the prelude for further hostilities, for within a short time, the forces of Zapata and Villa were aligned against those of President Carranza.

In the face of this renewed civil war, the leaders of the Casa del Obrero Mundial had a hard decision to make. Thus some of them, including a young lawyer Antonio Díaz Soto y Gama, joined forces with the Zapata-Villa armies. Then Díaz Soto y Gama himself became one of Emiliano Zapata's principal advisers.

However, the majority of the leaders of the Casa del Obrero Mundial entered into an agreement with General Alvaro Obregón, principal military leader of the Carranza forces. It was agreed that the Casa would have full freedom to carry on its organizational activities and establish unions among workers within the areas controlled by the Carranza forces. In return, the labor leaders would recruit soldiers to fight in the ranks of the Carranza armies.

As a result of this agreement, the leaders of the Casa del Obrero Mundial raised the so-called "Red Batallions." These made an important contribution to the ultimate military victory of the forces of President Carranza. At the same time, labor organizations affiliated with the Casa were established throughout the area controlled by the Carranza forces.

In spite of the agreement with the Casa and his decrees in favor of agrarian reform, President Carranza was essentially conservative. As a result, he soon ran into conflict with the labor movement.

In 1916 the electrical workers of Mexico City, led by Luis Morones, declared a strike. The Carranza government cracked down strongly on this walkout, by arresting its leaders and sentencing several of them, including Morones, to death. However, Carranza's vengeful hand was stayed by his military chief, Alvaro Obregón, who convinced the president to pardon the labor leaders.

THE CROM

The growth of the labor movement on a national scale made it inevitable that sooner or later the unions would be brought together in a central labor body. This occurred in 1918, when a congress of workers established the Confederación Regional Obrera Mexicana (CROM). Luis Morones was elected its secretary-general.

The name of the CROM reflected the anarchosyndicalist proclivities of many of its leaders; yet, within a very short time the Confederación lost whatever anarchosyndicalist orientation it might originally have possessed, and entered into an alliance with the government.

The CROM-government accord was made possible by the overthrow of the Carranza regime in 1919 by General Alvaro Obregón. During the following year, General Adolfo de la Huerta served as provisional president, after which General Obregón was finally inaugurated as constitutional president of the republic.

President Obregón, who had shown a deep degree of understanding of the social issues of the Mexican revolution virtually since its beginning, adopted a strongly prolabor position. In particular, he favored the newly established Confederación Regional Obrera Mexicana. Several of the leaders of the CROM were given important government jobs, Luis Morones himself becoming manager of the state munitions factory.

With the expiration of President Obregón's term in 1924, General Plutarco Elías Calles became president. During most of his administration, the position of the CROM was even more favorable than it had been under Obregón. Luis Morones served as Secretary of Labor and Industry under Calles, and other CROM leaders served as members of congress and state legislatures and even as state governors.

During this period the Confederación Regional Obrera Mexicana spread its organization throughout the republic. State federations were established in almost all areas. Generally, in conflicts with employers and with other trade-union groups, the CROM had the support of both the federal and state governments. Most important groups of workers were unionized, and collective bargaining agreements became commonplace.

The CROM, however, was faced with serious competition early in the Obregón administration. Those leaders of the CROM who were still loyal to anarchosyndicalist ideas objected to the alliance of the Confederación with the Obregón regime. As a result, they formed a rival organization, the Confederación General de Trabajadores, which affiliated with the anarchosyndicalist International Workingmen's Association.

The CGT, however, never rivaled the CROM in size or political importance, though it did among a number of labor groups offer serious competition to the government-backed group. There were also several important strikes during the 1920's—including one of the trolley-car workers of Mexico City—which were led by the CGT. Generally, such walkouts were opposed not only by the government but the CROM as well.

THE BREAKUP OF THE CROM

A split occurred between the Confederación Regional Obrera Mexicana and President Plutarco Elías Calles at the end of 1927.

The question at issue was the succession to the presidency. The CROM leaders felt that it was time that a civilian become president and, in addition, that it was Luis Morones who should be Calles' successor. However, ex-President Obregón had decided that he wanted to return to the presidency, and Calles not only supported him in his ambition, but he even arranged for a change in the constitution to make this possible.

So when Luis Morones resigned from the Cabinet, and the CROM in effect joined the opposition, virtual war was declared between the administration and the labor group. As a result, the CROM began to disintegrate. Various state governors brought about the disaffiliation of CROM state federations from their parent body. In addition, several nationwide groups of unions withdrew from the CROM as well.

One of these consisted of the unions under the control of the Communists. In conformity with the Third Period line of the Communist International, which called for the Communist parties to establish dual union groups under their own control, the Mexican CP established its own trade-union confederation, the Confederación Sindical Unitaria, in 1929.

This process of disintegration of the CROM continued for several years. One of the most important secessions was that led by Vicente Lombardo Toledano, who had been an important leader of the CROM virtually since its inception. This group established a new national labor group, the Confederación General de Obreros y Campesinos de Mexico.

As a result of this situation, the Mexican Labor movement of the early 1930's was divided into many rival organizations. The CROM itself was divided into at least two groups using the same name; the CGT continued to have certain influence, and several other national labor groups were carrying on bitter competition with one another. In addition, in several states the bulk of the labor movement was completely independent of any national central labor body.

THE FORMATION OF THE CTM

With the advent of President Lázaro Cárdenas to power at the end of 1934 the government again became interested in the unification of the labor movement. The President was faced with serious opposition from conservative elements, who opposed his intensification of the program of land redistribution, his economic nationalism (including the expropriation foreign-owned properties), and his support of organized labor. He felt a need for solidifying his support among workers and peasants, and to this end, he felt that it would be a good idea to establish once again a single large central labor organization.

President Lázaro Cárdenas selected Vicente Lombardo Toledano of the CGOCM as the man to bring about this unification. With the encouragement and support of Cárdenas, Lombardo Toledano began negotiations with leaders of other labor groups, looking towards the merger of all of them into a single powerful confederation.

The founding meeting of the new organization was held in Mexico City in 1936. All existing labor groups were invited to send delegates to this meeting; however, the CROM of Luis Morones and the CGT refused to participate. The congress therefore brought together the CGOCM, the Communists' CSU, various independent state groups, and several national industrial unions which had not hitherto belonged to any central labor group.

The new organization established at this congress, the Confederación de Trabajadores de Mexico (CTM), included at its inception the large majority of the country's organized workers. These included the railroad, electrical, petroleum, and mining workers, as well as a large part of the country's factory workers. The principal groups which did not participate in the founding of the CTM were the government employees and farm workers, which the Cárdenas regime had decided should remain outside of any central labor group.

Vicente Lombardo Toledano became secretary-general of the Confederación de Trabajadores de Mexico. The executive committee of the group was chosen with considerable care to include representatives of all the important elements which had drawn together to form the confederation.

THE DISINTEGRATION OF THE CTM

The trade-union unity achieved in the founding congress of the CTM soon began to be undermined. Several important national industrial unions, including those of railroad and mining workers, as well as one of the nation's three electrical workers' organizations, withdrew from the confederation during its first couple years.

A more important threat to CTM unity came early in 1937 when the Communists split the organization. Overestimating their own forces in the confederation, they attempted to take over the organization in March 1937, and when they failed, they withdrew the unions under their control from the CTM.

However, this split was soon brought to an end. As the result of the intervention of Earl Browder, secretary-general of the Communist party of the United States, who ordered the Mexican Communist leaders to end the schism they had started in the CTM, unity was quickly restored. In agreeing to the return of the Communist unions to the confederation, Vicente Lombardo Toledano overrode the opinion of an important group among his own followers.

In 1942 there was another significant division in the CTM. A number of unions, including most of those in the shoe industry as well as some groups of textile workers, building tradesmen, and miscellaneous industrial workers, withdrew from the CTM to form the Confederación Proletaria Nacional. These organizations claimed to be still loyal, at least to some degree, to anarchosyndicalist ideas. In subsequent years other small groups broke with the CTM.

The final split in the Confederación de Trabajadores de Mexico took place late in 1947. At this time, Vicente Lombardo Toledano was attempting to organize a new political party, the Partido Popular, in opposition to the government's Partido Revolucionario Institucional, to which the CTM was affiliated. Although Lombardo claimed that he had the support of the other CTM leaders in his efforts to launch a new party, when it came time for the CTM to decide whether or not to back the new group, its leaders refused to do so. When Lombardo Toledano refused to accept this decision, he was expelled not only from his post as secretary-general of the CTM but also from the CTM itself.

The small core of personal followers of Lombardo Toledano within the CTM, as well as the unions controlled by the Communist party, thereupon withdrew from the CTM. They established yet another small central labor group, the Unión General de Obreros y Campesinos de Mexico.

TENDENCY TOWARDS LABOR UNITY

During the first years of the 1950's the Mexican labor movement was more divided than it had been since before the formation of the CTM. The following central labor organizations were then in existence: the CTM, the CROM, the UGOCM, the Confederación Proletaria Nacional, the Confederación de Obreros y Campesinos de Mexico, the Confederación Nacional de Trabajadores, the Confederación Unica de Trabajadores, and the Federación de Agrupaciones Obreras. In addition, the Confederación General de Trabajadores was at that time split into three rival groups, each claiming to be the "authentic" CGT. Finally, there were several important national industrial unions, including the railroaders', miners', and one electrical workers' union which remained outside of all these central labor groups.

However, in 1952 there began a trend towards greater unity among the country's labor organizations. Subsequent to that date, no significant new split occurred in any of the more important central labor groups, and several of those existing at the beginning of 1952 were merged.

The first move was the unification late in 1952 of the Confederación Nacional de Trabajadores, the COCM, the Confederación Proletaria Nacional, and the Confederación Unica de Trabajadores. They formed a new group, the Confederación Revolucionaria de Obreros y Campesinos de Mexico, which immediately assumed the position of the second most numerous of the country's central labor bodies.

The CROM, first of the national labor groups, also participated in the trend towards greater unity. In the early 1950's important groups of unions in the states of Puebla, Tlascala, and Vera Cruz, which had formerly been outside of any central labor organization, joined the CROM. In the middle 1950's, the three rival factions of the Confederación General de Trabajadores also joined forces in a single group once again.

Early in 1963 a further and perhaps more important step towards labor unity took place. The CROC took the lead in bringing together several central labor groups and independent unions to form a new group, the Central Nacional de Trabajadores. Those participating included the CROC, the Confederación Revolucionaria de Trabajadores, the Federación Obrera Revolutionaria, and the independent unions of miners, railroaders, electrical workers, telephonists, and textile workers.

The leaders of the new CNT argued that they did not intend to merge their respective organizations into a new confederation. They claimed that they were merely forming a new political pressure group. However, at least the leaders of the CROC certainly hoped that the CNT would sooner or later develop into a national confederation which could rival in strength the Confederación de Trabajadores de Mexico.

By the early 1960's the CTM was still by all odds the largest of the nation's labor organizations. It was the only one which had substantial representation in every one of the country's states. It had in its ranks most of the country's national industrial unions. It was still politically the most potent of the country's labor organizations.

LABOR POLITICAL ACTIVITY

In the early 1920's, the Confederación Regional Obrera Mexicana established the tradition that the Mexican labor movement would actively participate in the country's political life. During most of the Calles administration, the Partido Laborista, closely associated with the CROM, was the principal party supporting the government.

With the split between the CROM leadership and President Plutarco Elías Calles, the role of the Partido Laborista declined. Calles organized a new party, the Partido Nacional Revolucionario, as the basis for the revolutionary administration. Although the labor movement generally continued to support the regime, the unions had no organic connection with the new government party.

President Lázaro Cárdenas reorganized the Partido Nacional Revolucionario. He changed its name to Partido de la Revolución Mexicana and set it up upon a new basis. Four separate "sectors" of the party were established: those of Labor, Peasants, Popular Organizations, and the Army. During the administration of Cárdenas' successor, President Manuel Ávila Camacho, the Army Sector of the party was suppressed, but the other three continued in existence. Under President Miguel Alemán (1946-52) the name of the government party was changed to Partido Revolucionario Institucional, but the form of organization originally established by President Cárdenas was maintained.

The Labor Sector of the government party has had as its objective the inclusion within its ranks of the whole labor movement. Since its inception it has included the great majority of the country's organized workers. In spite of the frequent schisms within the labor movement, most of the confederations as well as the independent national industrial unions have continued their association with the revolutionary party. In the early 1960's all of the important elements in the labor movement were affiliated with the PRI. The only central labor group remaining outside was the Unión General de Obreros y Campesinos de Mexico, which was dominated by members of Lombardo Toledano's Partido Popular Socialista and the Partido Comunista.

The PRI's Labor Sector is under the direction of the party's labor secretary. In the early 1960's this official was chosen from the ranks of the Confederación de Trabajadores de Mexico, and the party's assistant labor secretary was a leader of the Confederación Revolucionaria de Obreros y Campesinos (CROC).

During the administration of President Manuel Avila Camacho the CTM took the lead in trying to organize the whole labor movement so as to augment its influence within the government party. For this purpose, the Bloque de Unidad Obrera (BUO) was established. The role of the Bloque was to discuss questions of legislation and other political matters of interest to the labor movement, to reach agreement where possible among the various trade-union organizations on such issues, and to present a common front to other elements within the government party.

During the early 1960's the Bloque de Unidad Obrera included the considerable majority of the labor movement within its ranks. The organizations belonging to it include¹ the CTM, the CROM, the CGT, the Federación de Agrupaci⸱ ⸱es Obreras, and some of the independent unions. However, in ⸱ ⸱63 the Central Nacional de Trabajadores was established as a rival to the Bloque. There was at least some evidence that President Adolfo López Mateos encouraged the establishment of the CNT.

The influence of the organized labor movement within the government political party declined considerably in the quarter of a century following the Cárdenas administration. This was due largely to the stabilization of the country's political life, the economic development of the nation, and the expansion of membership of the so-called Popular Organizations Sector of the party.

As the security of the government became greater, and the possibility of armed insurrection against it declined, the regime came to depend less than in the past upon the potential military help of the organized workers. At the same time, the economic development of the country tended to increase the importance of various middle-class elements in society, particularly the industrialists. It was these groups which were principally represented in the Popular Organizations Sector of the government party. During the 1940's and 1950's increasingly numerous elements from this expanding middle class became affiliated with the Popular Organizations Sector.

ECONOMIC ACTIVITIES OF LABOR
MOVEMENT

Much of the attention of the organized labor movement of
Mexico is naturally taken up with the process of collective bargaining. The collective agreement has become standard in Mexico, and the tendency in recent decades has been for the national
contract to become typical. In those industries in which there exists a single large industry-wide union, it is this organization
which negotiates an agreement with the employer or employers in
its respective field. Where there are various competing unions in
the same industry, these sometimes join together to deal with the
employers.

The more important collective bargaining agreements in Mexico cover a wide range of issues. They not only include discussion of wages and hours, but also such issues as seniority, job
classification, social welfare, job tenure, grievance procedure, and
other matters.

Grievance procedure is a key element of collective bargaining
in Mexico. The employers and the unions establish an orderly
procedure through which the individual worker can present complaints against their treatment by the employer or alleged viola-
tions of the collective agreement. Normally, appeal to a government labor court is the last step in Mexican grievance procedure,
with the court being able to use both the law and the relevant
collective contract as basis of its judgments.

THE ROLE OF THE GOVERNMENT

The Mexican government has both an important formal role
and an equally significant informal participation in labor relations. On the former level, since the adoption of the Constitution
of 1917, the Mexican government has enacted a large body of
labor legislation. The Constitution itself outlined in great detail
of what this legislation should consist.

The country's labor laws were consolidated in a Labor Code
in 1929, one of the first such bodies of law to be enacted in Latin

America. It includes provisions for safety measures by employers to protect workers from accidents on the job, workmen's compensation, limitation of the working day, minimum wages, and special provisions for working women and children. In 1963 a constitutional provision for profit-sharing was enacted into law.

Mexican labor law provides less-strict formal government control over the trade unions than is the case in many of the Latin American countries. It allows the formation of unions with a great variety of kinds of jurisdiction, including national industrial unions, as well as those covering a single plant or firm or covering an entire industry on a local or regional level. The law puts very few impediments in the way of any group of workers wishing to establish a union.

However, in many ways the informal controls of the government over organized labor are more important than those set forth in the law. Because of the affiliation of most of the labor movement with the government political party, a peculiarly reciprocal relationship has existed between the administration and the trade unions for most of the history of Mexican organized labor.

The president and other government officials regularly consult the principal labor organizations concerning legislation and other matters of direct concern to the workers. But at the same time, the government is in a powerful position to influence the conduct of the leaders of the main trade-union groups.

This government influence is exercised through a variety of ways. In the first place, the country's most important labor leaders are in a very real sense members of the small group which in fact governs Mexico. They help to choose the government party's candidate for president every six years; they have marked influence on administration policy on a wide range of issues. There is a strong feeling of group solidarity among the members of this group which rules Mexico, and the labor leaders guide their own actions with this sense of solidarity in mind.

A second lever available to the government, and particularly to the president, in influencing the decisions and conduct of the labor movement is patronage. The principal leaders of the strongest trade-union organizations are candidates of the government party for congress and nomination by the government party is tantamount to election. Other lucrative posts in the public administration are often open to the labor chiefs. Lesser lights in the trade unions can become members of state legislatures or city councils. Labor officials at all levels are not anxious to lose these perquisites.

A third element through which the government can influence the labor movement is the latter's feeling of party solidarity and loyalty. Most trade-union officials regard the government party as the true spokesman of the Mexican revolution, to which all of them are loyal. The labor leaders therefore limit their actions so as not to undermine the position of the government party, or to create a situation which might strengthen the hand of the Communist and procommunist groups to the Left of the administration or the antirevolutionary parties to its Right.

This commitment to the government and its party has led to considerable complaint in the lower ranks of the labor movement from time to time. Such criticism became particularly vocal in the late 1950's. Elements hostile to the government party were able to gain control of several important unions, including the railroaders' and schoolteachers'. In 1958 and 1959 these elements led a series of major strikes, which were generally settled favorably to the unions. However, when the union leaders thereupon tried to push their advantage and launched other walkouts, the government of President Adolfo López Mateos cracked down on them very strongly. The strikes were broken and the principal leaders of the railroad workers' union were jailed, as were the chiefs of the Communist party. Soon afterwards a more accommodating group was chosen to lead the recalcitrant unions.

Summary and Conclusion

The Mexican labor movement has been an inherent part of the Mexican revolution. The Constitution of 1917, which gave institutional framework to the revolution, provided for extensive legal protection for the workers and their organizations. Since the 1920's the trade-union movement has been intimately linked to the government, and since the middle 1930's most labor organizations have been affiliated with the party in power.

Although the Mexican unions have organized most of the workers in the country's main industries—petroleum, transport, mining, metallurgy, textiles, and other manufacturing—as well as virtually all government employees, there are still sizable working-class elements outside of the labor movement. One of the principal weaknesses of organized labor in Mexico is the fact that the unskilled, uneducated, and largely migratory workers, who make up a very large part of the working class, have not been brought into the unions. Nevertheless, the unions have been able to defend effectively the interests of a large part of the working class, and have for more than a generation been one of the principal power centers of Mexican society.

SIXTEEN

Organized Labor in Central America

THE SIX SMALL COUNTRIES LOCATED BETWEEN MEXICO AND THE SOUTH
American continent—Guatemala, El Salvador, Honduras, Nicaragua, Costa Rica, and Panamá—are among the smallest nations
of Latin America. Until recently, their economic development
has been slow, and most of them have been plagued by political
problems which have made them tend to oscillate between dictatorship and chaos. Both economic underdevelopment and political instability have tended to militate against the growth of strong
labor movements in these republics.

EARLY BEGINNINGS OF ORGANIZED LABOR

As elsewhere in Latin America, the first workers' organizations
to be established were mutual-benefit societies, formed for the
purpose of providing a primitive type of insurance for their members against such things as unemployment and illness, and of providing small sums for the heirs of deceased members. Such organizations were found in all of these republics in the period before
the First World War.

The mutual-benefit societies had the advantage that they were
not organizations of class struggle, often had both workers and
their employers as members, and therefore did not give rise to
fear upon the part of dictatorial governments that they might be
focii of discontent or rebellion. In some instances, they were even
given some slight financial assistance by the various Central
American governments.

However, during the 1920's genuine trade unionism began to

make its appearance in these countries. In part this was due to the influence of the Pan-American Federation of Labor, which was faced in South America with the opposition of the already substantially organized labor movements under radical political leadership and which sought therefore to stimulate the development of labor groups in Central America which might become PAFL affiliates.

One of the earliest of these groups was one called Obrerismo Organizado of Nicaragua. Largely under the stimulation of the PAFL, Federaciones de Trabajadores were established in the three northernmost countries, Guatemala, El Salvador, and Honduras in the late 1920's. Although these groups joined for a while to form a Central American Federation of Labor, associated with the PAFL, they soon fell under Communist influence.

Under Communist leadership the labor federations of these three countries became a good deal more militant than they had formerly been. In Honduras the local federation made an unsuccessful attempt to organize the workers in the banana plantations of the country's north coast. Finally, in the early 1930's, the labor movement was destroyed by the three dictators who came to power at that time, Jorge Ubico in Guatemala, Maximiliano Hernández Martínez in El Salvador, and Tiburcio Carías Andino in Honduras. The same fate befell the Nicaraguan labor movement under the rule of General Anastasio Somoza, who seized power there in 1936.

A somewhat different situation prevailed in Costa Rica. The democratic conditions prevalent there made the task of organizing a labor movement somewhat less rigorous. The leadership in this direction was taken by the young Communist Party of Costa Rica, which had been established under the leadership of a recent law school graduate, Manuel Mora, in 1929.

Although the Communist party was established largely by young intellectuals, it immediately set to work to organize a labor movement. It had small success among the artisans of San José, the capital, but did better among the banana workers along the Caribbean coast. There by 1935 the Communists had established a small but militant union, and in that year they brought these workers out on strike, demanding union recognition, higher wages, and better living conditions.

The first reaction of the United Fruit Company was to resist any negotiation with their unionized workers. However, as a result of the intervention of Costa Rican President Ricardo Jiménez, they finally conceded to negotiate with them indirectly. As a result, they finally signed an agreement that, on one hand, conceded many of the workers' economic demands but, on the other, did not establish a regular channel for collective bargaining. It was another half decade before the United Fruit Company finally agreed to negotiate on a regular basis with the banana workers' union.

THE REBIRTH OF UNIONISM IN THE 1940'S

Organized labor revived in the four northern countries of Central America, and received a considerable impetus in Costa Rica and Panamá as a result of the events of World War II. All these countries were officially involved in the war, and although none of them actually sent soldiers to fight on the battlefields, they participated actively in providing goods which were much needed by the Allies. Furthermore, Allied war propaganda circulated widely in all of these nations, and its stress on the war's being a struggle for democracy and for the rights of the common people had considerable impact.

The result of this situation was that during and soon after the Second World War there began in most of these countries extensive political changes which were very conducive to the growth once again of an organized labor movement. In 1944, the dictatorships of Ubico in Guatemala and Hernández Martínez in El Salvador were overthrown. In 1948 the old dictator Carías Andino in Honduras passed power to a long-time civilian associate, Juan Manuel Gálvez, who was of considerably more liberal temperament and beliefs. In Nicaragua, fearful of being ousted if he remained a dictator, Somoza temporarily relaxed the rigors of his regime and, among other things, encouraged the development of a trade-union movement.

In Costa Rica and Panamá, too, although there did not exist dictatorial regimes to be overthrown, the war had its effect in stimulating organized labor. In the former country an administration came to power in 1940 which was frankly sympathetic to trade unionism, and in Panamá, too, the wartime regimes for the most part took a more sympathetic attitude towards organized labor than had governments in the past.

LABOR AND THE GUATEMALAN
REVOLUTION

As the result of the overthrow of General Ubico in Guatemala there came to power in October 1944 a provisional government of democratic orientation. Under its aegis a new constitution was written which instructed congress to write extensive labor legislation and bring about other basic reforms. Once the constitution went into effect, a university professor, Dr. Juan José Arevalo, was elected president of the republic.

The Arevalo administraion was frankly friendly to organized labor. It enacted a Labor Code which provided for legal recognition of trade unions, established a minimum wage, the eight-hour day, and other reforms, and established labor courts for hearing complaints of workers concerning violation of the Code. The Arevalo regime also established the beginnings of a social security system.

During this period between the revolution of 1944 and the end of the Arevalo administration in 1951, the labor movement grew extensively. In 1945 the first central labor organization of the period, the Confederación de Trabajadores de Guatemala (CTG), was established and was affiliated with the Confederación de Trabajadores de America Latina (CTAL).

However, the CTG soon split. Dissident elements in it charged that the leaders of the new group were Communist-inclined and that, in particular, the school which the CTG had established to train trade-union leaders was in fact carrying out through indoctrination in Communist ideas. As a result, a substantial group of unions, including the powerful Sindicato de

Acción y Mejoramiento Ferrocarrilero, the railroaders' union, withdrew to form a new organization, the Federación Sindical de Guatemala.

For some years the CTG had its main strength among some artisan groups in the capital, Guatemala City, and among farm workers in the environs of the capital. The Federación Sindical de Gutemala contained the railroaders' and most of the more important factory workers' unions. In addition there was a smaller group than either the CTG or FSG, known as the Federación Regional de Trabajadores, which included some artisans' unions and various white-collar workers' groups. Finally, there were a few autonomous labor groups in some of the provincial cities, particularly Quetzaltenango, the country's second largest town, as well as on the banana plantations of the United Fruit Company.

During these years the stronger Guatemalan unions established a system of collective bargaining with the employers. Collective contracts were signed, systems for processing grievances were organized. The government Labor Courts were sometimes called upon to decide disputed points in these contracts as well as to enforce the new code of labor laws.

The importance of the labor movement as a supporter of the Guatemalan revolution was demonstrated in July 1949, when a faction of the army arose in revolt against the Arevalo regime. At that time the government called upon the unions to support the administration, and they not only declared a general strike against the military insurrection, but also provided volunteers to whom the loyal military gave arms, and these labor militiamen fought alongside the loyal army units to defeat the rebellion.

The labor movement remained divided into various groups, however, until the advent of President Jacobo Arbenz to power at the end of 1951. Although Communist influence within the CTG had become complete, and the strength of the Communists had also been growing in the Federación Sindical de Guatemala, they had not been able to get complete control of the labor movement during the administration of Arevalo. The President himself was not sympathetic to Communist domination of organized labor which went far to explain the failure of the Communists to obtain it so long as Arevalo remained president.

However, such was not the case under President Arbenz. He had long been supported by the Communists as a candidate for president, and his relations with them were very close. He had been much impressed with the performance of the organized labor movement during the insurrection of 1949, and was convinced of the need to unify the trade unions under the leadership of his Communist allies. This guaranteed them success in their efforts completely to control organized labor, once he had moved into the presidential palace.

As a result, the three principal trade-union groups were merged in 1952 to form the Confederación General de Trabajadores de Guatemala. The United Fruit Company unions and most of the provincial labor groups also became affiliated with the CGTG.

That the CGTG was completely under Communist control, there is little doubt. Its secretary-general was Victor Manuel Gutierrez, a Communist member of the Chamber of Deputies. A second Communist deputy, Carlos Manuel Pellecer, was its Secretary for Agriculture Affairs; a third Communist Max Salazar, was Secretary of Organization of the CGTG.

During the remainder of the Arbenz regime, the Guatemalan labor movement remained completely under Communist domination. Near the end of his administration, attempts were made to establish rivals to the CGTG, in the form of the Unión Nacional de Trabajadores Libres and the Comité de Obreros Anticomunistas. They remained very small, however, and they were strongly persecuted by the government during the last months of the Arbenz regime—the head of the Comité de Obreros Anticomunistas being assassinated and the head of the UNTL being deported to Mexico.

The only organization remaining outside of the strict control of the Communist party was the Confederación Nacional Campesina de Guatemala. This was strictly speaking not a trade-union organization, but rather an organization consisting of organized groups of tenants, sharecroppers, Indian communities, and small farmers. There was considerable rivalry between the CNCG and the CGTG. Although an agreement was reached whereby rural wage workers would belong to the CGTG until they received land under the agrarian-reform program launched by the Arbenz administration—when they should be transferred to the Confederación Nacional Campesina—this agreement was not kept. The CGTG usually refused to give up any of its former affiliates even after they had become small landowners under the agrarian reform.

The CNCG was able to maintain some small semblance of independence of the Communists largely because it enjoyed the protection of Minister of Interior Augusto Charnaud MacDonald, the most important noncommunist politician in the Arbenz regime. However, even the CNCG found itself obliged to join the World Federation of Trade Unions and the CTAL and to adhere otherwise to the general Communist line.

When the final crisis of the Arbenz regime came in June 1954, with the invasion of the country by a small group of opponents led by Colonel Carlos Castillo Armas, the labor movement played little part in events. The leaders of the armed forces supporting Arbenz refused to allow a repetition of the 1949 pattern, and no arms were issued to the workers, in spite of urgent demands by the CGTG leaders and the Communists. In the end, the military leaders ousted President Arbenz and paved the way for the advent to power of Colonel Castillo Armas.

THE GUATEMALAN LABOR MOVEMENT
AFTER 1954

The labor movement of the revolutionary period was largely destroyed after Colonel Castillo Armas came to power. The CNCG was completely destroyed, and many of its lower-ranking leaders were murdered, by thugs associated with the Castillo Armas movement or by vengeful landlords. The CGTG was declared illegal, its leaders sought refuge abroad, and many of its affiliates ceased to exist.

One of the first acts of the Castillo Armas government was to suspend the legal recognition of all of the country's trade unions and peasant groups. Important employers thought that the time had come to destroy the labor movement completely. The International Railways of Central America and the United Fruit Company suggested that for six months there be no legally recognized unions.

However, President Castillo Armas resisted the more extreme suggestions of his supporters. Within about a month after he had taken power, he began the process of once again giving legal status to the workers' groups. One of the first unions to be re-established was the railway workers' SAMF.

Within a short while there appeared two new central labor groups. The first was the Federación Autonoma Sindical, established under the leadership of a former deputy and former Labor Judge, José García Bauer, one of the founders of the Christian Democratic party. It began the work of trying to reorganize the labor unions which had been badly demoralized by the sudden turn of political events.

García Bauer was soon elected to congress by the new Christian Democratic party. He then largely withdrew from the FAS, which nonetheless continued, and within a few years came largely under Communist and procommunist influence. It developed very friendly relations with the CTAL and the World Federation of Trade Unions, although it did not formally join these two groups. Its main strength was among factory workers' unions, and by 1959 it claimed to have seventeen organizations affiliated to it throughout all of Guatemala. The name of the organization was modified to Federación Autonoma Sindical de Guatemala (FASGUA).

About the same time that the FAS was established, another group, known first as the Comité Nacional de Reorganización Sindical, was set up in the former headquarters of the Confederación General de Trabajadores de Guatemala. It was headed by Ruben Villatoro, former chief of the Unión Nacional de Trabajadores Libres, and was supported by the ORIT and the ICFTU, as well as by the American Federation of Labor. Although Villatoro soon disappeared from the scene, the organization continued, being reorganized in time as the Consejo Sindical de Guatemala.

The CSG became a small, although relatively compact, group of unions. It included organizations of social security workers, public utility employees, dockers, and some agricultural workers' organizations. Most of its member unions established regular collective bargaining relations with the employers and were able to win substantial improvements for their members. However, the CSG suffered one considerable defeat when the Union of Workers of the Tropical Radio Corporation called an unsuccessful strike which resulted in the virtual liquidation of the union. What success the CSG affiliates had was due in no small degree to the help which the organization and its members received from the international free labor movement.

A number of unions remained outside of both the FASGUA and the CSG. The most important of these was the SAMF. It was generally reorganized after the counterrevolution of 1954, and succeeded in re-establishing collective bargaining with the International Railways of Central America, although the relations between the railway and the union remained basically difficult because of the recalcitrance of the IRCA management. In 1964 it joined the International Transport Workers' Federation.

Another important group of workers which remained outside of both FASGUA and the CSG consisted of the employees of the United Fruit Company. After resisting strongly, at first, the re-establishment of unions in its plantations, the company finally acquiesced, but for some time the workers' organizations there were more company unions than they were independent organizations. As a result of workers' resentment at this attitude by the company, the UFC unions ultimately came under extremist political influence.

THE UNIONS IN EL SALVADOR

With the overthrow of the dictatorship of General Hernández Martínez in 1944, a group of exiles who had spent some time in Mexico and had been associated with the CTAL returned to El

Salvador and began the work of rebuilding a labor movement. They established the Central de Unificación Sindical, which maintained friendly relations with the CTAL. However, when ex-police chief Ponce seized power a few months later, all labor organizations except mutual-benefit societies were suppressed.

Ponce was succeeded by General Castañeda Castro in 1945, who somewhat relaxed the government attitude towards the workers' organizations. Although he did not allow the formation of trade unions, he did give certain encouragement to the mutual-benefit societies, so that a few of these began acting more or less as *de facto* trade unions.

President Castañeda Castro was overthrown in December 1948, and after a period of provisional government Colonel Oscar Osorio assumed the presidency. During his administration, considerable labor legislation was passed and the workers were allowed to form local trade unions, but no legal regional or national labor federations were allowed.

The rebuilding of the labor movement was soon undertaken by a group which called itself the Comité de Reorganización Obrera Salvadoreña. It was allegedly under Communist influence, and was soon dissolved by the government. In its place in 1951 was established the Comité Pro Defensa de Derechos Laborales. It was also suppressed on the charge of being Communist controlled.

During the Osorio period, unions were established among groups of craftsmen in San Salvador, the capital, as well as among chauffeurs and some groups of factory and white-collar workers. The extremist political influence was more notable among the artisans than among other types of workers.

In spite of his tolerance for individual unions, President Osorio would not allow the establishment of a national labor confederation. It was not until Colonel José Maria Lémus became president in 1956 that this step was permitted by the government.

Within a year after the inauguration of President Lémus, the Confederación General de Trabajadores was established, and at its inception it included most of the country's unions. The charge, however, was soon raised that the leadership of the new group was in the hands of the Communists. As a result, a large number of unions, including the powerful chauffeurs' and railroad workers' organizations withdrew and established the Confederación General de Sindicatos. This group soon had within its ranks the great majority of the country's organized workers. It affiliated with the ORIT and the ICFTU.

The government of José Maria Lémus was overthrown in August 1960 after bloody student rioting in the capital. He was succeeded by a military junta which after three months was displaced by yet another Junta Cívico-Militar. During the year this group was in office, it enacted legislation providing for paid vacations and a minimum wage for urban workers, and a law setting forth the minimum diet that agricultural landlords must supply their laborers.

Early in 1962 a member of the Junta Cívico-Militar, Colonel Julio Rivera, was elected president. He enjoyed the support of most of the unions belonging to the Confederación General de Sindicatos. His administration took a generally reformist and prolabor attitude. In July 1964 it finally extended legal recognition to the CGS, which had been established six years before.

The CGS remained the country's principal trade-union group; however, the Christian Democratic party, which constituted the principal opposition to the Rivera administration, aided the formation early in his regime of a Christian Trade Union Federation, which affiliated to the CLASC and the International Federation of Christian Trade Unions.

THE GROWTH OF ORGANIZED LABOR
IN HONDURAS

With the inauguration of President Juan Manuel Gálvez in 1948 there began a relaxation of the dictatorship over which General Tiburcio Carías Andino had presided for a decade and a half. This relaxation, however, did not until 1954 go so far as to permit the establishment of a trade-union movement.

The contemporary Honduran labor movement had its origins in a spontaneous strike among the banana workers of the United and Standard Fruit Companies' plantations along the country's northern coast. Starting in May 1954 virtually without organization, this strike soon gave rise to a Central Strike Committee, which sought to bargain with the two fruit companies. President Gálvez refused to intervene to crush the walkout, and instead insisted that the two companies deal with their workers, as a result of which the strike was finally settled peaceably.

Once the strike was over, the workers set about to establish permanent unions. On the United Fruit Company's holdings there was established the Sindicato de Trabajadores de la Tela Railroad Company (this is the name of the UFC affiliate in Honduras), or SITRATERCO. A similar organization was formed among the Standard Fruit Company workers.

Since the strike had affected the workers in some of the industries of the northern city of San Pedro Sula, unions also appeared immediately afterwards in these factories. At the same time, the ORIT, which had given extensive moral and financial backing to the banana workers' walkout, sent in an organizer to help not only establish firm organizations in the northern part of the republic, but also to spark the setting up of a labor movement in Tegucigalpa, the capital. There a number of small mutual-benefit societies were converted quickly into trade unions, while in a number of other cases, entirely new unions were established.

It was some time before a national central labor body was established. The first move in this direction was the formation of the Federación de Trabajadores del Norte, which brought together the SITRATERCO and most of the smaller unions of the San Pedro Sula area. Subsequently there was established a counterpart, the Federación de Trabajadores del Centro de Sindicatos Libres, in the Tegucigalpa region. Finally, in September 1964 a national organization, the Confederación de Trabajadores de Honduras, was established. Its founding congress voted to join the ORIT and the ICFTU.

During the strike of 1954 the Liberal party, which was just reviving after having been long suppressed by the Carías Andino regime, threw its support behind the walkout. As a result, the newly organized labor movement was generally sympathetic to and closely associated with the Liberal party thereafter. The only major exception to this was the union of Standard Fruit Company employees, which early came under Communist influence.

In 1957 the Liberal party succeeded in electing its leader Ramón Villeda Morales as president of Honduras. During his administration the labor movement enjoyed very wide freedom and made considerable advances in terms of legislation. In 1959 a Labor Code was enacted, which had been drawn up with the advice of a mission from the UN's International Labor Organization. The government also laid the basis for a social security system. Generally, in labor disputes, the regime was sympathetic to the cause of the unions.

However, in September 1963 the government of President Villeda Morales was overthrown by the army shortly before elections which were to choose his successor. Although the labor movement had been closely associated with the Liberal party and the Villeda Morales regime, it did not suffer severe reverses at the hands of the military dictatorship which seized power. It continued to be a force of considerable consequence in the life of the country.

THE UPS AND DOWNS OF NICARAGUAN ORGANIZED LABOR

Under the democratic pressure engendered by World War II, Nicaraguan dictator Anastasio Somoza undertook to liberalize his regime. He had his puppet congress enact a Labor Code which provided for the legalization of trade unions as well as for setting forth various types of legislation in the benefit of the workers.

When it came to the actual organization of a trade-union movement, Somoza welcomed the cooperation of the Confederación de Trabajadores de America Latina which by that time was under Communist control. CTAL President Vicente Lombardo Toledano visited Nicaragua in 1943 and together with President Somoza reviewed a May Day parade. Soon thereafter, an arrangement was made whereby the exiled leaders of the so-called Partido Socialista de Nicaragua, the name used by the Communists, would not only be permitted to return, but would also be given a free hand to bring into existence a trade-union movement.

Within a short time, the Communists had succeeded in establishing the Confederación de Trabajadores de Nicaragua. It included within its ranks unions of transport workers, factory employees, artisans, and some white-collar workers. The cooperation of Somoza with the new group was symbolized by his turning over to the CTM the *casas sindicales* (trade-union houses), which the government had built in the capital city, Managua, and in one or two provincial towns.

All went well for the labor movement until the approach of the general election scheduled for the middle of 1946. At that time the Partido Socialista de Nicaragua negotiated with both General Somoza and his opposition, for the purpose of getting names of members of the party placed on lists of candidates for congress, in return for PSN support. Finally, the Communists made a deal with the opposition and threw their support behind it in the election campaign.

This decision proved disastrous for the Communists and, for the time being, all but annihilated the trade-union movement. General Somoza moved ruthlessly against the Communists and against the labor organizations under their control. The government arrested all of the members of the Partido Socialista de Nicaragua upon whom it could lay its hands, and after a while exiled them, while at the same time it outlawed the party. Simultaneously, the labor unions were all suppressed, many of their leaders were arrested, and their headquarters were closed.

It was several years before the government again allowed the re-establishment of a labor movement. By the early 1950's, however, there were several more or less well-organized groups of trade unions.

The single most important union was that of the chauffeurs, which was a nationwide group including principally truck drivers, but also having some bus and taxi drivers in its ranks. Aside from collective bargaining activities, the Federation of Chauffeurs maintained a cooperative, which sold gasoline and spare parts at reduced prices to union members as well as did repair work.

There were several central labor bodies. The largest was the Confederación Nacionalista de Sindicatos Democráticos. This group was more closely allied with the government than most others.

The Confederación General de Trabajadores was the second largest central labor group. In the early 1950's it was under the control of Peronista elements and for a short while formed a part of the Peronista continental labor organization.

The two smallest groups were the Unión General de Trabajadores, which did not enjoy official government recognition and which was controlled by the Communists; and the Federación de Trabajadores Democráticos, which was strongly critical of the government and the larger trade-union confederations.

By the early 1960's the Nicaraguan labor movement remained weak and divided. It seemed unlikely that it would be able to develop as an autonomous and strong element in the country's economic and society so long as the nation continued to be directed by the dictatorship of the Somoza clan.

ORGANIZED LABOR IN COSTA RICA

In 1940 a physician, Dr. Rafael Calderón Guardia, was elected president of Costa Rica. He had worked mainly in the poorer sections of San José and had some sympathy for the plight of the workers of the national capital. In addition, during the second half of his four-year administration he came to depend rather heavily on the support of the Communist party, since the popularity of his own National Republican party had declined considerably because of extensive corruption in the regime.

As a result of these factors, the Calderón Guardia administration enacted the country's Labor Code and established its social security system. At the same time, it encouraged the growth of the labor movement under Communist leadership.

The Communists were able to organize artisans, factory workers, and some white-collar workers in San José and other towns. They also unionized thoroughly for the first time the workers on the United Fruit Company's plantations, and the Banana Workers' Federation was the strongest single union in the country. Finally, they established the nation's first real central labor body, the Confederación de Trabajadores de Costa Rica, which became an affiliate of the CTAL.

In addition to the unions under Communist control, there appeared a small group of unions organized under the leadership of an energetic young priest, Padre Benjamín Nuñez. He had studied sociology at the Catholic University in Washington, D.C., and then had returned home to throw himself into the job of establishing a noncommunist labor movement. The result of his efforts was the Confederación Costarricense de Trabajadores "Rerum Novarum." Although Padre Nuñez' influence was great in this group, it was not particularly religiously oriented. It remained a minority group until 1948.

In that year presidential elections were scheduled. Ex-President Calderón Guardia sought to return to office, and his opponent was Otilio Ulate, publisher of the newspaper "Diario de Costa Rica." The campaign was a bitter one, and when it was over, congress, under the control of Calderón's followers, refused to recognize the victory of Ulate, which had been attested to by a majority of the members of the National Election Board.

The result of this attempt to thwart the will of the voters was a month-long civil war, in which the rebel forces were led by a new political figure, José Figueres, then a farmer and businessman. The ranks of his rebel army were swelled by students, young professional people, and workers belonging to the Rerum Novarum labor confederation. In the negotiations leading to the final surrender of President Teodoro Picado's forces, Padre Benjamín Nuñez served as spokesman for the forces of Figueres.

When the civil war was over the Figueres group established a provisional government that lasted eighteen months, presided over the writing of a new consititution, made certain basic reforms in the economy, and finally turned the government over to the victor in the 1948 election, Otilio Ulate. During this provisional government, Padre Nuñez served as Minister of Labor.

During this first government of José Figueres and for some time thereafter, the Rerum Novarum confederation was the only legal central labor body of Costa Rica. The Communists' Confederación de Trabajadores de Costa Rica was deprived of legal recognition, and the Communist party itself was outlawed by the Figueres regime. The result was a demoralization of Communist strength in organized labor and a unique opportunity for the Rerum Novarum group.

During this period the Rerum Novarum confederation succeeded in establishing strong unions among the railroad workers, employees of coffee plantations, the workers of a number of factories in San José. They also organized a new Banana Workers' Federation. However, due to stubborn resistance from the United Fruit Company which did not want to recognize this noncommunist labor group, and due to the personal ambitions of the leader of the federation, the banana workers were only partly unionized under Rerum Novarum influence, and the federation finally withdrew from Rerum Novarum.

At the expiration of President Ulate's term, José Figueres was overwhelmingly elected president. In his campaign, he had the strong support of the leaders of the Rerum Novarum confederation, which still remained the country's largest central labor body, a position it kept until the administration of Figueres' successor, Mario Echandi.

However, during the Ulate government, the Rerum Novarum confederation had been seriously challenged. Peronista influence spread within Rerum Novarum in 1950 and 1951, and at one point came very close to capturing the confederation. Although the Peronista bid for power was turned back, unions under Peronista control withdrew from the CCT Rerum Novarum to form a new confederation. Its principal base was among the municipal employees of San José and for some time it continued to have some influence in the ranks of Costa Rican organized labor.

In the late 1950's, the Communists were again successful in establishing a relatively strong labor group. They organized the Confederación General de Trabajadores de Costa Rica, which contained unions of artisans, factory workers, and a strong contingent of banana workers, and became the largest single central labor group in the country.

The rest of the labor movement remained divided. The CCT Rerum Novarum was reduced to a minority group, and the Peronistas disappeared altogether. Various unions remained independent, and the labor movement as a whole was weak.

The Federación de Trabajadores Bananeros, which had broken away from the CCT Rerum Novarum in 1949, remained independent during the next decade, and worked closely with the Communists in the latter part of this period. In 1962, however, it merged with several smaller groups, including some of the local unions which had formerly been under Communist control, to form a new banana workers' federaction free of Communist influence. This group joined the International Federation of Plantation Workers, one of the trade secretariats associated with the International Confederation of Free Trade Unions.

THE LABOR MOVEMENT OF PANAMÁ

During World War II the labor movement of Panamá began to develop with some rapidity. This development was stimulated by the efforts of the CIO's United Public Workers' Union to organize the Panamanian workers employed in the Canal Zone. Most of these became members of that union's Local 100, which entered into collective bargaining negotiations with the zone authorities. Local 100 also gave aid to the organization of workers in the Republic of Panamá outside the Zone.

When the United Public Workers was expelled from the CIO under the accusation of being Communist-dominated, Local 100 withdrew and became part of the CIO's new Government Employees' Organizing Committee. After the merger of the CIO and the A.F. of L. at the end of 1955, Local 100 became part of a union affiliated with the new federation.

Meanwhile, in the Republic of Panamá there had been established in the 1930's the Federación Sindical de Trabajadores de Panamá. It grew rapidly during the war, and came to include most of the country's relatively few factory workers, as well as transport workers, some white-collar employees, and artisans of various sorts.

During this period there was a struggle for control of the FSTP between Communist and Socialist elements. As a result of this struggle, the dismemberment of the Federación began. By the early 1950's there were several central labor groups in the country. Perhaps the largest was the Confederación de Obreros y Campesinos de Panamá, which included in its rank dock workers, a number of peasant and agricultural employees' organizations, and a scattering of factory workers' unions. This confederation was affiliated with the ORIT and the ICFTU. The Communists still dominated the FSTP, which was affiliated with the CTAL and World Federation of Trade Unions. For some time, there existed a Peronista-oriented group, the Confederación General del Trabajo de Panamá. There were also various unions which did not belong to any of these groups.

However, in spite of the multiplicity of central labor bodies, the Panamanian labor movement remained relatively small and weak. One cause for this was the fact that the economic development and industrialization of the country had remained relatively modest. In addition, few of the frequently changing governments took any particular interest in encouraging the growth of the labor movement.

Finally, in the early 1960's a move was made to bring most of the country's labor organizations together, with the formation of the Confederación de Trabajadores y Campesinos de Panamá. This group contained most of the nation's more important trade unions. It was affiliated with the ORIT and the ICFTU. It was hoped that with a unified organization, the labor movement would be able to present a good deal more solid front to the employers and the government.

One of the most serious labor problems in Panamá has been the reluctance of the United Fruit Company to allow any really independent trade unions to develop on its plantations in the northern part of the country. Upon several occasions during the 1950's unions were established, but they were generally either destroyed by the obduracy of the company or were virtually converted into company unions. Upon one occasion, Serafino Romuladi, Latin American secretary of the AFL-CIO and assistant secretary-general of the ORIT, was deported from Panamá on the insistence of the fruit company's officials when he sought to give aid to the banana workers' unions.

Another difficult situation has concerned the large number of ships which fly the Panamanian flag without really being owned or controlled by Panamanians. Both the local maritime unions in Panamá and the International Federation of Transport Workers and its affiliates have been interested in trying to unionize the workers on these ships, whose owners or lessees through paying low wages and having poor conditions are offering unfair competition to the world's other large merchant fleets. However, all the efforts of these unions and the IFTW to make progress in this direction have made but little headway.

By the early 1960's the Panamanian labor movement remained one of the smaller groups of organized workers in Latin America.

Summary and Conclusion

The labor movements of Central America have been relatively weak. The slowness of industry to develop in those countries, and the dictatorial nature of several their governments, have helped to explain the state of the labor organizations. However, the railroads and banana plantations became early centers of trade unionism, and in the decades since World War II organized labor has tended to spread more widely in all six of these countries. Even some of the dictatorial regimes have not been anti-labor.

SEVENTEEN

Organized Labor in
Nonrepublican Areas

ORGANIZED LABOR IN THE NONREPUBLICAN AREAS IN AND AROUND THE
Caribbean Sea is fundamentally the product of a revolutinary upsurge which took place in the region at the end of 1937 and during the early months of 1938. Although there were some trade
unions and labor political parties in the region before this period,
they were of relatively secondary significance. Since 1938, however, organized labor has been the single most important element
in the political life of the region and has played a major role in
the economy as well.

THE SITUATION BEFORE 1937

Before 1937 the British, Dutch, and French colonies in and
around the West Indies were virtually ignored by their metropol-
itan powers. Although in the seventeenth and eighteenth centuries, they had been prized as sources of great wealth and had been
fought over by the European powers, they had known little prosperity in the 150 years preceding the uprising of the late 1930's.
Poverty was all but universal, and the predominantly colored
population of these colonies had little to say about their administration.

Neither trade unions nor politcal parties were general in the
Caribbean area before 1937. Only in two territories had important labor movements existed before 1937. These were the British
colony of British Guiana on the northern coast of South America,
and the British island of Trinidad.

In British Guiana, a Negro dockworker, Hubert Critchlow,

organized the British Guiana Labor Union during World War I. It was both a trade union and a political party, and was for a time during the 1920's represented in both the International Federation of Trade Unions and the Labor and Socialist International. Critchlow visited Britain on various occasions, and received moral and financial aid from the British trade-union movement and the British Labor party. However, by the late 1930's the BGLU was a trade union representing only the dockworkers of the capital city of Georgetown.

THE 1937-1938 UPRISING

After a century and a half of abandonment and apparent somnolence, the Caribbean area was swept late in 1937 by a wave of spontaneous strikes. These spread from one area to another over a period of several months. They were both economic and political in nature.

The workers who participated in these walkouts had genuine grievances concerning their wages, hours, and working conditions, and they were seeking amelioration of their economic situation. However, there was more to these strikes than economic issues. The workers put forward political as well as economic demands. They insisted on an end to the lack of representation of the people of the colonies in their government. They protested the white racialism which characterized the social life of many of the areas.

In each of the territories, the strike was led by an individual or individuals who arose more or less spontaneously from the mass of the strikers. In a number of cases, these leaders were people with very colorful personalities such as Uriah Butler of Trinidad, William Alexander Bustamante of Jamaica, and Ayube Edun of British Guiana.

Although the Caribbean uprising began in the British territories, it spread beyond them. The Dutch West Indies and Surinam as well as the French territories of Guadeloupe and Martinique were also caught in the grip of the same movement.

The British government took action as the result of the

1937-1938 strike wave. A Royal commission, headed by Lord Moyne, was established to investigate the situation. It made its report shortly before the outbreak of the Second World War. This document recommended the granting of legal recognition to organized labor in the area, as well as of concessions in the direction of self-government for the various British territories of the Caribbean region.

The outbreak of World War II prevented the immediate enactment of legislation to carry out the recommendations of the Moyne Commission; however, during the last year of the war, and for the next two decades, they were put into effect. This process culminated in 1962 with the granting of independence to Jamaica and Trinidad.

DEVELOPMENTS IN JAMAICA

The events of 1937-1938 brought into existence two organizations in Jamaica, one a trade-union federation and the other a political party. The first of these was the Bustamante Industrial Trade Union, named after the most prominent leader of the strike movement. The second was the Peoples' National party, headed by Bustamante's cousin Norman Manley, one of the island's most outstanding lawyers.

During the Second World War, Bustamante was interned as a menace to the security of the island. When, he was released, early in 1944, he resumed his position of leadership of the Bustamante Industrial Trade Union. However, during the period of Bustamante's internment. strong differences of opinion developed between him and Norman Manley. As a result, the union leader broke with the Peoples' National party and established his own Jamica Labor party. Subsequently, labor unionists who sided with Manley in the dispute organized a rival, which was christened the Trade Union Congress, to the BITU.

In the meanwhile, in 1944 Jamaica was granted a new constitution, which established a wide degree of self-government and a largely elected legislature. In the first election the Jamaica Labor party defeated the Peoples' National party, and Bustamante became leader of the majority in the new house of representatives. A few years later, with further concessions in the direction of popular rule, Bustamante became First Minister, an equivalent of the title of Prime Minister in other countries.

Political quarrels brought a further split in the labor movement in 1951. At that time the principal leaders of the Trade Union Congress tended to take a procommunist position in the developing cold war, and as a result, they were expelled from the Peoples' National party, which was a Democratic Socialist party and was affiliated with the Socialist International.

As a result of this split in the PNP, trade unionists of that party organized a third national labor federation, named the National Workers' Union. In 1950 it became a member of the International Confederation of Free Trade Unions, and soon after its organization it became the second largest trade-union organization in the island, competing with the Bustamante Industrial Trade Union for dominance of the labor movement.

After the split in the Trade Union Congress that organization went through a strange political evolution. First, its more extremist leaders were expelled in the early 1950's. Thereafter, in search of international support, the TUC leaders turned toward the Christian labor movement, and finally joined the International Federation of Christian Trade Unions and the CLASC.

However, the TUC remained a small factor in the Jamaican trade-union movement. Fifteen years after the Trade Union Congress split with the PNP, the great majority of the organized workers of the island militated in the ranks of the Bustamante Industrial Trade Union and the National Workers' Union. The latter belonged to the International Confederation of Free Trade Unions, and the former had applied early in 1963 for membership in the ICFTU.

DEVELOPMENTS IN TRINIDAD

During the uprising of 1937-1938 the workers of Trinidad formed a movement headed by Uriah Butler; however, Butler's influence soon began to wane, and a new trade-union group, the

Trinidad Federation of Trade Unions was organized. This group was strongly influenced by procommunist leaders, notably Quentin O'Connor and José Rojas, leader of the Petroleum Union. The federation became a member of the World Federation of Trade Unions when that organization was established late in 1945.

Finally, a revolt within the ranks of the Trinidad FTU federation of Trade Unions occurred in the early 1950's. It was led by the Seamen and Waterfront Workers' Union (SWWU) headed by Cecil P. Alexander, a one-time close associate of Captain Cipriani and a former longshoreman. The SWWU joined the Confederación Interamericana de Trabajadores, and subsequently became part of the International Confederation of Free Trade Unions.

Under the leadership of the Seamen and Waterfront Workers' Union, which became a model for other unions in the island, a new federation of labor was established. It came to include most of the country's organized workers in its ranks, set about to organize the sizable groups of workers who were still outside of the trade unions, and did so with some success.

Several factors subsequently brought about the unification of the Trinidadian labor movement. One of these was the death of Quentin O'Connor, and the abandonment of procommunist orientation by the leadership of the Petroleum Workers' Federation. The second was the coming to power in 1956 of Dr. Eric Williams.

Williams was the country's most famous economist, had for several years taught in the United States, and then had been the chief economist for the Caribbean Commission. Early in 1956 he returned home to enter politics, and organized a new party, the Peoples' National Movement.

The appearance of Williams on the scene changed profoundly both the politics and the trade-union situation of Trinidad. He succeeded in establishing the first really national Trinidadian political party. Previously, all parties were little more than the personal following of relatively small-scale politicians; that of Williams was a good deal more than that.

In the election of 1956 the Peoples' National Movement won an overwhelming victory, and Williams became First Minister. He launched a vigorous program of economic development, and led the country step-by-step toward national independence, which was finally achieved in August of 1962. As a result of Williams' success, virtually all other elements in the political spectrum joined to form a single opposition party, the Democratic Labor party.

The impact of the People's National Movement was immediately felt in the labor movement. Almost all of the most important leaders of the trade unions joined the ranks of the new party. Partly under its inspiration, and partly because of the support of the ICFTU, virtually the whole labor movement of the island was brought together in the Trade Union Federation of Trinidad.

THE LABOR MOVEMENT OF BARBADOS

From several points of view, the economic and social situation of Barbados differed from that of most of the other colonial areas of the West Indies. It was the only British possession in which by the late 1930's there was still a sizable resident white element. Unlike the cases of Trinidad and Jamaica, the end of slavery in the 1830's had not meant the abandonment of the island by white plantation owners. A century later they were still the socially, economically, and politically dominant element in Barbados.

As a result of the continued residence in Barbados of a white ruling group, this was the only colony of the area which had not lost its institutions of self-government in the nineteenth century. The Barbados legislature continued to exist, although it was chosen by a very small electorate, confined almost exclusively to the resident whites.

However, economically, Barbados was very similar to the other British colonies of the Caribbean area. Sugar production was the overwhelmingly predominant source of livelihood for the overcrowded population of the island. Almost its only market and only source of imports was the United Kingdom.

The uprising of 1937-1938 brought into existence the Barbados Workers' Union, as well as the Barbados Labor party. The principal figure of the movement was a bright youngish lawyer, Grantley Adams, who concentrated most of his attention in the succeeding years upon his work in the political field.

The most important element in the Barbados Workers' Union was its sugar workers' section. It established a regular system of collective bargaining with the plantation owners, which was only occasionally marred by strikes in the quarter of a century which followed. The Union also entered into collective bargaining relations with the port administration, hotels, and the Cable and Wireless Corporation. In 1964 it was reported to have a membership of about twenty thousand workers, of whom about sixteen thousand were regular dues payers.

The Barbados labor movement also took a leading part in moves to unify the trade unions of the British Caribbean. They took part in the Caribbean Labor Congress in 1945, which was the first abortive effort toward this end. Almost a decade late, it also participated in the founding conference of the Caribbean Division of the ORIT, generally known as the CADORIT, which established its headquarters in Bridgetown, Barbados, with the Barbadian labor leader Frank Walcott as its general secretary.

For two decades after it was established the Barbados Workers' Union was closely associated with the Barbados Labor party. The party formed the government of the island after the introduction of universal adult suffrage in the late 1940's. Yet, after the resignation in 1958 of Grantley Adams from the leadership of the Barbados Labor party to become chief of the West Indian Labor party and Prime Minister of the new West Indies Federation, the Labor party lost the support of the island's organized labor movement.

In the early 1950's a dissident group had broken away from the Labor party to form the Democratic Labor party. In the election of 1961 the Democratic Labor party, under the leadership of Errol Barrow, defeated the Labor party, a victory which was mainly due to the support which the DLP received from the Barbados Workers' Union.

ORGANIZED LABOR AND POLITICS IN
BRITISH GUIANA

The workers of British Guiana, too, shared in the uprising of 1937-1938. However, there had existed a labor movement in the capital city of Georgetown for more than two decades before this upheaval. The British Guiana Labor Union was established in 1918 under the leadership of Hubert Critchlow. The principal strength of the BGLU, which served for some time as both a trade-union organization and a political party, was among the Negro dockworkers of the capital. It had no following among the workers in the country's principal industry, sugar, most of whom were of East Indian extraction.

It was the sugar workers who were principally effected by the 1937-1938 upheaval. As a result of it, the Man Power Citizens' Association was established to represent these workers. Subsequently, it also came to include workers in bauxite mining, rice growing and other industries. Its principal leader was Ayub Edun, an East Indian lawyer from Georgetown.

Under Edun's leadership, the MPCA was a militant trade union. It succeeded in negotating collective agreements with the Sugar Producers' Association which brought considerable gains for the sugar workers, including wage increases and a beginning toward renewal of miserable plantation housing, which dated from the days of East Indian indentured servitude, which had been abolished in 1917. However, subsequent to the death of Edun in 1947 the MPCA lost much of its militancy, and by the early 1950's some observers felt that it had become virtually a company union.

Unlike the situation in most of the other areas of the Caribbean, the 1937-1938 uprising did not immediately bring into existence a party as the political spokesman for the new labor movement. This was largely due to the rivalry of the two principal racial groups in the colony's population, the Negroes and the East Indians. Political groups continued for some time to be organized principally around this issue.

It was not until the late 1940's that steps were taken to form a labor-oriented political party by Cheddi Jagan, a young East Indian dentist who returned from receiving his university education in the United States soon after World War II. He was accompanied by his American wife, Janet. Soon thereafter, Cheddi Jagan ran successfully for one of the relatively few elective seats in the colonial legislature.

In 1950 the Jagans undertook to establish a new political group, the Peoples' Progressive Party. The PPP, unlike its competitors, ignored the racial issue, making an appeal to the citizenry on the basis of reform and anticolonialism. Seeking ultimate independence for British Guiana, they sought universal adult suffrage and complete internal self-government as first steps.

The Jagans had contacted political leaders in other Caribbean colonies before launching the PPP, and had made a considerable study of the Jamaican Peoples' National party, headed by Norman Manly. However, in spite of Jagan's contacts with Socialist-oriented political parties in the other colonies, opponents of the PPP alleged that the party and its leaders were of procommunist orientation—a claim denied for many years by the Jagans.

In 1952 the British government presented British Guiana with a new constitution, which established universal adult suffrage and greatly expanded the autonomy of the Guianese government; while control, though, of finances, the police, and the military remained in the hands of the governor, still appointed by London.

In the first election held under the new constitution in April 1953, the PPP won a stunning victory; however, it was not until early June that the PPP government took office, under the leadership of Cheddi Jagan—the delay being caused by a behind-the-scenes struggle for power within the party between the Jagans and the PPP's principal Negro figure, L. F. S. Burnham.

The first PPP government stayed in power only a little more than three months. It was removed, and the 1952 constitution was suspended early in October, when the governor charged that Jagan and his associates were trying to subvert the police and military. The immediate cause of the governor's action was the government's attempt to push through a new labor law.

The rise of the Peoples' Progressive party had brought about an upheaval in the trade-union movement. PPPers had organized a rival to the Man Power Citizens' Association, under the name of the Guiana Industrial Workers' Union, which was headed by an Indian medical doctor, Dr. Lachmansingh. The PPP had also won the overwhelming backing of the Indian sugar workers' in the 1953 election; yet, the party's trade-union group was unable to shake the position of the MPCA, which had both the collective contract in the sugar industry and the support of the Sugar Producers' Association. So the new legislation proposed by the PPP government was designed to make it possible for the GIWU to oust the MPCA from the sugar-labor field.

Subsequently, the ouster of the PPP government seriously weakened the efforts of the Guiana Industrial Workers Union to oust the MPCA. As a result, fifteen months after its ouster there was a split in the Peoples' Progressive party: L. F. S. Burnham led a dissident group to form a new party, the Peoples' National Movement. He cited the Communist proclivities of the Jagans as the principal reason for his break with the PPP. Dr. Lachmansingh joined the Burnham group. This left the PPP without any sugar workers' union under its control. With the death of Dr. Lachmansingh in 1957, the GIWU went out of existence.

In the meanwhile, the PPP had lost the influence which it had gained in other parts of the labor movement during the early 1950's. Jagan himself lost his post as leader of the Sawmill Workers' Union. The British Guiana Labor Union was lost to the PPP when its general-secretary Ashton Chase went to England to continue his legal education.

In 1956 most of the colony's unions were brought together in a new Trades Union Council. By 1964 the TUC had twenty affiliated unions, and was itself affiliated with the Caribbean Congress of Labor, the ORIT and the ICFTU. In the meanwhile, a fundamental change had occurred in the Man Power Citizens' Association. In 1954 a new president was elected in the MPCA, Richard Ishmael, a young East Indian who was principal of the most important private high school in Georgetown. Under his leadership, the MPCA gained a militancy that it had not had for a decade, was marked by several strikes, and made a serious effort to service the grievances of its rank-and-file members. Ishmael received financial help in his efforts to rebuild the MPCA from the British Trades Union Congress.

Although the PPP won two more elections, in 1957 and 1961, it did so by declining margins. In the latter poll, it received only 42 per cent of the total vote, compared with 41 per cent for Burnham's Peoples' National Movement, and 17 per cent for the third party, the United Force.

In spite of its electoral victories, however, the PPP continued to have relatively little influence in the labor movement. The TUC and the MPCA continued to be led by people opposed to the Peoples' Progressive party. After its third election victory in 1961, the PPP undertook once again to organize a rival sugar workers' union. This time it was led by Harry Lall, a former PPP member of the legislature, and was called the Guiana Agricultural Workers' Union. Even by 1964 it had failed to oust the Man Power Citizens' Association from its position as collective bargaining agent for the sugar workers.

Early in 1963 the Jagan government attempted to push a new labor law through the legislature, which would permit the Ministry of Labor to certify unions as agents for specific groups of workers. The opposition interpreted this as a move to break the MPCA, and in February 1963 it provoked a week-long wave of rioting in Georgetown which caused hundreds of thousand of dollars worth of damage and several deaths. This was the second such riot within a year, and imperiled the position of the Jagan government. It was brought to an end only after an agreement between the administration and the Trades Union Congress, whereby Jagan withdrew the proposed labor bill from legislative consideration and agreed not to introduce any other such legislation without approval by the TUC.

A year later, the Guiana Agricultural Workers' Union attempted to call a general strike of sugar workers, also in an effort to displace the MPCA as the official bargaining agent. Although this attempted walkout resulted in rioting and the deaths of numerous sugar workers and others, it did not succeed in its objective, and was finally canceled in August 1964, after five months.

In elections held in December 1964, the PPP lost control of the legislature. As a result Cheddi Jagan was succeeded by L. F. S. Burnham as premier, at the head of a coalition government. This change in administration seemed likely to greatly influence organized labor, although as this is being written it is too early to judge the nature and impact of this influence.

It was clear that the future of the labor movement of British Guiana would depend upon the future direction of the country's politics and government. If the Jagan government had remained in office, achieved the independence for British Guiana which it was seeking, and continued to move in the procommunist direction which became quite plain during 1963, it seemed likely that the free trade-union movement would not long survive. On the other hand, the movement's chances seemed considerably brighter after the Burnham government's accession to office. The fate of both labor and the general political situation then depended on the Burnham regime's ability to bring about rapid economic development and rising living standards and to overcome the deep racial cleavage between East Indians and Negroes.

LABOR IN THE DUTCH TERRITORIES

The Dutch part of the New World has been as affected by the revolutionary upsurge of the last quarter century as have the British territories. There have been basic economic, social, and political changes which have transformed the former Dutch colonies.

The Dutch areas are two in number. One is the mainland territory of Surinam, otherwise known as Dutch Guiana. The second consists of the islands of Aruba, Curaçao, Bonaire, and half of St. Martins in the Caribbean. Since World War II these areas have become self-governing and co-equal members of the Dutch kingdom. Their political evolution has been roughly similar to that of the British Caribbean territories.

The principal economic activity of the Dutch West Indies (or Netherlands Antilles as they are officially called) is oil refining.

Aruba and Curaçao both have large refineries, established by the international oil companies for processing petroleum from neighboring Venezuela. In Surinam the principal foreign exchange earner is the bauxite-mining industry, although most of the people of the territory are engaged in agriculture.

Since the achievement of internal self-government in the postwar period, both Dutch territories have carried out extensive economic development programs. In the Netherlands Antilles these have brought into existence a number of small consumers' goods industries and a stimulation of the tourist trade. In Surinam the development program has been considerably more extensive, involving the construction of a very large hydroelectric project which will provide power for industry and electrification, as well as providing the basis for what is hoped will become a sizable tourist industry.

The labor movement is one result of the changes in the Dutch territories. In Surinam a bauxite-company employee Leo Eleazar took the lead in the early 1940's in bringing into existence the Surinam Miners' Union. It organized most of the workers in the bauxite industry and entered into collective bargaining agreements with the mining companies.

On the basis of his success with the miners, Eleazar undertook the expansion of the organized labor movement. As a result of his organizing activities, the Surinam Workers' Union was formed soon after the establishment of the Miners' Union. For fifteen years these two organizations dominated the country's labor movement.

The Surinam Miners' Union and the Surinam Workers' Union became founding affiliates of the Inter-American Confederation of Workers (CIT), which was established in Lima, Peru, in January 1948. When the CIT gave way three years later to the ORIT, the two Surinam unions became members of the new group.

As in the case of the labor movements of the British Caribbean territories, the Surinam unions immediately became active in politics. They were from their inception closely associated with the Surinam Democratic party. So long as this party participated in the government, the position of the unions under Eleazar's leadership was virtually unchallenged.

In 1957, however, the Democratic party was defeated. Soon thereafter, the Surinam labor movement was split. Rival unions were formed in the mine fields and among the urban workers. However, the majority of the country's wage- and salary-earning employees continued to be members of the labor movement.

In the Netherlands Antilles, the largest unions have been those of the oil workers. In the late 1950's the Petroleum Workers' Federation of Aruba was established with the help of the ICFTU, the ORIT, and the International Petroleum Workers' Federation; however, its activities were fought vigorously by the oil companies. As a result of this opposition, a rival union known as the Independent Oil Workers' Union was established. In an election in August 1961 the workers voted by a slight majority for the independent group. Subsequently, the Petroleum Workers' Federation dissolved and urged its members to join the Independent Oil Workers' Union.

The only other unions in Aruba are a small Transport Workers' Union in Oranjestraadt, a Civil Servants' Association, and a Teachers' Union. None of these has international affiliation.

In Curaçao, the other major island of the Netherlands Antilles, the labor movement is stronger. The Petroleum Workers' Federation of Curaçao is the most important single union of the island, with about twenty-five hundred members in early 1964, and a collective agreement with the Shell Oil Refinery. Other labor groups include the United Miners' Union, the Civil Service Workers' Union, the Teachers' Union, and the Union of Stevedore Personnel. The oil and mine unions are affiliated with the Caribbean Congress of Labor, the ORIT, and the ICFTU.

ORGANIZED LABOR IN PUERTO RICO

The labor movement of Puerto Rico has existed virtually as long as the island has been under the United States flag. In the last years of Spanish occupation an attempt was made by a young Spanish immigrant, Santiago Iglesias, to organize trade unions, but Iglesias was jailed by the Spanish authorities, and was in prison at the time the Americans landed in June 1898.

The new colonial power was more sympathetic to organized labor than the Spaniards had been. Iglesias was released from jail, and the military government installed by the United States tolerated his labor-organization activities. Under his leadership, the island's first labor federation, the Federación Libre de Trabajadores de Puerto Rico, was established. It applied for affiliation with the American Federation of Labor and was granted a charter by the A.F. of L. as a state federation.

The Federación Libre grew slowly but steadily. By the time of World War I it had been successful in bringing a large segment of the workers in the sugar fields, the island's principal industry and source of employment, into its ranks. The sugar workers engaged in a successful strike in 1917, as a result of which the Federación Libre became the recognized bargaining agent of the sugar workers.

Santiago Iglesias organized a Socialist party as the political arm of the Federación Libre de Trabajadores. The party remained a small group in the island's political picture until after World War I. Although Iglesias was elected a senator in the state legislature in 1916, he was the party's only member of the legislature for a number of years.

In 1932 the Socialist party entered a coalition government with the Republican party, the principal spokesmen for the sugar interests. The union leaders and plantation owners had for a decade and a half been negotiating on a friendly basis in the economic field. During the decade of the 1930's they extended their cooperation to the area of politics.

However, the Republican-Socialist coalition, as well as events in mainland United States, tended to undermine the Federación Libre de Trabajadores during the 1930's. The Socialist party and Federación Libre leaders became increasingly separated from their constituents. At the same time, the appearance of the Congress of Industrial Organizations (CIO) on the continent stimulated the development of a similar rebel group in the Puerto Rican labor movement. This was the Confederación General de Trabajadores, which became associated with the CIO.

In 1938 a new political party, the Popular Democrats, was established under the leadership of State Senator Luis Muñoz Marín, formerly a leader of the Liberal party. Muñoz Marín had started his political career in the early 1920's as a member of the Partido Socialista, and he was widely popular among the workers and rural laborers who made up the majority of the population. The victory of Muñoz Marín's party in the election of 1940 further undermined the unity of the labor movement, since it signaled the collapse of the Socialist party and increased prestige for the CGT, which had supported his campaign.

The breakup of the previously united Puerto Rican labor movement continued during the 1940's. The CGT split into two rival groups, both of which used the CGT name, with one seeking legal incorporation and becoming known as the CGT Inc., the other ultimately taking the title CGT Autentica. The CGTA itself split when unions under Communist control broke away to from the Unión General de Trabajadores.

Finally, in 1952 the disintegration of Puerto Rican organized labor reached its limit with a new split in the Federación Libre de Trabajadores (FLT). The federation opposed the establishment of the semi-autonomous Estado Libre Asociado, or Commonwealth, carried out under Governor Luis Muñoz Marín's leadership in 1952. This was in conformity with the traditional position of the federation in favor of Puerto Rico becoming a state in the American Union. When a large part of the FLT's affiliated unions took exception to the FLT's position, they were supported by the American Federation of Labor, which canceled the charter of the Federación Libre and granted one instead to a newly organized Federación de Trabajadores de Puerto Rico, organized by the FLT dissidents.

Although the labor movement was split, various segments of it sought international affiliation. The Federación Libre de Trabajadores became a founding member of the Confederación Interamericana de Trabajadores (CIT). Subsequently, the FLT, the

Federación de Trabajadores de Puerto Rico, and the CGT Inc. all became members of the CIT's successor, the ORIT. At the same time, the CGT Autentica was for several years a member of the Peronista hemispheric labor confederation, the Agrupación de Trabajadores Latino Americanos Sindicalizados.

The process of reunification of the Puerto Rican labor movement got under way in the middle 1950's. The collapse of the Perón regime, and the resulting distintegration of the ATLAS removed one block to unity, since it meant that the various labor groups of Puerto Rico were no longer divided by affiliation with rival international groups. The unification of the A.F. of L. and the CIO on the continent also stimulated the sentiment for unity on the island.

A unification congress was finally held in 1959. Not only did the unions affiliated with the Federación de Trabajadores and the CGT Autentica participate in this meeting; the sugar workers' locals in the ex-CIO Packinghouse Workers' Union, and a number of local independent organizations were also there at this congress which organized the Federación de Trabajo de Puerto Rico. The only important group not participating was the Federación Libre de Trabajadores.

Another important development in the late 1950's was the tendency of national and international unions in the United States to seek affiliates in Puerto Rico. The most important sugar workers' union had already become affiliated with the Packinghouse Workers' Union. Furthermore, the International Ladies' Garment Workers, the Seafarers' International, the Carpenters', Machinists', and United Steel Workers' were among the other continental unions which acquired Puerto Rican affiliates.

Another important U.S. union which carried on organizing activities in Puerto Rico was the International Brotherhood of Teamsters. The organizing efforts of this union, which had been expelled from the A.F. of L., were opposed by the Federación de Trabajo of Puerto Rico as well as by the government of the island. However, in spite of this enmity, the Teamsters were successful in acquiring a dozen or more local union affiliates in various parts of the Puerto Rican economy by the early 1960's.

The moves toward the unification of the Puerto Rican labor movement which were made in the late 1950's proved to be short-lived. By the early 1960's new splitting had begun. A considerable number of local unions withdrew from the Federación de Trabajo, while some of the Puerto Rican affiliates of continental organizations withdrew once again. There was a good deal of raiding by rival unions upon one another.

Collective bargaining survived this further splitting of the labor movement, although the position of the unions at the bargaining table tended frequently to be weakened by their feuding. Union-management negotiation was encouraged by laws enacted by the insular government, along the lines of the continental Wagner Act. The sugar workers, longshoremen, garment workers, and employees of some parts of the construction industry were among the groups which had the most satisfactory bargaining relations with their respective employers.

LABOR IN THE SMALLER TERRITORIES

The Antigua Trades and Labor Union was established in 1939 and immediately became the most important organization on the island. By the early 1960's it had some eighteen thousand members of whom about twelve thousand regularly paid dues. It issued its own paper, "Voice of the Worker," and had collective agreements with all firms of any importance, including sugar plantations, hotels, dry-goods houses, and port services. The only other union on the island was the Civil Service Association.

The Antigua Trades and Labor Union from the beginning had a political committee, which supported candidates for public office. From the 1950's all members of the legislative council were men backed by the union, and the chief minister and all members of his cabinet were union members.

Organized labor in the Bahamas has met with strong opposition. Unions were only legalized in 1958, and by 1964 there were fifteen unions in the islands, with approximately forty-one hundred members. The largest organizations were those in the hotel

238 ORGANIZED LABOR IN LATIN AMERICA

and restaurant business, construction, and the Bahamas Civil Service Union. Most unions had collective agreements.

The labor movement was divided between the Bahamas Federation of Labor and the Trade Union Congress, established in 1958 as the result of a split in the BFL. Both of these central labor bodies were affiliated with the ORIT and the ICFTU, and the Trade Union Congress also belonged to the Caribbean Congress of Labor.

In Bermuda there were only five unions by 1964, the Bermuda Industrial Union, the Bermuda Teachers' Association, the Civil Service Association and two smaller teachers' groups. The BIU was the largest of these, with about one thousand members. It was affiliated with the Caribbean Congress of Labor, the ORIT, and the ICFTU. Moreover, an attempt in 1960 by the International Longshormen's Association of the United States to establish a local in Bermuda failed when a strike called by the ILA was broken.

In British Honduras, on the coast of Central America, there were in 1964 three recognized labor unions, the General Workers' Development Union, affiliated with the CCL, the ORIT and the ICFTU, the Public Officers' Union, and the Christain Workers' Union, belonging to the International Federation of Christain Trade Unions. In addition to these, there existed a number of small village unions, which, even though they were closely associated with the ruling Peoples' United Party, had no central federation. The largest organization there was the General Workers' Development Union, with a membership of about two thousand.

In the West Indian island of Dominica the labor movement consisted in 1964 of three organizations, the Civil Service Association, the Teachers' Union and the Dominica Trade Union. The last of these was established in 1945 and is a general workers' union. In 1964 it had about four thousand members, many of whom were small peasant farmers who had been given land under a government agrarian-reform program.

Five of the seven unions in Grenada belonged to the Trade Union Council; only the Teachers' Union and the Manual and Mental Workers' Union remaining outside. The TUC had some twenty-five hundred members in 1964, and was affiliated with the CCL, the ORIT, and the ICFTU. Its member unions had collective agreements covering port workers, electrical workers, government employees, and workers in commerce and factories. The Manual and Mental Workers' Union was the island's first labor organization, having been established in 1951. By 1964 it had a few collective agreements.

In Montserrat, the smallest of the West Indian territories, all organized workers in 1964 belonged to the Montserrat Trades and Labor Union, a general workers' union. It was active politically and controlled the government of the island.

In the territory of St. Kitts-Nevis-Anguilla the St. Kitts-Nevis-Anguilla Trades and Labor union was the strongest institution in the area, with some four thousand members, most of whom were in the sugar industry in 1964. It dominated the ruling political party, and most members of the government belonged to the union. It was affiliated with the CCL, the ORIT, and the ICFTU.

Six unions constituted the labor movement of St. Lucia. The largest of these was the St. Lucia Workers' Union, established in 1941, with approximately five thousand members in 1964—most of them employed on plantations and in the Public Works Department. The ruling St. Lucia Labor party was closely associated with the union, and the chief minister was also the union's president. Other important groups included the Vieux Fort Dock and General Workers' Union, and the Seamen and Waterfront Workers' Trade Union. Five of the island's six unions were affiliated with the CCL, the ORIT, and the ICFTU.

The St. Vincent Federated Industrial and Agricultural Workers' Union constituted the core of organized labor in St. Vincent. Most of its thirty-five hundred members worked on plantations, and it dominated the ruling Peoples' Political party. It, too, was affiliated with the CCL, the ORIT, and the ICFTU. Other unions included the Teachers' Union, Civil Service Association, and the Commerical Technical and Allied Workers' Union.

The labor movement in the French Caribbean territories of Martinique and Guadeloupe reflected the divisions in organized labor in the mother country. The Communist-controlled Confédération Général du Travail, the Socialist-oriented Force Ouvrière, and the Federation of Christian Workers all had local affiliates. The CGT was in 1964 the strongest of the three. The Force Ouvrière group maintained friendly relations with the ORIT and the CCL.

CARIBBEAN LABOR FEDERATIONS

During the last two decades several attempts have been made to bring together all of the labor organizations of the nonrepublican territories in and around the West Indies. The first group of this kind to be established was the Caribbean Labor Congress, set up during World War II. Most of the unions of the British West Indies belonged to this group, which became an affiliate of the World Federation of Trade Unions when that was established in 1945. However, because of the general procommunist cast of the CLC, it fell into inanition when the labor organizations of the area took an anticommunist turn at the end of the 1940's.

The second federation in the area was established as a consequence of the organization of the International Confederation of Free Trade Unions in 1951, and of its American regional grouping, the ORIT, in the following year. This new organization took the name of Caribbean Division of the ORIT or CADORIT. Its headquarters were established in Bridgetown, Barbados, and Frank Walcott, a leading figure in the Barbadian labor movement served as secretary-general of CADORIT during most of its existence. It included within its ranks not only the unions of the British territories, but also those of the Netherlands Antilles and Surinam.

The CADORIT was abolished with the organization in 1960 of the Caribbean Congress of Labor. The new group included virtually the same membership as the CADORIT. The activities of the CCL have been described by its Secretary-General Osmond Dyce as follows:

The CCL carries an Education Department and organizes and conducts trade union education courses for all the trade union organizations in the Area. It also assists individual unions with their organizing problems and acts as a center for disseminating useful trade union and economic information, to the affiliated organizations. It also coordinates the efforts of the scattered units in times of difficulties, stresses and strikes. In short, it performs the duty of a general handy organization for the affiliated unions.

Of some significance in the nonrepublican areas in and around the Caribbean area are two additional union federations. One of these is the Caribbean Union of Teachers, which was established as early as 1935. It holds a conference every two years. The second is the Caribbean Bauxite and Mine Workers' Federation. It was established in 1961, has its headquarters in Port-of-Spain, Trinidad, and includes affiliates from British Guiana, Jamaica, Surinam, and Trinidad. It held its second conference in Trinidad in February 1964.

In summation, one can say that the organized labor movements of the Caribbean area are relatively among the strongest labor groups of the hemisphere. Their role in the economy is of key importance, and they dominate the political life of many of the territories of the region.

EIGHTEEN

International Trade Union Organizations in the Americas

SINCE THEIR EARLIEST YEARS, THE TRADE UNIONS OF LATIN AMERICA have had connections with the world labor movement. By the early 1960's, the great majority of the workers' organizations of the area were affiliated with one or the other of the international labor groups.

As early as the 1860's and 1870's there existed Latin American affiliates of the International Workingmen's Association (IWMA) (the First International). Although most of these groups were not trade unions, many of them consisted of workers, often European immigrants. Not infrequently, these local units of the First International took a leading part in organizing the early trade unions of their respective countries.

Inasmuch as before World War I the majority of the Latin American trade unions were under anarchosyndicalist influence, it is understandable that the anarchosyndicalists were the first group to try to bring together the central labor organizations of Latin America. In 1907 the Federación Obrera Regional Argentina called a hemispheric conference to meet in the Argentine capital, Buenos Aires. Among those groups invited was the Industrial Workers of the World of the United States. However, only a handful of delegates from a few of the nations near Argentina were able to attend the Buenos Aires meeting.

Although the 1907 congress had as its purpose the establishment of a permanent hemispheric labor confederation, it did not succeed in achieving this objective. Such a confederation was not actually established until eleven years later, and this first effective

242

hemispheric labor group was of distinctly antianarchosyndicalist tendency.

THE PAN-AMERICAN FEDERATION
OF LABOR

The Pan-American Federation of Labor, established in 1918, was established on the initiative of the Confederación Regional Obrera Mexicana and the American Federation of Labor. The former was very concerned with rallying support for the Mexican revolution of 1910, which was then threatened by possible military intervention by the United States. For its part, the A.F. of L. was concerned both with supporting the efforts of Latin American workers to establish strong labor movements and with extending its own international influence.

The founding conference of the Pan-American Federation of Labor met in El Paso, Texas, in December 1918. During the next decade during which the PAFL was active, it consisted principally of national labor groups in the countries in and around the Caribbean Sea. At one time or another, it boasted affiliates in the United States, Mexico, Guatemala, El Salvador, Honduras, Nicaragua, Costa Rica, Panamá, Cuba, the Dominican Republic, and Haiti. Although delegates were accredited to its conventions from groups in Venezuela, Peru, and Chile, the organizations they supposedly represented were largely fictitious.

The PAFL had an important role in helping the organization of workers in countries in which it was weak. It also was important for the protests which it raised against the Dollar Diplomacy which was then the Inter-American policy of the United States. Finally, it was of significance because of the support which that federation was able to arouse in the United States for the cause of the Mexican revolution, in the face of strong pressure in the U.S. for armed intervention in that country.

The last congress of the Pan-American Federation met in Washington, D.C., in 1927. Thereafter, it virtually ceased to exist, although in theory it continued until the end of World War II.

RADICAL HEMISPHERIC GROUPS

The more radical elements in the Latin American labor movements were generally hostile to the Pan-American Federation of Labor. In 1926 the Socialist-controlled Confederación Obrera Argentina (COA) took the lead in trying to organize a purely Latin American labor confederation, which it was hoped would become an affiliate of the International Federation of Trade Unions, a largely European group under democratic Socialist influence. This move failed, however, when the Confederación Regional Obrera Mexicana refused to abandon the PAFL and to join the proposed new group.

In 1929 two new Latin American labor confederations were established. One of these was the Confederación Sindical Latino Americana, organized at a congress in Montevideo. It consisted of Communist-controlled labor groups from all over Latin America, and was established in conformity with the Third Period policy of the Communist International, which called for extreme sectarianism and the establishment of separate Communist-dominated labor movements in every country in which a Communist party existed. It was these national groups which were brought together in the CSLA.

The second hemispheric group to be established in 1929 was the Asociación Continental Americana de Trabajadores (ACAT). This confederation consisted of the hemisphere's anarchosyndicalist-controlled labor organizations. Although the anarchosyndicalists' influence had declined considerably since the early years of the century, the ACAT boasted affiliates in Argentina, Chile, Bolivia, Mexico, and several smaller Latin American nations. It continued to exist for at least two decades.

LATIN AMERICANS IN WORLD ORGANIZATIONS

The regional Latin American labor groups led by Communists and anarchosyndicalists were associated with broader international trade-union groups controlled by those elements. The Communists' Confederación Sindical Latino Americana was the regional federation of affiliates of the world-wide Red International of Labor Unions (RILU). The ACAT was the Latin American association of union groups belonging to the anarchosyndicalist International Workingmen's Association (IWMA). The national affiliates of the CSLA and ACAT were also members of the RILU and IWMA.

The third world-wide international trade-union group was the International Federation of Trade Unions. Established before World War I, it had had the American Federation of Labor as one of its founding members; however, after that war, the IFTU was dominated by the European Socialists, and maintained close relations with the Labor and Socialist International. As a result, the AF of L withdrew from the IFTU. Hence, few of the affiliates of the Pan-American Federation of Labor joined the IFTU. Only where labor movements were controlled by Socialist parties or by political groups aligned with the Socialists did the unions join the International Federation of Trade Unions.

During the 1920's, there were two principal national labor movements in Latin American countries which were members of the IFTU. One of these was the Confederación Regional Obrera Mexicana, which was closely associated with the Mexican revolutionary government, and the Mexican Labor party, which was closely associated with the CROM, maintained fraternal relations for some years with the Labor and Socialist International.

The other Latin American affiliate of the IFTU during the 1920's was the Confederación Obrera Argentina. This was the country's Socialist-controlled trade-union group, and the two powerful railroad workers' organizations were its principal affiliates.

In the 1930's, with not only the liquidation of the Red International of Labor Unions but also the merger of various national labor groups controlled by the Communists with other bodies in most of the Latin American nations, the IFTU obtained several more affiliates in the area. These included the Confederación General del Trabajo, which took the COA's place as the Argentine affiliate, the Confederación de Trabajadores de Chile, the

Confederación de Trabajadores de Mexico, and some smaller groups.

THE CTAL

In September 1938 an attempt was made to establish a Latin American central labor group which would include trade unions of all political colorations. This was the only important effort to establish such a broad united front of organized labor, and in the beginning at least, it was marked by considerable success.

The establishment of the Confederación de Trabajadores de America Latina was largely due to two factors. The first was the adoption by the Communist International of the Popular Front policy, which provided for the liquidation of separate Communist-controlled trade-union groups in each country and for the affiliation of their constituent unions to other existing central labor groups. This made possible at that time the collaboration on a hemispheric scale of Communist trade-union groups with those dominated by other political currents.

The second factor contributing to the launching of the CTAL was the particularly critical situation in which the Mexican government of President Lázaro Cárdenas found itself at that moment. In March 1938 the Cárdenas regime had nationalized the country's foreign-owned oil industry, an act which had aroused a hostile reaction in many political and financial circles abroad. The British government broke off diplomatic relations with Mexico as a result of the oil expropriation, and the international oil companies declared a boycott of the country, making it impossible for Mexico to purchase the machinery needed for continuing exploitation and expansion of its oil industry.

In the face of this situation, the Cárdenas regime was anxious to rally as much support elsewhere in Latin America as possible. The summoning of a hemisphere labor conference to meet in Mexico City six months after the oil expropriation was undoubtedly one effort to do this. There is little doubt that the costs of this conference were paid by the Mexican government.

The founding congress of the Confederación de Trabajadores

de America Latina brought together trade-union groups from virtually every country of the area. These included central labor organizations and individual unions under Communist control, the Socialist-dominated CGT of Argentina, and others led by Cuban Autenticos, Peruvian Apristas, Colombian Liberals, Chilean Socialists, and various other elements. The only significant element which did not participate was the anarchosyndicalists.

Vicente Lombardo Toledano, secretary-general of the Confederación de Trabajadores de Mexico, was elected president of the new Confederación de Trabajadores de America Latina. He was to remain in this post for the two and a half decades that the CTAL existed. An executive committee was elected which had representatives of most of the important labor groups of the hemisphere, and of most of the political elements represented at the congress.

In spite of this auspicious beginning, the CTAL was destined to become a completely Communist-dominated group, a development which was due to several causes. The first of these was the capture of the Argentine labor movement by followers of Colonel Juan Domingo Perón during 1943 and 1944, and the consequent withdrawal of the CGT from the CTAL. The second was the growth after the founding of the CTAL of the influence of the Communists in various national labor movements, including those of Chile, Peru, Cuba, Costa Rica, Bolivia, Panamá, and Nicaragua.

A third factor favoring the Communists during the first decade of the existence of the CTAL was the influence of President Lombardo Toledano. From the time he assumed the presidency of the organization, he collaborated particularly closely with the Communists within it. During the Second World War, he followed the vagaries of the Communist International line on the conflict—first denouncing it as a "war among imperialists" and then, after the Soviet Union was attacked, coming out strongly on the side of the Allies as "champions of democracy." He toured Latin America very widely during the latter years of the war, and in his voyagings gave considerable help to the Communists within the various national labor movements.

By the last year of World War II, the Communists were in complete control of the CTAL. At the Cali, Colombia, congress of the organization, in December 1944, a new executive committee was elected, consisting of seven declared Communists, three fellow travelers (including Lombardo Toledano), and only one member who was definitely anticommunist.

THE CIT

Soon after the end of World War II serious efforts began to organize a rival to the CTAL. Many Latin American trade-union organizations had come to feel alienated from the Communist leadership of that group, and to look for an alternative.

Moreover, as the result of the overthrow of several dictatorships in the period from 1944 to 1946, the position of the Communists in several national labor movements was undermined. The end of the Prado regime in Peru in 1945 and the legalization of the Aprista party resulted in these strong anticommunists assuming leadership of the Confederación de Trabajadores del Peru. The end of the first Batista government in Cuba, and its substitution by an administration of the Autentico party resulted first in a split in the Confederación de Trabajadores de Cuba between Communist and Autentico elements, and then in the subsequent disappearance (for all practical purposes) of the Communist-controlled labor group.

In several countries new labor movements arose which were not—as were the Peruvian and Cuban groups—affiliated with the CTAL. These included the Catholic-led Unión de Trabajadores de Colombia, the somewhat similarly oriented Confederación Costarricense del Trabajo "Rerum Novarum," and the Confederación de Trabajadores de Venezuela, which was controlled from its inception in 1947 by the strongly anticommunist Acción Democrática party.

Another factor contributing to the anti-CTAL developments in the Latin American labor movements was the renewed interest of the American Federation of Labor in the trade unions of that part of the world. For almost two decades the AF of L had paid but little attention to Latin America. Finally, though, in the Spring of 1946, the executive board of the federation appointed Serafino Romualdi, a member of the International Ladies Garment Workers' Union as Latin American Representative of the AF of L.

Romualdi began immediately to establish contacts with the anticommunist and noncommunist elements in the Latin American labor movements. With them he worked out plans for the establishment of a new inter-American labor group, which would not only include a large segment of the trade unions of Latin America, but would also have within its ranks the AF of L and its Canadian counterpart, the Trades and Labor Council.

The founding congress of the new group was held in Lima, Peru, in January 1948. Delegates attended from the Autentico-controlled CTC (Cuba), the CTV (Venezuela), the Unión de Trabajadores de Colombia, the CTP (Peru), the CCT Rerum Novarum (Costa Rica), the Socialist-controlled faction of the CTCh (Chile), as well as from other groups from Mexico, Argentina, Uruguay, and Haiti. In addition, there were delegates present from the Dutch territory of Surinam and from several British territories in and around the Caribbean, and from Puerto Rico. Finally, the AF of L and the Trades and Labor Council of Canada were well represented.

The Lima congress decided to establish the Confederación Interamericana de Trabajadores (CIT). It named Lima as the seat of the new group, although a few months later, after the miliatary *coup d'état* of October 1948, it was necessary to move it to Santiago, Chile.

From its inception, the CIT included an important segment of the most important trade-union groups of Latin America. Notably absent from the list was the Peronista-controlled Confederación General de Trabajo of Argentina, which the CIT refused to admit, and the largest trade-union groups of Mexico and Colombia, which did not affiliate with it for they chose to remain in the CTAL. However, the CIT was born as a formidable rival of the CTAL.

A year and a half after the formation of the CIT the World

Federation of Trade Unions, which had been established as a world-wide united front of labor right after World War II, split: for the West European anticommunist labor movements and the Congress of Industrial Organizations of the United States withdrew. This split paved the way for the amplification and transformation of the CIT.

At its second congress, in Havana, Cuba, in September 1949, the CIT made provision for its own demise. It approved a resolution providing for its liquidation if negotiations for a new confederation between CIT officials and leaders of organizations which had left the WFTU proved fruitful. When this came to pass, a new congress, called in Mexico City in January 1951, launched the Organización Regional Interamericana de Trabajadores.

The ORIT contained most of the union groups which had formerly belonged to the CIT. In addition, within a short time it came to include likewise the CIO of the United States, and its Canadian counterpart, the Canadian Congress of Labor; and a number of Latin American groups that had stayed in the WFTU and in its Latin American affiliate, the CTAL, so long as the WFTU remained united. These included the Confederación de Trabajadores de Mexico, the Confederación de Trabajadores de Colombia, and several federations in the British West Indies.

During the 1950's the ORIT had within its ranks the great majority of the most important trade-union organizations of Latin America. In 1951 it was joined by the three principal national labor groups of Brazil, the confederations of industrial, commercial, and land-transport workers. In the following year new central labor groups of Uruguay and Paraguay affiliated.

The only important national labor group that was not openly under Communist control and that remained in the CTAL in the 1950's was the Confederación de Trabajadores del Ecuador, which was nominally under Socialist party leadership. All the other national affiliates of the CTAL were openly Communist-dominated groups, and the Confederación de Trabajadores de America Latina itself was transformed virtually into the general staff of the Communists in the Latin American trade-union movement.

THE PERONISTA UNIONS

The most serious opposition to the ORIT in the early 1950's came from the Peronistas rather than from the Communists and the CTAL. With the refusal of the CIT and the ORIT to admit the Peronista unions of Argentina, and their acceptance instead of credentials of exiled and underground anti-Peronista unionists, the Perón government and the CGT attempted to build up a Latin American labor federation of their own. Since his inauguration in 1946, in fact, Perón had been dispatching Labor Attachés to the various Argentine embassies in Latin America. One of the principal functions of these officials was to flood local labor leaders in each country with Peronista propaganda, and to try to convince them of the feasibility of forming a Latin American trade-union confederation in competition with the CIT-ORIT and the CTAL.

These efforts bore fruit in 1951 when a congress was held in Asunción, Paraguay, which established the Comité Pro Unidad Sindical Latino Americana. This was a provisional committee both to coordinate the Peronista activities in various countries and to establish in each country a group which could be represented in a subsequent congress.

This second congress finally met in November 1952. It established the Agrupación de Trabajadores Latino Americanos Sindicalizados (ATLAS). Eventually the affiliates of the ATLAS, aside from the Argentine CGT, came to include small central labor groups in Uruguay, Chile, Puerto Rico, Colombia, Panamá, Costa Rica, Nicaragua, and Haiti. On the other hand, the Confederación Regional Obrera Mexicana (CROM) was the only significant group outside of Argentina which participated in it.

Although the Peronista continental labor group never was able to recruit as many affiliates as the ORIT, or as the CTAL in its heyday, for a short while it gave certain indications that it might be able to do so. The Peronistas challenged the leadership of the Costa Rican and Colombian affiliates of the ORIT. For a short while the Peronistas had the backing of the Ibañez government and it seemed possible that they might be able to develop an important central labor group in Chile, and they had the backing of the Odría dictatorship in efforts to establish a new national labor confederation in Peru.

In spite of these initial successes, the Peronistas failed in their efforts to establish a major competitor of the ORIT. Perón used the visit of Milton Eisenhower to Argentina in 1953, as an excuse to drop their violent campaign against the United States, and in the labor field against the AF of L and CIO. At the same time, many of the labor attachés were withdrawn from Argentine embassies in various Latin American nations.

At the same time, the Peronistas in the Argentine labor movement began to become aware that their "friends" in other Latin American countries were seeking to exploit their connection with the Confederación General del Trabajo to get free trips to Buenos Aires, and to be feted by important Argentine leaders, including President Perón, although many of these Latin American labor leaders had relatively little following.

The Peronista efforts in the inter-American labor movement finally collapsed with the overthrow of President Perón in September 1955. Yet, the ATLAS continued to maintain a somewhat phantom existence—having been kept alive largely by its Mexican affiliate, the CROM, which was the only affiliate of any significance by the end of 1964, when it *still* was officially in existence. Even the Argentine CGT was no longer a member of ATLAS.

ACTIVITIES OF THE ORIT

Meanwhile, the ORIT continued to be very active. It carried on a wider range of functions than any of its predecessors. These included organization, workers' education, lobbying in international organizations and national governments, as well as supporting the activities of various of its national affiliates.

The role of the ORIT in the field of organization was particularly important in those parts of the hemisphere in which the labor movement was relatively weak. For example, when a general strike broke out in 1954 among the banana workers of Honduras, where there had theretofore existed no labor movement, the ORIT rushed in financial aid. In the following months, it dispatched organizers to help the leaders of the new labor unions to consolidate their organizations. Somewhat similar activities were conducted in Guatemala after the fall of the procommunist regime of President Jacobo Arbenz in June 1954.

The ORIT organizer on the East Coast of South America also gave extensive aid to the labor organizations in that part of the hemisphere. His influence was of considerable importance in bringing together the free trade unions of Uruguay into the Confederación Sindical Uruguaya, and those of Paraguay into the Confederación Paraguaya de Trabajadores.

Labor education was also an important field of ORIT activity. The organization sponsored the establishment of a leadership-training school for Latin American trade unionists at the University of Puerto Rico, although shortly after its establishment the financing of this school was assumed by the foreign-aid program of the United States government. Thereafter, the ORIT conducted a series of labor-training seminars in various parts of the hemisphere.

The labor-education activities of the ORIT were intensified in the early 1960's with the establishment of the American Institute for Free Labor Development. Although this was fundamentally a United States institution, financed by U.S. unions and businessmen, it was headed by Serafino Romualdi, and its relations with Latin American national trade-union movements and the ORIT were very close. The American Institute set out to establish trade-union leadership-training schools in every major Latin American country.

Various congresses of the ORIT, as well as meetings of its executive bodies, adopted resolutions on a wide variety of problems facing the workers of the hemisphere. Delegations of the organization consulted with the government of the United States, to

urge broader aid to the economic development of the Latin
American countries, as well as to protest against U.S. support of
dictatorial regimes in various Latin American countries. At various times, similar representations on important issues were made
to one or another of the Latin American nations.

The ORIT was particularly persistent in its fight against certain of the Latin American dictatorships. In 1957 it organized in
Mexico a conference of representatives of exiled labor organizations of the Dominican Republic, Venezuela, and Peru. Upon
various occasions, the ORIT also presented protests against
dictatorships in the United Nations, the International Labor
Organization, the Organization of American States, and other
international bodies. On several occasions it was successful in getting annual conferences of the International Labor Organization
to refuse to seat workers' delegates named by Latin American
dictatorial regimes.

Finally, the ORIT supported the activities of its various affiliates. Moral and financial support was given to strikes of Chilean
copper miners, Central American banana workers, and other
groups. On the request of the Bolivian miners' federation it intervened with the United States government to continue to purchase Bolivian tin, even though the Bolivian labor movement was
not at the time affiliated with the ORIT.

THE CRISIS OF THE ORIT

In spite of these far-flung activities, the ORIT suffered a severe crisis during 1959 and 1960. This crisis arose largely from its
relations with the Cuban labor movement before and during this
period. For a short while, the crisis threatened the very existence
of the Organización Regional Interamericana de Trabajadores.

The Confederación de Trabajadores de Cuba had been one of
the founding members of the ORIT. At that time, it was controlled by members of the Autentico party. However, when General Batista seized power in Cuba in March 1952 and when a
general strike called by the Confederación de Trabajadores de
Cuba failed, a kind of armed truce was struck between the dicta-

tor and the labor leaders. This truce, whereby the dictator left the unions alone, and the labor leaders did not engage in overt opposition to Batista, lasted until the invasion of Cuba in November 1956 by the forces of Fidel Castro.

During the succeeding two years of civil war, the leaders of the CTC became among the most important allies of the Batista regime. Both Batista and the leaders of the confederation opposed a revolutionary strike, although for different reasons. Batista feared that such an event would overthrow his regime, the labor leaders that it would result in the destruction of the trade-union movement. The CTC leaders, therefore, did their utmost to suppress opposition to Batista within their organizations.

This kind of alliance between the CTC leaders and Batista tended to discredit the labor officials both inside Cuba and elsewhere in Latin America. Within the ORIT, there was strong sentiment in several national affiliates for expelling the Confederación de Trabajadores de Cuba from the ORIT. However, such a move failed, even at the congress of the ORIT held in Bogotá, Colombia, a few weeks before Castro's victory.

During the first months of the Castro regime, there was a prolonged discussion within the CTC, concerning whether it would remain in both the ORIT and the ICFTU. The first reaction of the new pro-Castro leaders of the CTC was to withdraw; however, as the result of long negotiations with officials of the ORIT, the CTC leaders decided to remain within the ORIT and the ICFTU and to attempt to modify these organizations' policies from within. This decision was confirmed by a national conference of the Confederación de Trabajadores de Cuba which met in Havana in September 1959.

This decision, however, was reversed by the first postrevolutionary congress of the CTC. That congress was the scene of a bitter struggle. Under exceedingly strong pressure from Fidel Castro and other high figures in the revolutionary regime, the congress decided to withdraw from the ORIT and the ICFTU and to issue an invitation for a congress to launch a new "revolutionary Latin American confederation of workers."

At that point in time, the initiative of the CTC promised to have a wide degree of success. The November 1959 CTC congress ratified a "defensive-offensive alliance" with the Confederación de Trabajadores de Venezuela, and the CTV at first expressed guarded support for the idea of a new Latin American confederation. Furthermore, there seemed considerable possibility that the Central Obrera Boliviana and the Peronista faction of the Argentine labor movement might join such a new hemispheric group. The Communist-dominated Central Unica de Trabajadores de Chile, which had never joined the CTAL, was certain to join the new Latin American group. The CTAL itself announced that it was willing to liquidate so that its national affiliates could join the new revolutionary group. Finally, it seemed distinctly possible that several long-time affiliates of the ORIT might also be willing to join forces with the new confederation.

However, these original prospects of the Cuban-sponsored Latin American confederation were not fulfilled. This failure was largely due to the CTC coming very soon under complete Communist domination. Therefore, it soon became clear to all that the new revolutionary Latin American group would be little more than a reconstitution of the CTAL, with only the addition of a few new national affiliates.

It had originally been proposed to summon the founding congress of the new group within a matter of months. However, its convocation was several times postponed. When it did finally convene in Santiago, Chile, in September 1962, the only groups that had not been part of the CTAL and that were represented by full-fledged delegates were the Cuban CTC and the Chilean CUTCh, both Communist-controlled. The meeting was such a disappointment for its organizers that it was converted into a "preliminary conference" instead of a full-fledged congress. The formal establishment of the new group was postponed for a further meeting.

REORGANIZATION AND EXPANSION
OF THE ORIT

The ORIT quickly recovered from its crisis. Uner the leadership of a new secretary-general, the Peruvian labor leader Arturo Jaúregui, the ORIT expanded its activities. Its corps of organizers in various parts of Latin America was expanded. For instance, in the Dominican Republic the ORIT gave extensive moral financial and personnel help in developing a free labor movement after the end of the Trujillo dictatorship in 1961. In several countries, the ORIT representatives worked closely with representatives of the International Trade Secretariats in helping to expand the local labor movements.

The labor-education work of the ORIT was also expanded. In Mexico, a residential labor-training school was established, which provided extensive courses for leaders from all over the hemisphere. In various nations, ORIT representatives worked closely with the leaders of the national labor movements and with the American Institute for Free Labor Development in developing training facilities for local trade-union leaders. The secretary-general of ORIT served as a member of the Board of Directors of the American Institute.

The ORIT also received several new members in the early 1960's. The Confederación de Trabajadores de Venezuela, which had stayed out of any international labor group after its reorganization in the wake of the fall of the Pérez Jiménez dictatorship in January 1958, finally rejoined the ORIT and the ICFTU in 1962. Individual national unions in Argentina, Bolivia, and Chile, which had joined their respective International Trade Secretariats also became members of the Organización Regional Interamericana de Trabajadores. The new Confederación Nacional de Trabajadores Libres of the Dominican Republic, established in 1962, also became an ORIT and ICFTU affiliate.

The ORIT also continued its policy of combating the remaining dictatorships in the Latin American countries. It supported the exiled leaders of the Confederación Paraguaya de Trabajadores in their struggle against the dictatorship of General

Alfredo Stroessner. It likewise gave strong backing to the exiled leaders of the Union des Travailleurs Haitiens against the tyranny of President François Duvalier. Finally, it strongly opposed the Communist dictatorship in Cuba, and gave its backing to various labor groups which were carrying on a struggle against the Castro regime.

Thus, the ORIT continued in the early 1960's to be the principal hemispheric labor organization. It had within its ranks the largest national central labor groups of Mexico, Honduras, El Salvador, Panamá, Colombia, Venezuela, Peru, Uruguay, Brazil, and the Dominican Republic, as well as those of the English- and Dutch-speaking areas in and around the Caribbean. It also had smaller central labor groups or important national industrial or craft unions affiliated to it in Guatemala, Costa Rica, Ecuador, Bolivia, and Argentina. Finally, exile labor groups from Haiti and Paraguay remained in the ORIT.

THE INTERNATIONAL TRADE SECRETARIATS

An important new development in the late 1950's and early 1960's was the greatly expanded activity of the International Trade Secretariats in Latin America. These international labor groupings are organized on the basis of particular industries or groups of industries. Individual national industrial unions in various countries are the affiliates of the ITS's, whereas in most cases the constituent organizations of the ORIT and ICFTU are national central labor bodies.

Until the late 1950's the International Trade Secretariats were principally European and North American bodies. At that time, however, many of them undertook to expand their activities into other parts of the world. Several of the ITS's established American regional headquarters, staffed with organizers, whose task was to help the free labor unions of their particular industries in the area, and to attempt to recruit as many of them as possible for their respective international groups.

Among the ITS's which became particularly active in the

Latin American area were the International Transport Workers' Federation, the International Miners' Federation, the International Plantation Workers' Federation, the International Union of Hotel and Restaurant Workers, the Post, Telephone, and Telegraph Workers' International, the International Federation of Clerical and Technical Workers, the International Petroleum Workers' Federation, and the International Federation of Factory and General Workers' Unions. Several of these organizations held Latin American regional congresses during the early 1960's.

The entry of the International Trade Secretariats into the Latin American field was of particular importance to the free trade union movement in the area. Although the ITS's are not officially part of the International Confederation of Free Trade Unions, they are closely associated with it, and the unions which are admitted to their respective ITS's are automatically eligible for membership in the ICFTU and its regional affiliates such as the ORIT.

In Latin America a number of national industrial unions which were affiliated with central labor bodies that were not in the ICFTU and ORIT found it impossible to enter their respective International Trade Secretariat. Some went further, and after joining their ITS, they also affiliated with the ICFTU and ORIT. This development was of particular importance in Chile, Bolivia, and Argentina.

THE CLASC

Another new aspect of the Latin American international labor picture in the early 1960's was the activity of the International Federation of Christain Trade Unions (IFCTU) in the area. Like the ITS's, the Christian Federation had never shown much concern with the Latin American labor movement until the late 1950's. However, at that time, anxious to convert itself from a largely European organization into a really world-wide grouping, it began activities in the Western Hemisphere.

In the late 1950's the IFCTU had only two or three affiliates in Latin America. With the encouragement, however, of the parent organization, they established in 1956 a regional organization for Latin America, the Confederación Latino Americana de Sindicatos Cristianos (CLASC). Subsequently, the CLASC undertook extensive organizational activities, seeking to bring about the establishment of affiliated central labor bodies in the various countries of the region.

The CLASC sought to recruit or organize two types of groups. One was national central labor bodies which shared its general orientation. The other was groups of Christian Democrats working within trade-union bodies that were not specifically Christian in tendency. However, it tended to regard the latter kind of group as merely a half-way station to the establishment of CLASC affiliated national trade-union confederations.

The hemisphere's two principal Catholic-oriented national central labor bodies, the Unión de Trabajadores de Colombia and the Confederación Costarricense del Trabajo Rerum Novarum did not affiliate with the CLASC. Rather, they maintained their membership in the ORIT and ICFTU. The only central labor bodies which belonged to the CLASC by the time of its Fourth Congress in Caracas in 1962 were small groups of Argentina, Chile, Venezuela, Panamá, Peru and Jamaica.

The leaders of CLASC became increasingly violent in the early 1960's in their attacks upon the ORIT and the ICFTU. They insisted that their organization was "purely Latin American" in spite of the fact that most of its funds came from European Catholic sources. It accused the ORIT of being a "tool of the State Department," and carried on considerable anti-Yankee propaganda.

Summary and Conclusion

The labor movements of Latin America have a long history of international association and membership. They have not only belonged to the various world-wide labor confederations, but they have also formed various organizations among themselves, and in conjunction with the labor movement of the United States and Canada.

Such international contacts have been very useful for the national labor movements of the Latin American area. They have helped to develop a more sophisticated type of union leadership than would otherwise exist. In addition, the Latin American unions have upon various occasions received important international support for strikes, demonstrations, and other activities. Finally, international labor backing has been of considerable importance in the Latin American labor movements struggle for more democratic regimes, economic development, and social change in their respective countries.

Postscript

ORGANIZED LABOR IN LATIN AMERICA IS REVOLUTIONARY. IT PROVIDES a means whereby the urban workers, who have previously been a weak and oppressed group, can have a voice in their nations' affairs. It is part of the broad movement to modernize the economy, society, and political life of the twenty republics as well as of the nonrepublican territories of the region.

Most Latin American unions are under the control of one or another of the parties that are working for revolutionary change in the area. These include not only the Communists and their variants, but also the National Revolutionary parties, the Christian Democrats, and such indigenous groups as the Mexican Partido Revolucionario Institucional, the Partido Peronista of Argentina, and the Partido Trabalhista of Brazil. In most cases, the unions are used by the political parties, rather than being able to convert the parties into union vehicles.

However, the Latin American labor movements are an element of great potential power. When well-led and disciplined, they possess the ability to challenge the military as the ultimate determinant of power in Latin American politics. Through street demonstrations, partial and general strikes, and in the ultimate instance taking up arms, the union members are able to bring powerful support to those governments they favor or to imperil the position of those which they oppose.

The unions have been able to use their political power effectively in many cases to gain concrete advantages for their members. Thus, most Latin American countries have extensive labor legislation, covering minimum wages, the limitation of working hours, the protection of workers against dangerous machinery, and special provisions dealing with the labor of women and juveniles. They also possess wide social security systems covering workmen's compensation, illness, and retirement pensions.

Nevertheless, the principal function of the trade unions is not in politics, but in the economic field. Here, organized labor has been able to make collective bargaining a widespread phenomenon in Latin America. Through negotiations with employers, the labor unions have been able to achieve wage increases and a wide range of fringe benefits. The latter have included housing, commissary privileges, medical care, loans from employers, and other things which in the United States might be considered as unwarranted and unwanted employer paternalism.

Collective bargaining machinery has also been developed for presenting the grievances of individual workers. Thus, the unions have frequently been able to assure respect for the individual workers' rights. They have been able to achieve a status which they had never before enjoyed.

Latin American governments frequently supervise the collective bargaining process. They usually limit the right of certain kinds of workers to strike or even to engage in collective bargaining. Frequently, too, they require unions and employers to submit to government conciliation and mediation. In some countries, as a result of these nations' peculiar political history, collective bargaining has been largely superseded by government labor courts.

Most Latin American countries also have legislation governing the organization and functioning of the workers' and employers' organizations. Such laws often provide for control over the unions' jurisdiction as well as for control of their finances and elections.

Latin American organized labor is part of the world trade-union movement. Since before World War I, some Latin American unions have been a part of international labor groups. During the interwar period, the number of such international affiliations increased, and since World War II most of the Latin American labor groups have become members of one or another of the world-wide trade-union confederations, the Communist-controlled World Federation of Trade Unions, the International Federation of Christian Trade Unions, or the International Confederation of Free Trade Unions, by far the largest number belonging to the last of these.

For more than half a century, too, the Latin American unions have organized regional labor confederations. These have been under either anarchosyndicalist, Communist, Peronista, or Catholic control or have been of straight trade-union orientation.

The future of organized labor in Latin America depends fundamentally on the future trend of the Latin American Revolution. If this Revolution proceeds along a democratic path, the trade-union movement in these countries will become stronger and more capable of defending the interests of its members, while its influence in the economic, social, and political life of the Latin American nations will continue to expand. However, if the other republics and the nonrepublican territories of the area follow the lead of Castro's Cuba, and take the totalitarian path, the labor movement will become little more than an arm of the government.

The labor movements themselves will play a major role in determining the direction which the Latin American Revolution will take. In recent years, their influence has been predominantly on the side of political democracy and they have generally been aligned with the parties of the democratic Left.

If the development of the economies of the Latin American nations goes forward, this will make it possible for the organized workers of Latin America to raise their living standards and to get justice through the medium of their unions' grievance procedures. Under these circumstances, organized labor will in all likelihood continue to be aligned on the democratic side of the political struggles of the area. However, if the economies of Latin America do not expand, and it proves impossible to continue to raise their real wages through the process of democratic collective bargaining, the workers will find the siren calls of the totalitarian Left increasingly attractive.

Bibliographical Note

RELATIVELY LITTLE HAS BEEN WRITTEN CONCERNING LABOR RELA-
tions in Latin America, at least so far as the English language is
concerned. Much of what appears in the foregoing pages, therefore, is based upon nearly twenty years of observation and personal contact with the labor movements of the area.

The best book on the subject to appear in English heretofore
has been the volume by Ben G. Burnett and Moises Poblete
Troncoso entitled "The Rise of the Latin American Labor Movement." All other books have dealt with the unions or labor
relations in only a limited part of the Latin American area.
Among those available are Marjorie Clark's "Organized Labor in
Mexico," published in the mid-1930's, and the present author's
"Labor Relations in Argentina, Brazil, and Chile," put out in
1962.

A reader interested in keeping up with current developments
in Latin American labor has several sources available to him. Until November 1964 one of the best was *Hispanic American Report,* published at Stanford University each month. Its files are
still an invaluable source of information for a period of almost
two decades. Other more specialized periodicals include *The Inter-American Labor Bulletin,* the monthly publication of the
Organización Regional Interamericana de Trabajadores; *Free
Labor World,* published by the International Confederation of
Free Trade Unions; and the *World Trade Union News,* the
periodical of the World Federation of Trade Unions. Of some use,
too are the *Monthly Labor Review* of the U.S. Department of
Labor and the ILO's *International Labor Review.*

Other publications carry occasional news on Latin American labor. Such dailies as the *New York Times, Christian Science Monitor,* and *Washington Post* are useful in this connection, as are such journals of opinion as *New America, Nation, New Republic.* Even extreme left-wing periodicals such as the Communists' *The Worker* and the Trotskyites *The Militant* occasionally carry news on Latin American organized labor, and particularly concerning political trends in the labor field.

Index